D1431042

THE S.S. HUEBNER FOUNDATION

FOR INSURANCE EDUCATION

Publications of
THE S. S. HUEBNER FOUNDATION
FOR INSURANCE EDUCATION

LECTURE SERIES

STUDIES SERIES

Insurance To Value

GEORGE L. HEAD, CPCU, CLU

Director of Educational Publications
The American Institute for
Property and Liability Underwriters, Inc. and
The Insurance Institute of America

Published for
**The S. S. Huebner Foundation for
Insurance Education**
University of Pennsylvania

by

RICHARD D. IRWIN, INC.
Homewood, Illinois   60430
Irwin-Dorsey Limited, Georgetown, Ontario

© 1971
THE S. S. HUEBNER FOUNDATION FOR INSURANCE EDUCATION
University of Pennsylvania

First Printing, October, 1971

Library of Congress Catalog Card Number 70–158046
Printed in the United States of America

HG
8065.
H43

To my
Mother and Father

THE S. S. HUEBNER FOUNDATION
FOR INSURANCE EDUCATION

The S. S. Huebner Foundation for Insurance Education was created in 1940, under the sponsorship of the American Life Convention, the Life Insurance Association of America (then the Association of Life Insurance Presidents), and the Institute of Life Insurance, and operated under a deed of trust until 1955 at which time it was incorporated as a Pennsylvania nonprofit corporation. Its primary purpose is to strengthen and encourage insurance education at the collegiate level. Its activities take three principal forms:

a) The providing of fellowships to teachers in accredited colleges and universities of the United States and Canada, or persons who are contemplating a teaching career in such colleges and universities, in order that they may secure preparation at the graduate level for insurance teaching and research.

b) The publication of research theses and other studies which constitute a distinct contribution directly or indirectly to insurance knowledge.

c) The collection and maintenance of an insurance library and other research materials which are made available through circulating privileges to teachers in accredited colleges and universities desirous of conducting research in the insurance field.

Financial support for the Foundation is provided by contributions from more than one hundred and twenty life insurance companies and proceeds from the sale of Foundation publications.

The program of activities is under the general direction of a Board of Trustees representing the life insurance institutions. Actual operation of the Foundation has been delegated to the University of Pennsylvania under an administrative plan submitted by the University and approved by the Board of Trustees. The University discharges its responsibilities through an Administrative Board consisting of five officers and faculty members of the University of Pennsylvania and four academic persons associated with other institutions. Active management of the Foundation is entrusted to an Executive Director, appointed by the University of Pennsylvania.

BOARD OF TRUSTEES

J. McCall Hughes, *Chairman*
  President, Mutual Life Insurance Company of New York
J. K. Macdonald, *Vice-Chairman*
  Chairman of the Board, Confederation Life Association
Earl Clark, President & Chief Executive Officer, Occidental Life Insurance Company of California
William D. Grant, Chairman of the Board and President, Business Men's Assurance Company of America
Robert L. Maclellan, President, Provident Life & Accident Insurance Company
Donald S. MacNaughton, Chairman of the Board and Chief Executive Officer, Prudential Insurance Company of America
James R. Martin, President and Chief Executive Officer, Massachusetts Mutual Life Insurance Company
John S. Pillsbury, Jr., Chairman of the Board and Chief Executive Officer, Northwestern National Life Insurance Company
Benjamin N. Woodson, President, American General Life Insurance Company

OFFICERS OF THE CORPORATION

J. McCall Hughes, *Chairman*
J. K. Macdonald, *Vice-Chairman*
Dan M. McGill, *Secretary*
Harold E. Manley, *Treasurer*
(Vice President for Business and Financial Affairs,
University of Pennsylvania)
William Lowery, *Counsel*
(Dechert, Price and Rhoads)

ADMINISTRATIVE BOARD

Dan M. McGill, *Chairman and Executive Director*
Edison L. Bowers   D. J. O'Kane
Charles C. Center   John D. Long
Herbert S. Denenberg   C. Arthur Williams, Jr.
Robert D. Eilers   Willis J. Winn

ix

Foreword

Property insurance companies have long recognized that there is a fundamental relationship between the ratio of insurance to value and the price that should be charged for the insurance protection. This relationship derives from the fact that the great majority of losses in the property insurance area are partial and, indeed, most constitute only a relatively small percentage of the value of the insured property. If this phenomenon were not recognized in either the rate making process or the loss adjustment procedures, an individual could obtain full coverage for the most probable loss by carrying insurance to only a fraction of the value of the insured object. To discourage this practice and to seek an equitable distribution of the burden of insured losses, the companies have followed the practice of requiring a specified percentage of insurance to value or adjusting the premium rate for amounts of insurance less than that contemplated in the computation of the basic rate.

Despite the prevalance and importance of this practice, virtually no attempts have been made to establish the theoretical and statistical validity of the insurance companies' approach to the problem of underinsurance. This book fills that void in insurance and actuarial literature. It offers a rigorous examination of the theory of insurance to value and its application to current coinsurance requirements—including agreed amount endorsements and periodic reporting forms—in fire, extended coverage, sprinkler leakage, water damage, and earthquake insurance in the United States.

The theory of insurance to value is presented in a series of mathematical equations showing the relationship between the pure premium rate and the policy face when it is possible for the losses to be smaller than the amount of insurance. The rate criteria of equity, adequacy, and reasonableness are explored mathematically in terms of a minimum requirement of insurance to value. The author concludes that the coinsurance concept is an essential ingredient in any equitable system of sharing the burden of partial losses. Recognizing the inadequacy of presently available data, he urges insurers to compile and disseminate statistical data needed to validate or correct coinsurance credits now based exclusively on judgment.

Based on a doctoral dissertation, this book is not for the casual reader. It tells more than most people want to know about coinsurance and other devices to deal with inadequate insurance to value. On the other hand, it should be an invaluable reference for serious students of the subject. It is a truly definitive work, well organized and logically developed to the last detail.

The author is a native of the state of Washington. He graduated magna cum laude from the University of Washington in 1963 and did one year of graduate work at that institution in the business area. He studied under a Huebner Foundation grant at the University of Pennsylvania from 1964 to 1967, receiving his Ph.D. in 1968. Since 1967 he has been with the American Institute of Property and Liability Underwriters, Inc., currently serving as Director of Educational Publications. He has already had several articles published in scholarly journals and promises to be a prolific writer.

The nature of the purposes for which the Foundation was created precludes it from taking an editorial position on controversial insurance theories or practices. It does not, therefore, detract in any way from the quality of this volume to state that the findings of fact and the conclusions derived therefrom are those of the author and not of the Foundation.

Philadelphia, Pennsylvania   Dan M. McGill
June, 1971   *Executive Director*

Preface

A mathematician with dreams of empire would be fascinated with coinsurance and insurance to value. Armed with a very simple actuarial theory, published as early as 1904 but never rigorously applied, this mathematician could remake the world—or at least a very small part of it. True to his theory and blind to practical considerations, he could campaign for a coinsurance clause in every property insurance policy where losses less than the policy face were possible. He could expose state rating bureaus for promulgating coinsurance rate credits without having statistics on the size of losses as percentages of property values as a basis for these credits. (He could ignore the difficulties in getting reliable data on property values before loss.) He could lobby in the state legislatures for repeal of laws restricting the use of coinsurance and for enactment of statutes prescribing coinsurance, thus striving to bring greater equity and financial strength to the operations of property insurers. Wide publicity for his campaign slogan—"Everyone's Pure Premiums Should Equal His Expected Indemnity Payments"—could guarantee his public status as a "crackpot."

This campaign slogan is true, the author believes, and is the theoretical heart of this dissertation. This study examines the implications of this slogan for the theory and practice of property insurance premium rates as they depend on the relationship between property values and amounts of insurance. If the author escapes the "crackpot" label, and if the reader is not subjected to a tract, substantial credit must go to Dr. Gerald R. Hartman, the supervisor of this study when it was presented as a doctoral dissertation. His jovial discipline and keen mind kept this study within the bounds it so badly needed and led its author back from his grosser errors of fact and judgment.

The author wishes to thank Dr. Clyde M. Kahler for his expert review and corrections of Chapter 10 and Appendix 5. Of course, any errors which remain in this or any other chapter are solely the author's responsibility.

Several officers of the Insurance Company of North America, whose contributions are documented in the text, have assisted the author greatly. He also gratefully acknowledges the help of those other employees of the Company who listened to his questions, usually answered them correctly, and then cleared his path to the officer able to give the most authoritative answer.

The staff of the Department of Statistics and Operations Research of the University of Pennsylvania gave generously of their time and facilities in expediting the statistical work which this study required.

Without the financial support of the S. S. Huebner Foundation for Insurance Education, this dissertation and the author's study at the University of Pennsylvania would not have been possible. The editorial advice of the Foundation's Administrative Assistant, Mildred A. Brill, has been invaluable.

Finally, and most important, inexpressible gratitude to my wife Anne for her help with this study as with so much else.

Bryn Mawr, Pennsylvania   GEORGE L. HEAD
June, 1971

Contents

List of Tables and Figures

FIGURE

Table of Notation

The mathematical formulas in this study use the following notation:

A Dollar amount of a stated amount coinsurance requirement in an agreed amount endorsement

B Dollar amount of a coinsurance limit in an open-stock burglary policy

c Coinsurance percentage in a percentage-of-value coinsurance clause (expressed as a decimal fraction)

C Dollar amount of a percentage-of-value coinsurance requirement ($C = cV$)

D Dollar amount of a deductible for each loss

$E(I)$ Expected value of indemnity payments per policy period

$E(I|x < L \leqq y)$ Expected value of indemnity payments per policy period for losses greater than x but not greater than y

f Probability of loss per policy per period (expressed as a decimal fraction)

F Dollar amount of policy face

F_n Dollar amount of face of an insured's n^{th} policy

g A subscript identifying quantities associated with a policy not written as a provisional reporting form policy (see r, below)

i A subscript identifying quantities associated with an individual insured

I Dollar amount of indemnity

k Any constant for all insureds

L Dollar amount of a particular loss

M Number of insured properties in a class which are expected to suffer some loss during a policy period

N Total number of insured properties in a class $(f = M/N)$

$p(L)$ Unconditional probability of a loss of L to a given insured property during a policy period $[p(L) = fs(L)]$

P Dollar amount of pure premium per policy period

r A subscript identifying quantities associated with a provisional reporting form policy (see g, above)

R Pure premium rate per dollar of face amount of insurance per policy period

$R/\$100$ Pure premium rate per $100 of face amount of insurance per policy period

$s(L)$ Percentage of all losses exactly equal to L, or the conditional probability of a loss of L to an insured property during a policy period, given some loss to that property greater than zero

V Insurable value of an insured property, i.e., the full value of that property on the same basis as that on which insured losses are paid

V^* True insurable value of an insured property at the reporting date of the last report filed prior to a loss under a provisional reporting form policy

VLR Insurable value of an insured property according to the insured's last report filed prior to a
loss under a provisional reporting form policy

Every major formula, except those appearing in the appen-
dixes, is identified by a number indicating the location of its first
appearance. For example, Equation 2–4 is the fourth major equation in Chapter 2. If a formula is repeated, it retains its original
number. Some equation numbers end with a lower case letter.
Any equation so designated is a specific example of a more general equation. Thus, Equation 7–3b is the second numerical application of the third major equation in Chapter 7.

CHAPTER 1

Introduction

*Go ye into all the world
and preach the gospel of coinsurance.*[1]

Coinsurance clauses have confused many American insureds, insurance agents and brokers, and insurance students since these provisions were introduced in the United States in industrial fire policies about 1870.[2] Many readers of "nontechnical" explanations of coinsurance "for the layman" apparently have failed to understand the theoretical need for coinsurance.[3] Coinsurance—or some essentially equivalent device such as graded premium rates

---

[1] William A. Louis, "Some Observations on Co-Insurance," *Proceedings of the Fifteenth Annual Meeting of the Fire Underwriters' Association of the Pacific* (San Francisco, 1926), p. 137.

[2] Edward R. Hardy, *The Making of the Fire Insurance Rate* (New York: The Spectator Co., 1926), p. 278. Coinsurance provisions were incorporated in fire insurance policies written abroad at much earlier dates. Such clauses have been found in English fire policies on movable property issued as early as 1728. H. S. Bell, *Average and Contribution in Fire Insurance* (London: Charles and Edwin Layton, 1911), p. 2. In ocean marine insurance and in fire insurance underwritten by tax-supported municipal funds in many European towns, evidence of the application of the coinsurance principle exists in the earliest historical records. Cornelius Walford, *The Insurance Cyclopaedia* (London: Charles and Edwin Layton, 1871), vol. I, p. 232.

[3] "The coinsurance clause is without doubt one of the least understood clauses used in the insurance business. It is, nevertheless, one of the most important ones." James L. Athearn and Cameron S. Toole, *Questions and Answers on Insurance,* 2nd ed. (Englewood Cliffs, N.J.: Prentice-Hall, Inc., 1960), p. 117.

1

for larger policies—theoretically is necessary for any insurance policy under which the insurer's liability for a loss may be less than the full face amount of insurance. If this theoretical need is not met, premium rates may be inadequate for insurers and inequitable for insureds. The author believes that much of the current confusion and ignorance about coinsurance and about the problem of insurance to value to which coinsurance is one solution is due to the absence of a firm analytical foundation for the largely superficial treatment of these subjects in current insurance literature. Therefore, this study attempts to go beyond the standard explanations of coinsurance in order to answer some of the questions left by these rudimentary discussions.

This study begins, however, with a brief review of these elementary explanations.

THE RUDIMENTS OF COINSURANCE

A simple coinsurance clause is the "Average Clause," which was once mandatory in all fire policies on real property in New York City.

This company shall not be liable for a greater proportion of any loss or damage to the property herein described than the sum hereby insured bears to ———% of the actual cash value of said property at the time such loss shall happen.[4]

The mechanics of this clause can be expressed in a formula in which

I = the indemnity received by the insured for a loss
L = the dollar amount of a loss
F = the face amount of insurance
V = the actual cash value of the property
c = the coinsurance percentage (inserted in the blank space in the above clause).

---

[4] William N. Bament, "Co-Insurance," an address to the Insurance Society of New York, March 30, 1920, p. 11. Other, more modern, provisions known as "average clauses" have somewhat different wording. Modern "average clauses" also vary somewhat in phrasing.

The above clause provides that

$$I \leq L \left(\frac{F}{cV} \right). \tag{1-1}$$

Verbally, Equation 1–1 states that the foregoing clause limits an indemnity payment for a loss to no more than the loss multiplied by a fraction made up of the policy face divided by the coinsurance requirement (i.e., the coinsurance percentage, c, times the property value at the time of the loss, V).

If the fraction F/cV were to exceed 1, as it would if the insured purchased a policy greater than the above "Average Clause" stipulates, Equation 1–1, standing alone, would prescribe that the indemnity payment exceed the loss—allowing the insured an illegitimate profit on his insurance. Similarly, for a loss greater than the coinsurance requirement (so that L/cV exceeds 1) Equation 1–1 would mathematically imply that the indemnity payment would be more than the policy face. Because in practice an indemnity payment is limited by the lesser of the loss or the applicable insurance, a logically complete and yet realistic algebraic model of the effect of the above "Average Clause" requires that Equation 1–1 be subject to two constraints:

$$I \leq L, \tag{1-2}$$

that is, the indemnity payment cannot exceed the loss, and

$$I \leq F, \tag{1-3}$$

the indemnity payment is never greater than the applicable policy face.

Equations 1–1 through 1–3 describe the mechanics of one type of coinsurance clause in the absence of any deductible, pro rata distribution clause, or other limitation on the insurer's liability. As explained in Chapter 4, only slight modification of these formulas is required to describe the operation of all types of coinsurance clauses.

As an illustration of these equations, if a $10,000 building, insured for $6,000 subject to an 80 percent coinsurance clause like that above, suffers a $5,000 loss, the insured receives no more than

$3,750. A $1,250 coinsurance penalty is deducted from the $5,000 the insured would have received had he met the $8,000 coinsurance requirement, because the insured carried less coverage than the insurer assumed in computing a premium rate (price per $100 unit of insurance) which would be just adequate to pay fully all losses up to the assumed amount of insurance. In this example, Equation 1–1 indicates

$$I \leqq 5,000 \left(\frac{6,000}{0.8 \times 10,000} \right) = \$3,750. \qquad (1\text{–}1a)$$

If the insurance policy has no other provisions—such as a deductible or pro rata distribution clause—which would limit the insured's recovery, Equation 1–1a, solved as a strict equality, gives the indemnity payment.

The constraints imposed on indemnity payments by the amount of the loss and the face amount of the applicable insurance can be illustrated in the context of the same example. If the policy face is $9,000 instead of $6,000, but the coinsurance requirement (cV) remains $8,000, the insured collects only $5,000 for a $5,000 loss—not $5,625.00 (9/8 of $5,000). Similarly, if the loss is $8,400, instead of the $5,000 in the original example, the indemnity payment is only the $6,000 policy face—not $6,300 (6/8 of $8,400). To generalize these results, any type of coinsurance clause reduces an indemnity payment below that which would otherwise be paid *only if* (1) the policy face is less than the coinsurance requirement (here, cV, the coinsurance percentage of the property value at the time of loss) *and* (2) the loss is less than the coinsurance requirement. In all other cases, either Equation 1–2 or Equation 1–3 becomes binding as a strict equality, and the loss is paid as if no coinsurance clause existed in the policy.

The way in which coinsurance achieves the purposes assigned to it by various writers is not intuitively clear, and many elementary discussions give weak justifications of coinsurance. At this point, it need only be noted that the possibility of losses less than the policy face forces the insurer to make an assumption about the amount of insurance purchased in order to set a premium rate which equates the expected indemnity payments with pure premiums.[5] This assumption establishes the coinsurance requirement, an 80 percent coinsurance requirement meaning that the pure premium rate calculation assumes that all properties are insured to exactly 80 percent of value at the time of any loss. If an insured buys only 50 percent coverage at a premium rate based on 80 percent protection, he pays 5/8 of the assumed premium and, by the coinsurance clause, receives no more than 5/8 of any loss.[6] For 80 percent or larger losses, the insurer expects to pay the face on all policies not greater than the coinsurance requirement, and this result is achieved for these losses regardless of the presence or absence of any coinsurance clause. Thus, at one level, the purpose of coinsurance is to balance pure premiums with expected indemnity payments on all policies not exceeding the coinsurance requirement. This balance, in turn, promotes other objectives.

In the United States, coinsurance clauses frequently are available or required in policies against fire (except on dwellings[7]), burglary, business interruption, sprinkler leakage, and ocean marine perils. But in insurance on certain types of property in certain states insurers do not permit coinsurance. Statutes in some states prescribe procedures to be followed when coinsurance is used in specified policies; other states forbid coinsurance on some risks.

In most instances the premium rate for insurance subject to coinsurance (a coinsurance rate) is lower than that for coverage not subject to coinsurance (a flat rate). Usually a higher coinsurance requirement brings a lower coinsurance rate.[8] Coinsur-

---

[5] Pure premium is premium for paying losses—gross premium less allowances for expenses and profits.

[6] An insured buying 90 percent coverage at the 80 percent rate pays more pure premium than his expected losses and theoretically is overcharged.

[7] However, the replacement cost provisions of coverage for dwelling structures in homeowners' policies, discussed on page 31, employ an adaptation of the coinsurance concept.

[8] The usual explanation is that, larger losses being less likely, larger amounts of insurance have a lower average cost per $100 of coverage (a lower premium rate). In actual fact, even if large losses were more likely than small ones, pure premium rates should fall with larger coinsurance requirements (see pages 14 and 16). The *possibility* of losses less than the policy face, not their *predominance*, makes coinsurance necessary.

ance rate credits differ from state to state, some states giving credits where others give none. Some states offer credits for lower coinsurance requirements than do others. In Europe and Great Britain, insurers uniformly require 100 percent coinsurance on nearly all types of coverage.[9]

PURPOSES AND OUTLINE OF STUDY

The foregoing discussion of the rudiments of coinsurance raises a number of questions. The purpose of this study is to answer these questions or to find that, as yet, no answers exist. Hence, the following questions outline this study.

What is the significance of insurance to a specified percentage of value? More specifically, how does the amount of insurance affect the premium rate? What occurs if policyholders insuring to different fractions of value pay the same premium rate for policies without coinsurance clauses, and how does coinsurance change these results? What proportion of insureds meets coinsurance requirements? What are the alternatives to coinsurance? Chapter 2 explores these questions.

What is coinsurance? The above explanation does not define it. In Chapter 3, coinsurance and related terms are defined.

What clauses provide for coinsurance? The clause quoted on page 2 was called an "Average Clause," but policy captions are not uniform. Chapter 4 classifies coinsurance clauses, giving them unambiguous titles.

For what purpose(s) does an insurer insert a coinsurance clause in a policy? The several answers to this question are enumerated in Chapter 5. Hopefully, this discussion will clarify some of the inconsistent statements made by various text writers regarding the purposes of coinsurance.

In theory, how should coinsurance rates be computed for different coinsurance requirements? The key to this computation is a distribution of losses by size—either by dollar amounts or percentages of value, depending on the form of coinsurance requirement—for the peril and type of property insured. Chapter 6

---

[9] Letter from David C. Tausche, Manager for Europe, Insurance Company of North America, October 6, 1966.

deals with these distributions. In Chapter 7, two of these distributions—one of dollar size of loss, the other of loss relative to value—are used in models for theoretically proper coinsurance rates.

In practice, how are coinsurance rates determined, and how do they differ among states? These matters occupy Chapter 8.

How do insurers decide what types of insurance on what types of property should be subject to coinsurance, either as a strict requirement or at the insured's option? If the insured is given a choice of coinsurance requirements, what should be the range of that choice? Chapter 9 covers these underwriting questions.

Do any difficulties in settling losses interfere with the theoretically precise operation of coinsurance? Problems of loss adjustment are taken up in Chapter 10.

Why and how do the states regulate the use of coinsurance clauses by statutes or administrative rulings? Regulation is the topic of Chapter 11.

The conclusions and recommendations of this study are summarized in Chapter 12.

SCOPE OF STUDY

No attempt is made to deal with all types of insurance subject to coinsurance. The major perils discussed—fire, sprinkler leakage, water damage, earthquake, and the perils grouped under the extended coverage endorsement—differ sufficiently to pose most of the questions relevant to coinsurance wherever it is used. The loss statistics in this study cover only fire damage, because figures for others perils are not readily available. A final limitation is that this study makes only passing reference to the history of coinsurance and to its use aboard.

METHOD OF STUDY

In addition to texts, articles in academic and trade journals, and insurance rate manuals, this study draws upon correspondence and interviews with officers of property insurers, rating bureaus, and rating advisory organizations. Another important source is the unpublished, detailed records of the Oregon Fire Marshal on every insured fire loss in Oregon during 1964 and 1965. Index cards for each loss are the basis for a distribution of losses as percentages of sound value for frame structures with public fire protection. This distribution, to which a function has been fit by an IBM 7040 computer, may be one of the most significant results of this study.

CHAPTER 2

Survey of Insurance to Value

PURPOSE

In order to provide a foundation for a detailed treatment of coinsurance throughout the rest of the study, this chapter explores "insurance to value," the phrase generally associated with the concept that the equitable, adequate, and reasonable[1] price per $100 of property insurance (the gross premium rate[2]) should vary with the amount of insurance (the policy face). The chapter's four parts (1) define insurance to value with a model of the theoretical relationship between the pure premium rate and the policy face; (2) examine the effects of deviations from insurance to value; (3) review data on the extent of existing deviations; and (4) enumerate insurers' means of coping with these deviations. One of the most important of these means is coinsurance.

---

[1] In practically every state, the statutes regulating property insurance premium rates direct that "rates shall not be excessive, inadequate, or unfairly discriminatory." Spencer L. Kimball and Allen L. Mayerson, *Cases and Materials on the Law of the Insurance Enterprise* (Ann Arbor, Mich.: By the authors, 1965), p. 298 (mimeographed).

[2] The gross premium rate is made up of the pure premium rate plus a loading for administrative expenses, contingencies, and profit. This chapter focuses on pure premium rates; gross rates are discussed in Chapter 7.

THE POLICY FACE AND THE
PURE PREMIUM RATE

Determinants of the Pure Premium Rate

The aggregate pure premium which an insurer collects from an individual policy in a policy period (usually one year) should equal the indemnity payments which an insurer expects to pay under that policy during the same period. Such a total pure premium is just adequate and is equitable to the individual insured in relation to all other insureds. The pure premium collected from each policy is the product of the policy face (typically in $100 units) and the pure premium *rate* per unit. The determinants, or parameters, of a pure premium rate are: (1) the probability of some loss of whatever size; (2) a distribution of losses by size; and (3) the amount of insurance. The probabilities and dollar amounts underlying the first two parameters establish the expected value of losses to each property. The third parameter is needed to determine the insurer's limit of liability for these losses.[3] The policy face and the loss may be less than the full property value. The possibility of losses less than the policy face creates the pricing problem known as "insurance to value."

General Pure Premium Rate Equation

The general equation relating the pure premium rate to these determinants uses the following notations:

$$F = \text{the policy face expressed in dollars}$$
$$P = \text{the pure premium charged each insured per policy period}$$

---

[3] A property insurer is liable for no more than the amount of a loss or the amount of insurance, if less. The first limit is known as the principle of indemnity. See William R. Vance, *Handbook on the Law of Insurance,* ed. Buist M. Anderson, 3d ed. (St. Paul, Minn.: West Publishing Co., 1951), p. 102. Other policy clauses may further limit an insurer's liability.

$R =$ the pure premium rate per dollar of face amount per policy period ($R = P/F$)

$L =$ a particular dollar amount of loss

$f =$ the probability of any loss, of whatever size greater than zero, to each insured property per policy period. The unit exposed to loss is an individual property. By assumption, each property is insured under only one policy, and no policy insures more than one property.

$s(L) =$ the percentage of losses exactly equaling L, or the conditional probability of a loss of L, given some loss greater than zero

$fs(L) =$ the unconditional probability of a loss exactly equal to L to each insured property per policy period

$E(I) =$ the expected value of the insurer's indemnity payments for insured losses of whatever size greater than zero to each insured per policy period

$E(I|x < L \leq y) =$ the expected value of the insurer's indemnity payments to each insured per policy period for losses greater than x but not greater than y.

If pure premium equals expected indemnity

$$P = FR = E(I)$$

or

$$R = \frac{E(I)}{F}. \tag{2-1}$$

An insurer's expected indemnity payments can be divided into two parts.[4] First, for losses not exceeding the policy face, the expected value of these losses is the sum of the products of the

---

[4] Only the loss and the policy face are assumed to limit the insurer's liability.

amount of each loss times the unconditional probability of each loss. This expected value[5] can be expressed as

$$E(I|0 < L \leq F) = \sum_{L=1}^{L=F} Lfs(L)$$

if L can take on only discrete values, or

$$E(I|0 < L \leq F) = \int_0^F Lfs(L)dL$$

if the values of L are continuous. The second element of an insurer's expected indemnity payments, the portion for losses exceeding the policy face, is equal to the policy face times the probability of all losses greater than the policy face. This probability is the unconditional probability of any loss of whatever size greater than zero, that is, f, multiplied by the difference between one and the percentage of losses not exceeding the policy face. In notation, this expected value is

$$E(I|F < L \leq \infty) = Ff\left[1 - \sum_{L=1}^{L=F} s(L)\right]$$

if L can take only discrete values, or

$$E(I|F < L \leq \infty) = Ff\left[1 - \int_0^F s(L)dL\right]$$

if L is a continuous variable.

Combining the above expressions, the total of an insurer's expected indemnity payments under one policy during one policy period can be expressed as

$$E(I) = f\left(\sum_{L=1}^{L=F} Ls(L) + F[1 - \sum_{L=1}^{L=F} s(L)]\right)$$

if the values of L are not continuous, or .

---

[5] For the computation of expected values of joint events (e.g., the occurrence of some loss and a loss of a particular size, given some loss), see Robert Schlaifer, *Introduction to Statistics for Business Decisions* (New York: McGraw-Hill Book Co., Inc., 1961), pp. 125–130.

$$E(I) = f\left(\int_0^F Ls(L)\,dL + F\left[1 - \int_0^F s(L)\,dL\right]\right) \quad (2\text{-}2)$$

if the values of L are continuous.

The calculations leading up to the continuous Equation 2–2 have been presented in both discrete and continuous form in order to clarify the derivation of this equation. The author prefers the continuous expressions because they simplify manipulation, and continuous equations will be used in the rest of this study. However, the theoretical problem in the assumption that the values of losses are continuous should be noted.

The heart of the difficulty is that the continuous equations, and the derivatives based on them, are justified in theory only if all conceivable amounts of loss between zero and any maximum loss are possible—losses such as three hundred sixty-seven thousandths of one cent, $10,082.6789423, $10,082.6789424, and an infinitely large number of possible different values of loss between these last two figures. In fact, the United States monetary system makes one cent the smallest unit for measuring losses and dictates that all losses be integer values expressed in pennies. Therefore, the theoretical requirement of continuity cannot strictly be met. Perhaps more important for practical purposes, the human tendency to use round figures results in clusters of losses at certain amounts such as $5,000, $10,000, or $10,500. Very few losses are evaluated at $10,000.01, $10,001.00, or even $10,010.00; insurers and insureds usually round all three of these amounts to $10,000. Even when an insurer could document a loss to be only $9,950, the insurer may meet the insured's demand for $10,000 rather than spend, say, $200 to win a $50 dispute.

The theoretical difficulties imposed by the monetary system and by the common affinity for round numbers should be kept in mind and bowed to when the data require. But the author chooses to make the assumption that L is a   continuous variable because this assumption clarifies some relationships which might be nearly unintelligible in discrete notation.

To continue the derivation of a general expression for a pure premium rate, the substitution of Equation 2–2 into Equation 2–1 shows that the pure premium rate for each unit of face amount F is

$$R = f \left(\frac{\int_0^F Ls(L)dL + F\left[1 - \int_0^F s(L)dL\right]}{F} \right). \quad (2\text{--}3)$$

The following simple example illustrates Equation 2–3. Assume that a building is expected to have one loss every forty years ($f = 1/40 = 0.025$). Only two sizes of loss, L_1 and L_2, are possible, namely \$40,000 and \$60,000. (This example is a very rough discrete approximation of the continuous functions postulated in Equations 2–2 and 2–3. It should be noted that the presently available data on loss severity are insufficient to support the assumption of a continuous function.) One-fifth of all past losses have been \$40,000, so $s(L_1) = 0.20$. Four-fifths of all past losses have been \$60,000, so $s(L_2) = 0.80$. For \$50,000 of insurance, the pure premium rate per \$100, $R/\$100$, is

$$R/\$100 = 0.025 \left(\frac{(0.20)(40{,}000) + (0.80)(50{,}000)}{500} \right) = \$2.40.$$

$$(2\text{--}3a)$$

The pure premium rate per \$100 for an \$80,000 policy is

$$R/\$100 = 0.025 \left(\frac{(0.20)(40{,}000) + (0.80)(60{,}000)}{800} \right) = \$1.75.$$

$$(2\text{--}3b)$$

The principle that the pure premium rate decreases as the policy face increases—in this example, despite the greater probability of the larger loss—is shown on page 16 to be mathematically necessary.

Equation 2–3 applies to four broad types of rate calculations. First, as given above, it applies where the loss to the insured is unlimited, but the policy face limits the insurer's liability. General liability insurance is an example. Second, if both the insured's loss and the insurer's aggregate liability are unlimited, as in workmen's compensation insurance, the numerator on the right-hand side of Equation 2–3 is the expected value of losses from zero to infinity. Since policies of this second type lack a face amount, F moves from the right-hand denominator to the left-hand side of Equation 2–3. The modified Equation 2–3 then yields a *total* premium ($P = FR$) rather than a premium *rate* per unit of coverage. Third, if, as is typical in automobile physical damage insurance, the insured's loss and the insurer's liability are limited only by the property value, the right-hand side numerator is the expected value of losses from zero to full value. Finally, if the insured's loss is limited by the property value and the insurer's liability cannot exceed the policy face, which may be less than the property value, Equation 2–3 requires no change.

This fourth case—where property values and amounts of insurance are definite and separable—raises the topic of insurance to value. Given that (1) each insured has some choice of policy face and (2) a premium rate is proper only if each insured chooses the policy face assumed in the rate calculation, what is to be done if insureds select a policy face different from that assumed? This is the problem central to insurance to value; coinsurance can be one solution to this problem.

"Insurance to value" can now be defined. In this study, insurance to value exists if property is insured to the exact extent (dollar amount or percentage of value) assumed in the premium rate calculation. Underinsurance is coverage less than that assumed, and overinsurance is coverage beyond that assumed. Insurance to value means insurance to full value only if 100 percent coverage is assumed in the rate computation. Throughout this study, "value" means the value of the property on the same basis used in indemnifying losses—usually actual cash value or replacement cost. If the premium rate is based on 80 percent insurance to replacement cost, neither coverage to 80 percent of actual cash value nor coverage to 90 percent of replacement cost is insurance to value. In the first case, the property is underinsured if actual cash value is less than replacement cost; in the second instance, the property is overinsured relative to the insurance to value relationship assumed in the premium rate.

Change of Rate with Face

Whenever losses less than the policy face are possible, the pure premium rate should fall as the policy face increases—either absolutely or relative to value—even if large losses predominate. In the words of the 1911 *Merritt Committee Report:*

The principle that the rate falls as the ratio of insurance to value increases holds whatever the figures that are used, even though large losses were relatively more frequent than small ones.[6]

Proof of this principle is that the first derivative of the premium rate with respect to the policy face in Equation 2–3 is negative if losses less than the face are possible. This derivative is:

$$
\frac{dR}{dF} = \left(\frac{1}{F^2}\right) fF \left[Fs(F) + \right.
$$

$$
\left(1 - \int_0^F s(L)dL\right) - s(F)F \right] - \left(\frac{1}{F^2}\right) f \left[\int_0^F Ls(L)dL + \right.
$$

$$
\left. F\left(1 - \int_0^F s(L)dL\right) \right]
$$

$$
= \left(\frac{1}{F^2}\right) f \left[F^2 s(F) + \right.
$$

$$
F - F \int_0^F s(L)dL - F^2 s(F) \left[\right.
$$

$$
- \left(\frac{1}{F^2}\right) f \left[\int_0^F Ls(L)dL + \right.
$$

$$
\left. F - F \int_0^F s(L)dL \right]
$$

$$
= \frac{-f \int_0^F Ls(L)dL}{F^2} . \qquad (2\text{–}4)
$$

[6] *Report of the Joint Committee of the Senate and Assembly of the State of New York, Appointed to Investigate Corrupt Practices in Connection with Legislation, and the Affairs of Insurance Companies, Other than Those Doing Life Insurance Business,* Assembly Document No. 30 (Albany, N.Y., February 1, 1911), p. 85.

This derivative, illustrated arithmetically in Appendix 1, is the negative of the expected value of losses less than the policy face divided by the policy face squared.

EFFECTS OF DEVIATIONS FROM
INSURANCE TO VALUE

If an insurer computes and applies a pure premium rate based on one standard of insurance to value but one or more insureds exceeds or fails to meet that standard, then—in the absence of coinsurance or some adjustment of premium rate or coverage—use of the original premium rate can create inequitable and either inadequate or excessive premiums.

Since pure premium rates should fall as the assumed policy face increases, the insured with less than the assumed coverage pays less pure premium than is needed for the indemnity he can expect if losses up to the policy face are fully paid. The insured with more than the assumed coverage pays unnecessary premiums. If most policyholders purchase less than the assumed coverage, the insurer's premium income tends to be inadequate. If most policyholders buy more than the assumed coverage, the insurer's premium income tends to be excessive.

Inequities arise between any two insureds with equally hazardous properties who insure for different amounts or percentages of value at the same premium rate. The possibility of losses less than the policy face implies that the increase in the pure premium cost of indemnity is less than proportional to the increase in the policy face, but a constant premium rate fixes a constant proportionality between policy face and total premium. The more fully insured policyholder is discriminated against, to some extent, relative to the insured with less coverage obtained at the same rate. The underinsured policyholder receives some subsidy from the insurer's surplus if all his losses up to the policy face are paid fully.

In sum, if pure premium rates are to be just adequate for the insurer and equitable for all insureds in the absence of coinsurance or some equivalent device, each insured must have just the amount or percentage of insurance assumed in the premium rate computation.[7] But this condition cannot be maintained in practice. Even if, at the beginning of the policy period, each insured paid a premium precisely calibrated to the exact ratio of insurance to the value of his property at that time, that property value almost certainly would change during the policy period, thereby creating a tendency toward inadequate or excessive premiums. Hence, some device, such as coinsurance, must balance each insured's pure premium and expected indemnity by changing the rate to reflect the actual policy face and/or by reducing indemnity payments to the underinsured. This necessity underlines the importance of this study.

EXTENT OF DEVIATIONS FROM INSURANCE TO VALUE

The importance of coinsurance is great if deviations from insurance to value are great; coinsurance is less significant if deviations are small. Precise evaluation of these deviations requires knowledge of (1) the amounts of insurance assumed in premium rate calculations and (2) the amounts of insurance actually carried. But neither type of information is readily available in reliable quantities or workable form. Numerous sources make general statements that few insureds are "adequately" or "fully" insured against at least one peril, fire. However, the significance of most of these statements cannot be evaluated because they (1) do not define "adequately" or "fully"; (2) fail to specify the standard of value, such as actual cash value or replacement cost, used as a measure of insurance to value; or (3) are silent on the size or other characteristics of the sample from which the conclusion is drawn.[8] The only meaningful information the author

---

[7] Aggregate rate adequacy could be achieved if more policyholders overinsured than underinsured, but inequities among insureds would result in this case.

[8] See, for example, Hartford Fire Insurance Company, *The Co-Insurance Clause* (Hartford, Conn., 1909), p. 7; A. F. Dean, *The Philosophy of Fire Insurance*, ed. W. R. Townley (Chicago: Edward B. Hatch, 1925), vol. I, p. 129; George G. Traver, "Under-Insurance a Vital Matter that Agents

has found on current differences between actual and assumed insurance to value pertains to fire insurance and is in (1) a survey by the Safeco Insurance Company of America; (2) a Homeowners insurance study by the St. Paul Fire and Marine Insurance Company; (3) evidence from the Roseburg, Oregon disaster; and (4) annual reports of the Oregon Fire Marshal.

Previously Published Data

In a letter dated May 18, 1966, to its Northwest Division agents, the Safeco Insurance Company of America stated:

If our estimate of the situation and trend is correct . . . the insurance industry has a book of commercial property business underinsured by perhaps 20%. . . . Companies are protected by coinsurance clauses in most commercial building and equipment policies, which means that the principal burden of underinsurance falls on your customers.

In setting premium rates for policies subject to coinsurance, the coinsurance requirement is the assumed policy face. Since, according to this passage, the "principal burden" of underinsurance in on insureds, presumably as coinsurance penalties, the quotation seems to use "underinsurance" in the sense of coverage less than that assumed in the premium rate. Because the statement applies to insurers' "book" of commercial property insurance, the statement may be an indication of the combined severity and frequency of underinsurance.

Fail to Stress," *The Weekly Underwriter*, vol. CLIV, no. 7 (February 16, 1946), p. 435; F. P. O. Potter, "Insurance to Value," *The Casualty and Surety Journal*, vol. IX, no. 9 (November 1948), p. 10; John D. C. Roane, then President, National Association of Independent Insurance Adjusters, "Appraisals and Underinsurance," an address to a meeting of Maryland insurance agents, Ocean City, Md., June 1952, p. 5; "Underinsurance Trend Is Accented by Sampling," *The National Underwriter*, vol. LVI, no. 37 (September 11, 1952), p. 14; Lumbermen's Mutual Casualty Company, *A Study of Under-Insurance in American Industry* (1951), p. 2; "Catastrophe Cover Gap Called Widespread," *The Journal of Commerce and Commercial*, May 7, 1969, p. 9; Alexander Picone, "Homeowners Need Insurance to Avoid Damaging Effects of Underinsurance, Inflation," *The Journal of Commerce and Commercial*, August 14, 1969, p. 7; and Joseph M. Zangerle, "Inflationary Pressure on Homeowners Insurance," *Best's Review* (Property and Liability Edition), vol. LXX, no. 6 (October 1969), p. 20.

Prior to a 1964 mail survey of 7,400 homeowners in a nationally representative sample, the St. Paul Fire and Marine Insurance Company concluded from a pilot study that insureds with Homeowners policies could estimate the replacement cost of their dwellings within 2 percent of the true value. The survey indicated that (1) over 55 percent of all dwellings with Homeowners insurance were covered to less than 80 percent of replacement cost; (2) the average ratio of insurance to replacement cost was 70.8 percent; (3) dwellings insured for less than 80 percent of replacement cost averaged 54.2 percent coverage; and (4) newer homes of younger, better educated owners with annual income above $4,000 in areas with a population of over 50,000 tended to be the most fully insured.[9] Actual cash value Homeowners coverage is not subject to coinsurance, but the Homeowners study points out the extent to which policyholders insure to different percentages of value. These differences require some device to preserve equity among insureds. The cited article's title suggests that higher ratios of coverage to value would generate enough pure premium to pay losses.

From General Adjustment Bureau records and a mail questionnaire sent by a United States district court, Mark R. Greene studied 405 physical damage and business interruption losses resulting from a 1959 dynamite truck explosion in Roseburg, Oregon.[10] Coinsurance penalties averaging $1,641.17 were assessed on 23 losses, 15 losses exceeded the policy face, and 5 losses were completely uninsured. The coinsurance penalties indicate underinsurance, but their significance depends on two unreported facts: (1) the number of policies subject to coinsurance; and (2) the number of losses at least equal to coinsurance requirements (for which the policy face is paid and no coinsurance penalty appears).

---

[9] "Adequate Insurance to Value Would Have Put Homeowners in the Black," *The National Underwriter,* vol. LXVIII, no. 45 (November 6, 1964), pp. 1, 35–36.

[10] Mark R. Greene, "The Effect of Insurance Settlements in a Disaster," *The Journal of Risk and Insurance,* vol. XXXI, no. 3 (September 1964), p. 385.

New Data

The author has compiled statistics from the 1953 through 1966 issues of *The Annual Statistical Report of the Office of the Fire Marshal of the State of Oregon.*[11] These *Reports* contain data, summarized by occupancy class, on the damage, total fire insurance of all insurers, sound value before loss, and indemnity payments for all insured Oregon fire losses from 1942 through 1965. Insurers provide these data to the fire marshal's office, which acts merely as a compiler and publisher.[12] These statistics measure the dispersion of actual ratios of insurance to sound value in 1952[13] and 1965 (important to equity among insureds if no coinsurance is used) and the 1942–1965 trend in the aggregate ratio of insurance to sound value (important to the adequacy of insurers' premium income in the absence of coinsurance).

The fact that the information on losses and sound values comes from reports of insurance loss adjusters—whose lack of appraisal training sometimes makes their valuations suspect for actuarial purposes[14]—does not appear to be a weakness in the data. The author believes that, for the most part, insurers view losses through the eyes of their adjusters. The premium rates charged to pay these losses must take account of any systematic bias in adjusting—such as the apparent tendency to equate amounts of insurance with sound values—which produces high reported ratios of insurance to sound value. If these high reported ratios are better evidence of adjusters' reluctance to impose coinsurance penalties than they are of true relations of coverage to value, this reluctance is an aspect of the loss which must be considered in a workable rating formula, at least until insurers modify their adjusting practices to obtain more accurate property values before loss.

---

[11] Salem, Ore.: State Printing Office.

[12] Letter from Norbert J. Lecher, Statistician, Office of the Fire Marshal, State of Oregon, September 9, 1966.

[13] The earliest year for which these ratios by occupancy class are available.

[14] Interview with L. H. Longley-Cook, retired Vice President and Actuary, Insurance Company of North America, September 20, 1966.

Since the Oregon Fire Marshal has no special definition of "sound values,"[15] the definition by two authorities—"sound value is the actual cash value of the property just before its damage or destruction"[16]—is presumed to have been used. Because most policies pay actual cash value indemnity, sound value generally is value determined on the basis on which losses are paid.

Table 1 gives the average ratios of fire insurance to full sound value for various classes of insured Oregon property suffering fire losses in 1952 and 1965. The division of aggregate insurance by

TABLE 1. Weighted* average ratios of fire insurance to full sound value among properties in Oregon damaged by fire, classified by occupancy, 1952 and 1965

(1) Occupancy	(2) 1952	(3) 1965
Amusement halls	n.c.†	0.959 (6)
Apartments	n.c.	0.986 (368)
Bakeries	n.c.	0.975 (4)
Bakeries, candy, cracker manufacturers	0.852 (6)	n.c.
Barns	n.c.	0.942 (67)
Bowling alleys	n.c.	1.000 (2)
Breweries & bottling works	0.937 (6)	0.909 (1)
Canneries	n.c.	0.992 (6)
Canneries & dehydrators	0.910 (5)	n.c.
Chemical works	1.000 (1)	—— (0)
Churches	0.965 (28)	0.980 (28)
Clubs	n.c.	0.989 (26)
Colleges	n.c.	0.976 (8)
Creameries	0.792 (3)	1.000 (1)
Docks & piers	n.c.	1.000 (2)
Dryers (nut, prune, & h..p)	0.625 (5)	1.000 (2)
Dwellings	n.c.	0.947 (8,923)
Dwellings, apartments, & flats	0.849 (10,541)	n.c.
Educational institutions	0.977 (35)	n.c.
Farm barns, outbuildings, crops, etc.	0.847 (272)	n.c.

[15] Letter from Norbert J. Lecher, Statistician, Office of the Fire Marshal, State of Oregon, September 9, 1966.

[16] The quoted definition is from Prentiss B. Reed, *Adjustment of Property Losses,* 2nd ed. (New York: McGraw-Hill Book Co., 1953), p. 11. A later edition of this text, Prentiss B. Reed and Paul I. Thomas, *Adjustment of Property Losses,* 3rd ed. (New York: McGraw-Hill Book Co., 1969), does not appear to use the term "sound value." However, a definition of "sound value" equivalent to that quoted in the text appears in Mark R. Greene, *Risk and Insurance,* 2nd ed. (Cincinnati, O.: South-Western Publishing Company, 1968), p. 236, n. 1.

TABLE 1. (*Continued*)

(1) Occupancy	(2) 1952	(3) 1965
Fraternity & sorority houses	n.c.	1.000 (5)
Fruit & nut packing	0.958 (2)	0.949 (2)
Garages (public)	0.944 (63)	0.967 (17)
Grain elevators	0.954 (11)	0.968 (11)
Hospitals	n.c.	1.000 (5)
Hotels	n.c.	0.944 (54)
Hotels, rooming houses, & auto courts	0.940 (520)	n.c.
Ice & cold storage plants	0.926 (12)	1.000 (1)
Laundry & dry cleaning plants ...	0.985 (18)	0.996 (17)
Linen & woolen mills	0.999 (2)	0.878 (1)
Meat packing	0.520 (32)	—— (0)
Mercantile & office buildings	0.923 (543)	n.c.
Metal products	0.933 (43)	0.848 (14)
Mining risks	n.c.	1.000 (6)
Miscellaneous manufacturing	0.925 (38)	0.995 (39)
Miscellaneous nonmanufacturing .	0.852 (22)	n.c.
Motels	n.c.	0.965 (122)
Motor vehicles	0.989 (693)	0.995 (1,297)
Nursing homes	n.c.	0.974 (9)
Office buildings & banks	n.c.	0.983 (32)
Other farm property	n.c.	0.902 (90)
Oil risks	0.902 (42)	1.000 (1)
Outbuildings	n.c.	0.943 (75)
Paper & pulp mills	1.000 (18)	1.000 (2)
Printing establishments	0.998 (12)	0.999 (5)
Public buildings	0.965 (32)	0.984 (9)
Restaurants	0.916 (166)	0.971 (119)
Rooming houses	n.c.	1.000 (2)
Self-service laundry & dry cleaning plants	n.c.	0.966 (11)
Service stations	n.c.	0.924 (8)
Schools	n.c.	0.951 (30)
Shopping centers	n.c.	0.922 (2)
Stores	n.c.	0.929 (260)
Theatres	0.926 (15)	0.984 (5)
Trailer homes	n.c.	0.959 (95)
Utilities	0.986 (27)	1.000 (1)
Warehouses	n.c.	0.961 (21)
Warehouses, including docks	0.981 (15)	n.c.
Wood products	0.906 (194)	0.957 (137)
All properties	0.901 (13,422)	0.955 (11,953)

° Weighted by value of properties in each occupancy class.

† n.c. denotes "not classified." Between 1952 and 1965 the Office of the Fire Marshal expanded the classification system, so that the same classes are not used in both years. This table includes all classifications used in either year.

Source: *Annual Statistical Report of the Office of the Fire Marshal of the State of Oregon* (Salem, Ore.: State Printing Office, 1953 and 1966), p. 35 of each edition.

aggregate values produces averages for each class weighted by the sound values of the properties. The numbers in parentheses indicate the number of damaged properties in each class.

These ratios are higher than those in any previous study, perhaps because many adjusters tend to equate property values with the amount of insurance available. Note that several ratios in Table 1 are exactly one. If premium rates were to be based on only one ratio of insurance to value for all occupancy classes, 90 to 95 percent would be the most appropriate ratio, according to Table 1.

Fire insurance rates traditionally assume 80 percent coverage,[17] but only three classes of Oregon properties in either 1952 or 1965 were insured for less than this percentage. This evidence, if representative, implies that fire insurance rates are slightly higher than they would be if adjusters' reported ratios of insurance to value were recognized in rate making. But fire insurance premium rates have not been excessive over all. In fact, during the years 1951 through 1969, national overall ratios of incurred fire losses and fire loss adjustment expense to premiums earned rose rapidly —from 47.0 to 61.6 percent for stock insurers, and from 37.6 to 54.5 percent for mutual companies.[18]

The dispersion among the class average ratios of insurance to value indicates that those more fully insured will be discriminated against if premium rates are based on only one ratio. In 1952, the occupancy class averages ranged from 52.0 (meat packing) to 100.0 percent, with a standard deviation of class averages of 10.2 percentage points. The 1965 range was 84.8 (metal products) to 100.0 percent, with a standard deviation of 3.6 percentage points. Premium rates computed on a single assumed ratio of insurance to value could have been adequate, but they would have been

[17] Francis C. Moore, *Fire Insurance and How to Build* (New York: The Baker & Taylor Co., 1903), p. 709; A. B. Roome, "Coinsurance under Fire Policies," *Annual of American Insurance Thought: Fire, Casualty, Surety,* 6th ed. (New York: Convention Yearbook Co., 1926), p. 184; F. E. Wolfe, *Principles of Property Insurance* (New York: Thomas Y. Crowell Co., 1930), p. 143; and Laurence E. Falls, "Coinsurance," *Best's Insurance News, Fire and Casualty Edition,* vol. XLIX, no. 6 (October 1948), p. 94.

[18] See *Best's Fire and Casualty Aggregates and Averages* (New York: Albert M. Best Co., 1951–1969).

inequitable unless some adjustment, such as through coinsurance, had been made for individual variations in ratios of coverage to value.

The trend in the aggregate ratio of insurance to sound value for all Oregon properties is explored in Table 2. From 1942 through

TABLE 2. Aggregate weighted average ratios of fire insurance to full sound value among all properties in Oregon damaged by fire, 1942 through 1965

Year	Ratio	Year	Ratio
1942	0.907	1954	0.934
1943	0.895	1955	0.923
1944	0.913	1956	0.931
1945	0.916	1957	0.926
1946	0.897	1958	0.902
1947	0.916	1959	0.929
1948	0.889	1960	0.929
1949	0.922	1961	0.914
1950	0.936	1962	0.926
1951	0.906	1963	0.952
1952	0.901	1964	0.961
1953	0.925	1965	0.955

Source: *Annual Statistical Report of the Office of the Fire Marshal of the State of Oregon* (Salem, Ore.: State Printing Office, 1953 through 1966). The ratios for years prior to 1952 are calculated from the ten-year summary in the earliest available *Report*.

1965, the average ratio of 92.11 percent increased 0.18 percentage point annually, on the arithmetic average, and the coefficient of variation of the annual average for all occupancy classes was 0.02. At least in Oregon, the reported ratio of aggregate insurance to aggregate value seems to have been quite stable.

TECHNIQUES FOR PROMOTING INSURANCE TO AN ASSUMED PERCENTAGE OF VALUE

Although coinsurance requirements and credits recognize most directly that premium rates ought to vary with the policy face, insurers have other techniques for guarding against insurance above full value or coverage to very small fractions of value.

These techniques indirectly promote insurance in the amount or to the percentage of value assumed in the premium rate.

Discouraging Insurance beyond Full Value

Limit of Recovery to Loss. The fact that the principle of indemnity limits the insurer's liability to no more than the loss— usually without refund of premium for coverage beyond full value —presumably deters policyholders from insuring above value in the hope of profit. However, valued policies and some state statutes requiring payment of the policy face for a total fire loss are exceptions to this limit.

Special Restrictions in Fire Policies. Two provisions, found mainly in fire policies on rural property—(1) the three-fourths value clause, voiding any insurance beyond three-fourths of total value, without any return of premium on the voided coverage; and (2) the three-fourths loss clause, limiting the insurer's liability to three-fourths of any loss (in effect, a deductible of 25 percent of the loss)— preclude full coverage and allegedly motivate insureds to prevent and minimize fires where public fire protection is unreliable.[19] These clauses are becoming rare. In fact, Mississippi law forbids three-fourths value clauses with insurance of real property against fire.[20]

Underwriting Surveillance. Insurers' underwriters and agents watch for applications for policies which seem excessive in light of the insured's description or the agent's examination of the property. Unless further inquiry justifies the request, the application is rejected, or the underwriter suggests less coverage.[21]

Discouraging Insurance to Low Fractions of Value

Insurers' methods of discouraging slight coverage relative to value are found both outside and within the policy.

---

[19] S. S. Huebner and Kenneth Black, Jr., *Property Insurance,* 4th ed. (New York: Appleton-Century-Crofts, Inc., 1957), pp. 136–137.

[20] *Mississippi Code of 1942,* as amended, section 5693.

[21] Interview with C. Neville Wight, former Assistant Executive Manager, Middle Department Association of Fire Underwriters, September 22, 1966.

Techniques Outside the Policy. These techniques include education and advertising, premium rate reductions, minimum premiums, and underwriting rules.

Education and Advertising. Especially during inflation, insurers periodically conduct promotional campaigns among agents and the public, stressing that coverage should keep pace with rising values and that additional coverage brings lower premium rates (usually through coinsurance credits).[22] Letterheads and postage meter slogans admonish the policyholder to "Be Sure to Fully Insure," and advertisements often portray the homeowner with less than full coverage as an unwitting gambler.

Premium Rate Reductions. Coinsurance credits reduce the price per $100 of insurance as coverage approaches full value. Alternatively, bands of graded rates lower the price per $100 of coverage for larger face amounts not limited by any property value. Coinsurance credits and graded rates can be mathematically equivalent ways of recognizing losses less than the policy face.[23] Under either system, the lower price attracts insureds, but graded rates involve nothing analogous to coinsurance penalties.

---

[22] See, for example, "National Board's Program to 'Lick' the Under-Insurance Problem," *The Local Agent,* vol. XVIII, no. 3 (March 1946), pp. 15–16; Safeco Insurance Company of America, Interoffice Correspondence to Northwest Division Agents, May 18, 1966; the Philadelphia Contributionship for the Insurance of Houses from Loss by Fire, *Co-Insurance Briefly Explained* (Philadelphia: The Contributionship), pp. 3–4; Alexander Picone, "Retail Credit Co. Introduces New Residential Replacement Cost Reporting Service in 4 States," *The Journal of Commerce and Commercial,* March 19, 1969, p. 10; and Alexander Picone, "Homeowners Need Insurance to Avoid Damaging Effects of Underinsurance, Inflation," *op. cit.,* p. 7.

[23] Edward A. Ketcham and Murray Ketcham-Kirk, *Essentials of the Fire Insurance Business* (Madison, Wis.: By the authors, 1922), pp. 370–371; Robert Riegel and H. J. Loman, *Insurance Principles and Practices,* rev. ed. (New York: Prentice-Hall, Inc., 1942), p. 368; Robert Riegel and Jerome S. Miller, *Insurance Principles and Practices,* 5th ed. (Englewood Cliffs, N.J.: Prentice-Hall, Inc., 1966), pp. 496–497; C. Arthur Williams, Jr. and Richard M. Heins, *Risk Management and Insurance* (New York: Mc-Graw-Hill Book Co., 1964), p. 197; S. S. Huebner, Kenneth Black, Jr., and Robert S. Cline, *Property and Liability Insurance* (New York: Appleton-Century-Crofts, 1968), pp. 95–96; and Albert H. Mowbray, Ralph H. Blanchard, and C. Arthur Williams, Jr., *Insurance, Its Theory and Practice in the United States,* 6th ed. (New York: McGraw-Hill Book Co., 1969), p. 147.

Minimum Premiums. Rate manuals often stipulate minimum annual gross premiums—for example, a $25.00 fire premium.[24] If a $75,000 property carries a $0.04 per $100 annual gross rate, the policyholder should not buy less than a $62,500 policy—the amount $25.00 will purchase. Minimum premium requirements may even force some insureds to pay more than they would for full coverage.[25]

Underwriting Rules. Requirements that certain properties be appraised or scheduled before insurance is written or renewed, that some policies be at least as great as a minimum amount, and that other coverages be "packaged" with fire insurance are underwriting rules which forestall low ratios of insurance to value.

Insurer appraisal of each property is feasible when policies cover large values at few locations.[26] For example, Associated Factory Mutual companies, which specialize in insurance for large industrial firms, rely on appraisals almost exclusively and use very few coinsurance clauses.[27]

With scheduled insurance, specific items of property are described in the policy and assigned a given amount of insurance. By comparing the requested amount of coverage with the property description, the underwriter can single out properties which seem underinsured relative to the coverage assumed in the premium rate. If the unduly low request is not increased, coverage is refused. Hence scheduling prompts the policyholder to insure fully.[28]

Minimum policy amounts, common in fire insurance,[29] can be

[24] Washington (State) Surveying and Rating Bureau, *General Rules,* (Seattle, Wash.: The Bureau, loose-leaf, revised and supplemented periodically), p. 63, effective March 28, 1966.

[25] Specific fire rates, subject to 80 percent coinsurance, can be as low as $0.022 per $100 of coverage on buildings in Washington. *Ibid.,* p. 79-I, effective March 22, 1963. The Washington minimums are not unusual.

[26] Letter from P. G. Buffinton, Vice President, State Farm Fire and Casualty Company, October 21, 1966.

[27] Joseph Finley Lee, Jr., "The Functional Operations and Competitive Role of the Associated Factory Mutual Insurance Companies" (doctoral dissertation, University of Pennsylvania, 1965), p. 59.

[28] William H. Rodda, *Inland Marine and Transportation Insurance,* 2nd ed. (Englewood Cliffs, N.J.: Prentice-Hall, Inc., 1958), p. 65.

[29] "Fire Companies Progressing in Requiring Insurance to Value," *Insurance Advocate,* vol. LXXII, no. 3 (April 1, 1961), p. 14.

stated dollar sums or specified percentages of the agent's estimate of the property value. With properties of nearly equal value, the minimum dollar amount of insurance provides coverage approximating a predetermined percentage of value. When property values vary, the agent must be relied on to adjust the policy minimum to achieve a given percentage of coverage to value.

Coverages overlooked by most insureds, purchased only in small amounts by others, and used heavily by insureds with extra-hazardous exposures can be marketed more widely for larger average amounts as parts of a "package" of coverages in minimum amounts or minimum ratios of amounts. The most obvious example is the indivisible group of coverages against windstorm, hail, explosion, civil commotion, riot, riot attending a strike, aircraft, vehicles, and smoke in the extended coverage endorsement to fire policies insuring industrial, commercial, or residential structures. Because the amount of insurance for each extended coverage peril equals the amount of fire insurance, the average amount of insurance for these perils is substantially larger than it would be if each peril were separately insured at the insured's option.[30] As another example, Homeowners policies provide coverage for contents in the amount equal to 50 percent of the coverage on the dwelling structure. It should be noted that the insured usually can buy more than the prescribed minimum amount or ratio of coverages which have been packaged in order to achieve acceptable levels of insurance to value.[31]

Techniques within the Policy. These techniques include policies with no face amount, price level adjustment clauses, encouragement of large deductibles, distribution of insurance, and coinsurance.

Actual Cash Value Coverage. Some policies—such as typical automobile physical damage contracts and workmen's compensa-

---

[30] S. S. Huebner, Kenneth Black, Jr., and Robert S. Cline, *Property and Liability Insurance, op. cit.,* p. 107.

[31] John Eugene Pierce, *Development of Comprehensive Insurance for the Household* (Homewood, Ill.: Richard D. Irwin, Inc., 1958), p. 364; and William H. Rodda, "Multiple Line Underwriting: Rating Methods," *Readings in Property and Casualty Insurance,* ed. H. Wayne Snider (Homewood, Ill.: Richard D. Irwin, Inc., 1959), pp. 356–357.

tion (not employers' liability) coverage—lack a face amount but pay all losses in full. The insured, with no policy face to select, cannot underinsure. The premium rate can be computed as if the policy face equaled full property value (of the automobile) or infinity (the largest possible workmen's compensation claim). Although called actual cash value insurance, this type of policy can provide replacement cost coverage.

Price Level Adjustment Clauses. European fire insurance policies on business and residential properties often tie the amount of insurance and the insured's total premium (but not the premium rate) to a construction price index.[32] This European provision may increase the amount of coverage, but typically it cannot reduce coverage without the insured's consent.

In the United States, the actual cash value coverage provided by Homeowners policies is not subject to coinsurance. But some insurers have recently been experimenting with three variations of price level adjustment clauses in an attempt to keep pace with inflating property values.[33] First, some insurers give each insured ninety days' notice that the building and contents coverage in his Homeowners policy will be increased 8 to 12 percent (depending on the insurer) when the policy is renewed, and the insured's premium will be increased accordingly, unless the insured objects to this increase. Second, some insurers offer an optional "inflation guard" endosement to each Homeowners policy at no initial extra cost. Every three months, this endorsement increases the insured's building and contents coverage by 1 percent of the original coverage, and the insured is billed annually for the increased coverage. Third, at least one large insurer writing Homeowners coverage provides that its limits of liability for building and contents losses under all Homeowners policies except the

---

[32] Letter from David C. Tausche, Manager for Europe, Insurance Company of North America, October 6, 1966.

[33] Joseph M. Zangerle, *op. cit.*, pp. 22, 24, and 26; "HO Coverage Increased 10 PC," *The Journal of Commerce and Commercial*, January 30, 1969, p. 8. For more information on the "inflation guard" endorsement, see the *Fire, Casualty, and Surety Bulletins* (Cincinnati, O.: The National Underwriter Company, loose-leaf, revised periodically), pp. Dwellings Ae-3 to Ae-4, Second Printing, February 1969.

tenants' form, HO-4, will increase proportionately with increases in the Composite Construction Cost Index of the Department of Commerce. Under HO-4, which insures tenants' contents but not losses to leased structures, increases in the contents insurance are linked to increases in the Department of Labor Consumer Price Index. Should either of these indexes decline, coverage cannot fall below the original policy face without the insured's consent.

Each of the European and American forms of price level adjustment clause has weaknesses and disadvantages. None of them compensates for underinsurance if the original policy is inadequate; they can only prevent any original underinsurance from growing proportionately larger. Those clauses which provide a fixed percentage of additional coverage at specified intervals will function as intended only if the actual increase in the value of each particular property during that interval equals the predetermined percentage increase in coverage. Finally, clauses relying on national price indexes are based on the implausible assumption that the change in the value of each residence will correspond to that particular index. Thus, regional differences in rates of price changes are ignored.

Offer of Replacement Cost Indemnity. A policy which ordinarily pays the actual cash value of losses may provide replacement cost indemnity if the insurance is at least a specified percentage of replacement cost at time of loss. The Homeowners policy does this for damage to dwelling structures at least 80 percent insured. The actual cash value protection remains in force, free of coinsurance.[34] For maintaining insurance to value, the insured's reward is the restoration of damage with new for old.

Encouragement of Large Deductibles. A deductible reduces premiums by at least part of the cost of paying and adjusting small, usually budgetable losses. If an insured with a limited insurance budget can be persuaded to adopt a substantial deductible and to apply the premium saving to the purchase of higher limits of coverage, the decreasing premium rate for larger policies permits him to obtain a greater total amount of insurance and

---

[34] Homeowners Policy, "Extensions of Coverage," 3(b) through 3(f).

more complete insurance to full value than without a deductible. This approach is feasible only for insureds who view insurance primarily as protection against catastrophes and who are eligible for large deductibles.[35]

Distribution of Insurance. One item of insurance on separable values may be distributed among those values (1) by the ratios of the values, (2) in equal amounts over each value, and (3) evenly over time (for loss of use). These "internal limits" for a loss to any one value force the policyholder to insure to full aggregate value for full protection.

A pro rata distribution clause distributes many forms of property insurance according to ratios of values:

This policy shall attach in each building or location in the proportion that the value of each is to the value of all.[36]

For example, three buildings worth $200,000, $300,000, and $500,000, insured for a total of $600,000 by one item of insurance, are apportioned $120,000, $180,000, and $300,000 of coverage, respectively.

When values of separate properties are presumed to be equal, such as are the parts of a standing crop, the insurance can be spread equally over each small part (square foot of field) to achieve the same result as a pro rata distribution clause. Crop insurance typically pays a fraction of the policy face equal to the portion of the crop destroyed.[37] When separate values are unknown but are presumed to average a given amount (e.g., the contents of safe-deposit boxes), payment for loss to one unit may be restricted to a small percentage of the policy. Custodians' safe-deposit box policies once paid no more than 10 percent of the face for one box.[38]

Time value coverages often are spread evenly over the period

---

[35] Lee, *op. cit.,* p. 353.

[36] Robert I. Mehr and Emerson Cammack, *Principles of Insurance,* 4th ed. (Homewood, Ill.: Richard D. Irwin, Inc., 1966), p. 231.

[37] George F. Rutledge, "Farm and Crop Insurance," *Property and Liability Insurance Handbook,* eds. John D. Long and Davis W. Gregg (Homewood, Ill.: Richard D. Irwin, Inc., 1965), pp. 155–156.

[38] C. A. Kulp, "Non-Insured and Non-Insurable Loss," *Journal of American Insurance,* vol. V, no. 6 (June 1928), p. 12.

underwriters judge to be the longest foreseeable loss of use or maximum indemnity period. For example, one form of business interruption policy provides that no more than one three-hundredth of its face is paid for each day's stoppage.[39] Landlords' rental value coverage may be apportioned weekly or monthly, with a higher premium rate when a larger fraction of the policy face applies to one week or month.[40]

Coinsurance. Coinsurance can adjust precisely the premium rate to the amount of insurance (a dollar sum or a percentage of value) and, thus, can be the most exact method of promoting insurance just sufficient to balance each insured's pure premiums with his expected indemnity. Coinsurance penalties and premium rate reductions can prompt insureds to take just the amount of insurance assumed in the rate computation. The remainder of this study examines coinsurance in detail.

SUMMARY

This chapter (1) defines insurance to value with a model of the theoretical link between the pure premium rate and the policy face; (2) outlines effects of deviations from insurance to value; (3) presents data on the extent of such deviations; and (4) catalogues insurers' means of promoting insurance to value.

The pure premium rate which equates pure premiums and expected indemnity falls as the policy face increases, regardless of whether small or large losses predominate. A property is insured to value if the policy face equals that assumed in the rate calculation, which only coincidentally would be to full value.

Underinsurance and overinsurance are deviations from insurance to value. Underinsurance by many insureds may produce premium inadequacy; general overinsurance may generate excessive premiums. If one policyholder is more fully insured than

---

[39] John D. Phelan, "Business Interruption Insurance," *Property and Liability Insurance Handbook, op. cit.,* p. 121. This assumes 300 working days in a one-year maximum stoppage. Plans are available for other work schedules and maximum stoppages.

[40] Sidney G. Behlmer, "Other Consequential Loss Insurance," *Property and Liability Insurance Handbook, op. cit.,* p. 133.

is another with an equally hazardous property who pays the same premium rate, the more fully insured policyholder suffers some price discrimination. Thus, insurance to value is closely connected with the regulatory goals of adequate, reasonable, and equitable premium rates.

Information on existing ratios of insurance to full value is limited to fire insurance and is largely inconclusive. But it seems clear that individual policyholders insure to different percentages of value, creating the need for some device to eliminate price discrimination.

Insurers may prevent coverage beyond full value by limiting recovery to the amount lost, with three-fourths value and loss clauses, and through underwriting surveillance. Insurers may discourage unduly low insurance through educational and advertising campaigns, minimum premium and policy requirements, graded premium rates, appraisals, scheduling, and packaging—all means outside the policy. Policy provisions promoting insurance to high percentages of value are actual cash value protection, price level adjustment clauses, replacement cost extensions of coverage, large deductibles, distribution of insurance, and—for the most precise treatment of insurance to value—coinsurance.

CHAPTER 3

Definition of Coinsurance and Related Terms

PURPOSE

This chapter defines coinsurance, coinsurance clause, coinsurance deficiency, coinsurance penalty, and coinsurer as they are used in this study. These definitions, clarifying the scope and operation of coinsurance, provide useful terminology.

DEFINITION OF COINSURANCE

"Coinsurance" has several meanings not connected with the effect of insurance to value on premium rates, and scholars disagree on the meaning of coinsurance in relation to insurance to value.[1] Therefore, the definition used in this study is prefaced by a review of usages in other aspects of insurance and of existing definitions related to insurance to value.

Definitions Unrelated to Insurance to Value

Coinsurance—in the context of health insurance, credit insurance, life insurance, apportionment of losses among insurers, loss

---

[1] Robert Riegel, "Coinsurance," *Journal of American Insurance,* vol. XXXII, no. 6 (June 1945), p. 4; and Commission on Insurance Terminology of the American Risk and Insurance Association, *Bulletin,* vol. II, no. 1 (March 1966), pp. 4–5.

participation clauses generally, and self-insurance—is not relevant to insurance to value.

In health insurance policies a coinsurance clause, also called a percentage participation clause, is a deductible, expressed as a fraction of the loss, under which the insured bears a fraction of all eligible expenses.[2]

A coinsurance clause in a credit insurance policy requires the businessman insuring against abnormal bad debts to absorb a fraction of these credit losses, the fraction decreasing as the premium rate or customers' credit standing rises.[3]

A life insurer reinsuring policies under the coinsurance plan transfers to the reinsurer a share of the liability for death claims, for nonforfeiture values, and for any dividends—not just for the death claims beyond the ceding insurer's retention, as under yearly renewable term reinsurance.[4]

When an insured has more than one policy which might pay a loss, courts called upon to apportion liability among insurers sometimes refer to these insurers as "coinsurers." The following passage is illustrative:

A careful reading of both policies discloses that, in some instances at least, they cover the identical liability that may ensue. Both policies carry provisions for other insurance which in their meanings are identical and by which they both have agreed to be co-insurers. Although the policy of the [first] Company covers the insured for liability for any accidental injury on the insured's premises, the natural and necessary implication of the other insurance clause, without some specific language to the contrary, is that in case of such liability as appears in the instant case, the two policies constitute coinsurance for the same liability.[5]

---

[2] See O. D. Dickerson, *Health Insurance*, 3rd ed. (Homewood, Ill.: Richard D. Irwin, Inc., 1968), pp. 210–211.

[3] See William H. Rodda, *Fire and Property Insurance* (Englewood Cliffs, N.J.: Prentice-Hall, Inc., 1956), p. 468.

[4] See Dan M. McGill, *Life Insurance*, rev. ed. (Homewood, Ill.: Richard D. Irwin, Inc., 1967), pp. 437–438.

[5] *Ranallo v. Hinman Brothers Construction Company, et al.*, 49 F. Supp. 920 (1942), at 925. A more recent case is *United Services Automobile Association v. Russom*, 241 Fed. (2d) 296 (1957), at 302. Hyphenation of "co-insurance" or "co-insurer" has no special significance.

Coinsurance sometimes is said to be the common characteristic of all loss-participation clauses—clauses under which the insured bears part of his otherwise insured losses. One text, after describing limits of indemnity for certain losses, various deductibles, and three-fourths value and loss clauses, definies coinsurance as

. . . the obligation of the insured to share in losses. And in this sense several of the above types of clauses are coinsurance clauses, . . .[6]

One authority has described deductibles as embodying "the coinsurance idea."[7]

Occasionally, coinsurance is said to be synonymous with self-insurance, which means "conscious retention of risk"[8] by one who insures only partially. Echoing an earlier writer,[9] one author has stated:

The word coinsurance means that if the policyholder does not carry enough insurance, he self-insures a part of each loss. . . . If the insured does not carry enough insurance, the amount he collects will not, of course, cover his entire loss, *whether or not his policy contains a coinsurance clause.*[10]

Definitions Related to Insurance to Value

Below are four of the most precise definitions of coinsurance related to insurance to value:

Coinsurance is that called for by a provision imposing an obligation upon the insured to keep a specific amount or percentage of insurance in force, failing which he becomes a coinsurer to the extent of the omitted insurance.[11]

---

[6] Robert Riegel and Jerome S. Miller, *Insurance Principles and Practices,* 5th ed. (Englewood Cliffs, N.J.: Prentice-Hall, Inc., 1966), p. 494.

[7] C. A. Kulp and John W. Hall, *Casualty Insurance,* 4th ed. (New York: The Ronald Press Co., 1968), p. 48. The same wording appears in the third (1956) edition of the same text, authored by Kulp alone, p. 51.

[8] Robert C. Goshay, *Corporate Self-Insurance and Risk Retention Plans* (Homewood, Ill.: Richard D. Irwin, Inc., 1964), p. 21.

[9] F. E. Wolfe, *Principles of Property Insurance* (New York: Thomas Y. Crowell Co., 1930), p. 134.

[10] Allen L. Mayerson, *Introduction to Insurance* (New York: The Macmillan Co., 1962), p. 233. Emphasis supplied.

[11] *Oppenheim v. Fireman's Fund Insurance Company,* 119 Minn. 417, 138 N.W. 777 (1912), at 779. The *Oppenheim* definition has been ex-

Coinsurance: . . . specif., as in fire insurance, a system in which the insured is treated as insuring himself to the extent of that part of the risk not covered by his policy.[12]

Coinsurance is an arrangement under which the insured bears a share of certain losses if the amount of his insurance is less than a specific percentage of the value of the property insured.[13]

The term "coinsurance" denotes a relative division of risk between the insurer and the insured, depending upon the relative amount of the policy and the value of the property insured.[14]

These definitions seem faulty because they do not identify clearly the class of things to which coinsurance belongs[15] and the scope of coinsurance.

In order, the above definitions classify coinsurance as "that called for" by a policy provision, a "system," an "arrangement," and a "relative division of risk." The first phrase leads to circular definitions, and the other three are vague. What is being arranged or systematized is not clear, and "risk" is ambiguous.[16]

With respect to the scope of coinsurance, the third definition

---

plicitly adopted by the courts of Alabama, Delaware, Minnesota, South Carolina, Texas, Utah, and Washington. A recent use of the *Oppenheim* definition was in *American Insurance Company v. Iaconi,* 47 Del. 167, 89 Atl. (2d) 141 (1952), at 144.

[12] *Webster's New International Dictionary of the English Language,* unabridged, 2nd ed. (Springfield, Mass.: G. & C. Merriam Co., Publishers, 1958), p. 522. This definition is similar to the above definitions of coinsurance in connection with all loss-participation clauses and with self-insurance.

[13] Albert H. Mowbray, Ralph H. Blanchard, and C. Arthur Williams, Jr., *Insurance, Its Theory and Practice in the United States,* 6th ed. (New York: McGraw-Hill Book Co., Inc., 1969), p. 144. The same definition appears on page 83 of the fifth edition of this text, published in 1961, with Mowbray and Blanchard as the only authors.

[14] Among legal scholars who have adopted this definition are Henry Campbell Black, *Black's Law Dictionary,* 4th ed. (St. Paul, Minn.: West Publishing Co., 1951), p. 326; George J. Couch, *Cyclopedia of Insurance Law,* ed. Ronald A. Anderson (Rochester, N.Y.: The Lawyers Co-operative Publishing Co., 1962), section 37:1375; and John Allan Appleman, *Insurance Law and Practice* (Kansas City, Mo.: Vernon Law Book Co., 1942), vol. VI, p. 218. Each author cites supporting cases.

[15] To be most useful in academic work, a definition should place the thing defined in a class and then distinguish it from all other members of that class. See Irving Pfeffer, *Insurance and Economic Theory* (Homewood, Ill.: Richard D. Irwin, Inc., 1956), pp. 12–14.

[16] For discussion of this ambiguity, see Commission on Insurance Terminology of the American Risk and Insurance Association, *op. cit.,* pp. 3–4.

is restricted to a percentage of value coinsurance requirement, while the first definition, referring to a "specific amount or percentage of insurance," is broad enough to include an agreed or guaranteed amount clause.[17] The second and fourth definitions relate the insured's recovery to the amount of "his policy" or "the policy," while the first and third mention "insurance in force" or "his insurance," perhaps in more than one policy. These different wordings correspond to the difference between a so-called "average" clause (". . . the sum hereby insured . . .") and a so-called "coinsurance" clause (". . . the total amount of insurance . . .").[18] A complete definition of coinsurance should include the mechanisms found in agreed amount, "average," "coinsurance," and all other coinsurance clauses.

Definition of Coinsurance in This Study

In this study,

coinsurance is an apportionment of losses between an insurer and its insured such that the insurer pays—within other restrictions stated in the policy or arising from the nature of property insurance—a fraction of each loss equal to the ratio (called the coinsurance apportionment ratio), not greater than one, of a designated amount of insurance to (1) a stated sum or (2) the whole, or a specified percentage, of the value of the insured property. The designated insurance may be (1) the face amount of the policy requiring coinsurance, (2) the total face amounts of the insured's applicable policies, or (3) under provisional reporting form policies, full insurance on the property values last reported before loss.

This definition classifies coinsurance as an apportionment of losses, differentiates coinsurance from all other such apportionments, and is definite in scope.

---

[17] One such clause reads: "In consideration of the rate and form under which this policy is written, the company shall not be liable for a greater proportion of any loss than the amount hereby covered bears to $_____." Middle Department Association of Fire Underwriters Agreed Amount Endorsement (Form No. TE-22, edition date 6/59).

[18] Prentiss B. Reed and Paul I. Thomas, *Adjustment of Property Losses,* 3rd ed. (New York: McGraw-Hill Book Co., Inc., 1969), pp. 404–405. The full wording of these clauses, which do not always produce equivalent effects, is given on pages 49 and 56.

Coinsurance is an apportionment of losses between insurer and insured (not between insurers) according to a coinsurance apportionment ratio.[19] Although for the majority of insureds, who meet coinsurance requirements, this ratio is one (its maximum relevant value)—the insurer paying the whole loss—the loss still has been apportioned by the ratio of an amount of insurance to a determinable sum. All loss-participation clauses apportion losses between insurer and insured, but only coinsurance does so by an insurance to value (or to stated sum) ratio.[20]

In property insurance, a 90 percent coinsurance clause does *not* mean that the insurer pays only 90 percent of any loss. Instead, its liability depends on the ratio of insurance to 90 percent of value.

The coinsurance apportionment ratio applies "within other policy restrictions," such as the policy face, the amount of loss, any deductible, and any pro rata liability clause. An insurer never pays more than the face of its policy. Because no insured may collect more than the amount of his loss, an insured with 100 percent coverage subject to 80 percent coinsurance is not entitled to 125 percent of his loss even though his coinsurance apportionment ratio is 100/80. When coinsurance is subject to both percentage coinsurance and a per loss deductible, coinsurance is applied first, and then the deductible is subtracted[21] even though, as shown in Appendix 2, applying the deductible first would be more favorable to insureds who do not meet coinsurance requirements. Pro rata liability clauses in concurrent policies[22] generally apportion liability by the ratios of (1) amounts each policy would pay (its limit of liability) for the loss without contribution from

---

[19] Chapter 4 classifies coinsurance clauses by the components of this ratio.

[20] A pro rata distribution clause apportions coverage among properties by the ratios of their values only. A pro rata liability clause apportions losses among insurers by ratios of amounts of insurance only.

[21] *Guiding Principles—Casualty, Fidelity, Fire, Inland Marine—First-Party Property Losses and Claims* (New York: Association of Casualty and Surety Companies *et al.*, November 1, 1963), p. 16. This work is referred to as the *1963 Guiding Principles*.

[22] Concurrent policies are alike except for face amount, date, duration, insurer, coinsurance clauses, or deductibles. See *1963 Guiding Principles*, p. 37. Nonconcurrent apportionments involving coinsurance are discussed in Chapter 10 and Appendix 5.

other policies to (2) the sum of the limits of liability. Failure to meet a coinsurance requirement in one policy reduces its limit of liability and shifts more of the loss to other policies, until their limits of liability are reached. The losses of some insureds not meeting coinsurance requirements may be paid fully by contribution from other policies.

DEFINITION OF COINSURANCE CLAUSE

A coinsurance clause is any policy provision which establishes coinsurance as defined above. This definition gives a blanket term covering provisions sometimes labeled "average" clauses (under which the coinsurance apportionment ratio is the face of *one* policy divided by a percentage of value); "coinsurance" clauses (ratio equal to *all* insurance divided by a percentage of value); agreed amount endorsements (ratio equal to the face of one policy divided by a stated sum); full reporting clauses (ratio equal to value last reported divided by true value at time of report under provisional reporting form policies); a few other special provisions; and other clauses, virtually identical to the above, with various policy captions. All these clauses are described and classified in Chapter 4.

DEFINITION OF COINSURANCE REQUIREMENT

A coinsurance requirement is the least amount of insurance which raises to one the coinsurance apportionment ratio in a given coinsurance clause. This insurance may equal a percentage of value, a stated sum, or the true value at the date of the latest report under a provisional reporting form policy. When the coinsurance requirement is met, the coinsurance clause does not reduce indemnity for any loss.

DEFINITION OF COINSURANCE DEFICIENCY

A coinsurance deficiency is the amount by which a coinsurance requirement exceeds the insurance presently applicable to that requirement. For example, if a clause in a $70,000 policy binds the insurer to pay no greater portion of a loss than the ratio which "the amount hereby insured" bears to $100,000, the coinsurance deficiency is $30,000. The purchase of a concurrent $30,000 policy would not lessen the deficiency, because the second policy does not increase "the amount hereby insured" by the first. But, if the first policy had read ". . . the insurance on the property hereby insured . . .," the second policy would have removed the coinsurance deficiency under the first.

DEFINITION OF COINSURANCE PENALTY

A coinsurance penalty is the amount, greater than zero, by which an indemnity payment for a loss is reduced by the operation of a coinsurance clause. If no loss occurs when a coinsurance deficiency exists, no coinsurance penalty arises.

A coinsurance penalty equals the indemnity payment of a policy lacking a coinsurance clause minus the indemnity payment the same policy would make if subject to coinsurance. As illustrated by the four examples below, this definition implies that coinsurance penalties (1) rise until the loss equals the policy face, where the penalty reaches a maximum; (2) fall for larger losses; and (3) equal zero for losses equal to or greater than the coinsurance requirement.

Assume a $250,000 policy with a $300,000 coinsurance requirement imposed by a 75 percent coinsurance clause on coverage of a $400,000 building. For a $60,000 loss (which is less than the policy face), the coinsurance penalty is $10,000, because the full $60,000 would have been paid by a $300,000 policy, but only $50,000 (250/300 of $60,000) is paid by the $250,000 deficient policy. For a loss equaling the $250,000 policy face, only $208,-333.33 (250/300 of $250,000) is paid by the $250,000 policy, resulting in a $41,666.67 coinsurance penalty from the full loss which the $300,000 policy would pay. For a loss greater than the deficient policy's face, but less than the coinsurance requirement, say $270,000, the $250,000 policy pays $225,000 (250/300 of $270,000), while the $300,000 policy would pay the whole loss. Here, a $25,000 penalty results. For a loss equal to or greater than the $300,000 coinsurance requirement, the $250,000 policy pays its face, because 250/300 of $300,000 or more is at least the policy face. No coinsurance penalties are assessed for losses at least equal to a coinsurance requirement, because any deficient policy, with or without a coinsurance clause, pays its face.

DEFINITION OF COINSURER

A coinsurer is an insured who has failed to meet a coinsurance requirement, thus exposing himself to possible coinsurance penalties. He is a coinsurer of his property because he is providing more "self-insurance" than if he had met the coinsurance requirement.

A loss need not occur to make an insured with a coinsurance deficiency a coinsurer. Such an insured provides his own protection for the maximum coinsurance penalty—$41,666.67 in the previous example, or, in the general case where C replaces cV as the coinsurance requirement,

$$F \left(1 - \frac{F}{C} \right).$$

The insured provides his own protection even if no losses occur. For losses less than the coinsurance requirement, the insured with a coinsurance deficiency contributes the amount of the coinsurance penalty to the payment of his own loss. For losses not less than the coinsurance requirement, for which the face of the deficient policy is paid, the insured bears a portion of the loss, not as a coinsurer but as an insured with less than full coverage. As an insured with less than full coverage, he receives the full face amount of his policy for such large losses with or without a coinsurance clause. He is liable for no coinsurance penalties.

SUMMARY

This chapter defines coinsurance, coinsurance clause, coinsurance requirement, coinsurance deficiency, coinsurance penalty, and coinsurer for purposes of this study.

Coinsurance is an apportionment of losses between an insurer and its insured such that the insurer pays—within other restrictions stated in the policy or arising from the nature of property insurance—a fraction of each loss equal to the ratio (called the coinsurance apportionment ratio), not greater than one, of a designated amount of insurance to (1) a stated sum or (2) the whole, or a specified percentage, of the value of the insured property. The designated insurance may be (1) the face amount of the policy requiring coinsurance, (2) the total face amounts of the insured's applicable policies, or (3) under provisional reporting form policies, full insurance on the property values last reported before loss.

From the definition of coinsurance, the definitions of related terms follow directly. A coinsurance clause is any policy provision which establishes coinsurance as defined above. A coinsurance requirement is the least amount of insurance which raises to one the coinsurance apportionment ratio in a given coinsurance clause. A coinsurance deficiency is the amount by which a coinsurance requirement exceeds the insurance presently applicable to that requirement. A coinsurance penalty is the amount, greater than zero, by which an indemnity payment for a loss is reduced by the operation of a coinsurance clause. A coinsurer is an insured who has failed to meet a coinsurance requirement, thus exposing himself to possible coinsurance penalties. He is a coinsurer of his *property*, not necessarily of every *loss*.

CHAPTER 4

Classification and Mechanics of Coinsurance Clauses

PURPOSE

This chapter classifies coinsurance clauses, regardless of their policy captions, by the components of their coinsurance apportionment ratios, tracing these ratios' effects on the insured's indemnity payment and the distribution of liability among insurers.

The classification of coinsurance clauses presented in this chapter should dispel some of the confusion about the differences between provisions captioned "Coinsurance Clause" and those titled "Average Clause." To clear the ground for discussion of these differences, those meanings of average and of average clause which have no relevance to insurance to value should first be put aside.

THE MEANINGS OF AVERAGE AND OF AVERAGE CLAUSE

In maritime insurance, average, according to one authority, means *contribution* to a total or partial loss.[1] Another authority

---

[1] Cornelius Walford, *The Insurance Cyclopaedia* (London: Charles and Edwin Layton, 1871), vol. I, p. 224.

states that average means a *partial* loss itself.[2] Average clause was once widely synonymous with pro rata distribution clause,[3] and the term has been used in this sense by some modern writers.[4] But, according to modern usage, a pro rata distribution clause apportions coverage in a blanket policy among the properties insured in proportion to their values. Average clauses once were distinguished from pro rata contribution clauses—both of which stipulate a percentage of value coinsurance requirement—on the grounds that only pro rata contribution clauses contain (1) a recital of legal consideration given the insured for accepting coinsurance and (2) a passage prorating liability among policies by their face amounts.[5] Pro rata liability now is provided for elsewhere in most policies, and only one overruled court decision[6] holds that an insurer waives contribution from other policies by not specifying pro rata liability in a coinsurance provision. Since recital of consideration is rarely significant, no important distinctions between these two coinsurance clauses exist. As explained below, this study classifies both average clauses and pro rata contribution clauses as policy to percentage of value coinsurance clauses.

---

[2] William D. Winter, *Marine Insurance, Its Principles and Practices*, 2nd ed. (New York: McGraw-Hill Book Co., Inc., 1953), p. 2.

[3] *Dahms & Sons Company v. German Fire Insurance Company*, 153 Iowa 168, 132 N.W. 870 (1911), at 872.

[4] See George Richards, *Law of Insurance*, ed. Rowland H. Long, 4th ed. (New York: Baker, Voorhis & Co., 1932), p. 352; John Allan Appleman, *Insurance Law and Practice* (Kansas City, Mo.: Vernon Law Book Co., 1942), vol. VI, p. 223; Robert Riegel and H. J. Loman, *Insurance Principles and Practices*, rev. ed. (New York: Prentice-Hall, Inc., 1942), p. 371; and Philip Gordis, *Property and Casualty Insurance, A Guide Book for Agents and Brokers*, 4th ed., rev. (Indianapolis, Ind.: The Rough Notes Co., Inc., 1956), p. 50.

[5] William N. Bament, "Co-Insurance," an address to the Insurance Society of New York, March 30, 1920, p. 11.

[6] *Buse v. National Ben Franklin Insurance Company of Pittsburgh, Pa.*, 164 N.Y.S. 1088, 123 N.E. 858 (1916). To the contrary are *Farmers' Feed Company v. Scottish Union and National Insurance Company*, 173 N.Y. 241, 65 N.E. 1105 (1903); *Stephenson v. Agricultural Insurance Company*, 116 Wis. 277, 93 N.W. 19 (1903); *Commodity Credit Corporation v. American Equitable Assurance Company*, 198 Ark. 1160, 133 S.W. (2d) 443 (1939); and *Aetna Insurance Company v. Eisenberg*, 188 F. Supp. 415 (1960).

BASIS FOR CLASSIFICATION OF
COINSURANCE CLAUSES

A coinsurance clause can be classified by the numerator or denominator of its apportionment ratio or, as in Table 3, cross-
classified by both numerator and denominator. Possible numerators—(1) the face of one policy, (2) the insured's total applicable
insurance, or (3) the value last reported before loss under a provisional reporting form policy—are listed across the top of Table
3. Alternative denominators—coinsurance requirements of (1) a

TABLE 3. Classification of coinsurance clauses by the numerator and denominator of their coinsurance apportionment ratios

Denominator of Ratio	Numerator of Ratio		
	Policy Face	Total Insurance	Value Last Reported
Stated amount	Policy to stated amount	Insurance to stated amount	Not found in practice
Percentage of value	Policy to percentage of value	Insurance to percentage of value	Value reported to percentage of value

stated amount or (2) a percentage of value—are given at the left
side of Table 3. The cells contain suggested descriptive titles
of coinsurance clauses. With three exceptions,[7] all coinsurance
clauses seem to fit into one of the cells of Table 3. The remaining sections of this chapter correspond to the organization of
Table 3.

---

[7] The institutional property form, the open stock burglary policy, and
Iowa fire insurance contracts issued before 1955 contain coinsurance requirements which may be either a stated amount or a percentage of value,
as explained on pages 53, 51, and 58.

CLAUSES WITH NUMERATOR
EQUALING POLICY FACE

Denominator Equaling Stated Amount

One example of a policy to stated amount coinsurance clause is:

In consideration of the rate and form under which this policy is written, this company shall not be liable for a greater proportion of any loss than the *amount hereby covered* bears to $———.[8]

Generally, a clause with this coinsurance apportionment ratio is captioned "Agreed Amount (or Guaranteed Amount) Endorsement."

The operation of this clause is shown by a formula (in which the agreed amount is designated A) for indemnity under a policy which limits the insurer's liability by only the loss, the policy face, and the agreed amount endorsement. This indemnity equation is:

$$I \leqq \frac{F}{A} L \qquad (4\text{-}1)$$

subject to

$$I \leqq L \qquad (1\text{-}2)$$

and

$$I \leqq F. \qquad (1\text{-}3)$$

Specifically, if the agreed amount is $300,000, a $275,000 policy pays $55,000 of a $60,000 loss. For a loss of $300,000 or more, this policy pays its face.

The fact that this coinsurance requirement is a stated sum—usually set at full property value after the insurer's, or other authoritative, appraisal[9]—makes a policy to stated amount clause

---

[8] Clause captioned "Agreed Amount Endorsement" in Middle Department Association of Fire Underwriters Form No. TE-22 (edition date 6/59). Emphasis supplied.

[9] Interview with John B. Davis, Assistant Vice President, Insurance Company of North America, December 22, 1966.

the easiest coinsurance clause for the insured to fulfill.[10] Only by error would the policy face differ from the coinsurance requirement. If the property value rises during the policy period, the insurer assumes the risk of inadequate premiums; losses up to the policy face are paid fully. Agreed amount endorsements, however, are attached to property damage policies only where valuation difficulties, competition, or the insured's bargaining power require them (see pages 156–57).

Denominator Equaling Percentage of Insurable Value

The following provision, mandatory in New York State fire policies subject to coinsurance, illustrates a policy to percentage of value coinsurance clause.

This Company shall not be liable for a greater proportion of any loss or damage to the property described herein than *the sum hereby insured bears to the percentage* specified on the first page of this policy (or endorsed thereon) *of the actual cash value* of such property at the time such loss shall happen, nor for more than the proportion which this policy bears to the total insurance thereon.

In the event that the aggregate claim for any loss is both less than $10,000 and less than 5% of the total amount of insurance upon the property described herein at the time such loss occurs, no special inventory or appraisement of the undamaged property shall be required, provided, however, that nothing herein shall be construed to waive application of the first paragraph of this clause.

If the insurance under this policy be divided into two or more items, the foregoing shall apply to each item separately.[11]

---

[10] P. D. Betterley, *Buying Insurance, A Problem of Business Management* (New York: McGraw-Hill Book Co., Inc., 1936), p. 105.

[11] "New York Standard Coinsurance Clause," Form No. 819, New York Fire Insurance Rating Organization, *General Rules* (New York: The Organization, loose-leaf, revised and supplemented periodically), p. 20, effective August 2, 1965. Emphasis supplied. Strictly, only that part of the first paragraph before the comma is a coinsurance clause. The last part of the first paragraph prorates liability among insurers, as discussed on page 40. The second paragraph (a waiver of undamaged inventory) and the third paragraph (applying the coinsurance requirement to each item of insurance in a policy with more than one item) are treated on pages 169–70 and Appendix 5, respectively.

Some writers call a *policy* to percentage of value clause an "average" clause—or a "pro rata contribution" clause if, as in New York, the clause also prorates liability among insurers. For these writers, a "coinsurance" clause is an *insurance* to percentage of value coinsurance clause, under which all the insured's applicable coverage can be used to meet a coinsurance requirement in one policy.[12] The discussion on pages 00 and 00 and in Appendix 5 points out how "coinsurance" clauses can be more liberal to insureds than "average" clauses.

The indemnity formula for a policy to percentage of value coinsurance clause (c percent of value, V) is:

$$I \leqq \frac{F}{cV} L \qquad (4\text{-}2)$$

subject to

$$I \leqq L \qquad (1\text{-}2)$$

and

$$I \leqq F \qquad (1\text{-}3)$$

on the assumption that the amount of loss and the policy face are the only other limitations on indemnity. Thus, an 80 percent policy to value clause in a $500,000 policy on a $750,000 risk implies a $600,000 coinsurance requirement. For a $100,000 loss, the policy pays $83,333.33, or 500/600 of any loss less than the coinsurance requirement. The policy face is paid for larger losses.

Any coinsurance requirement expressed as a percentage of value makes the insured responsible for maintaining insurance to value as values change. If rising values cause a coinsurance deficiency, coinsurance penalties keep the insurer's premium income

---

[12] "Average Clause: A clause providing that the insurer shall be liable in the event of loss for not more than that proportion of the loss which the amount of *insurance under the policy* bears to a specified percentage of the *actual cash value* of the property insured." "Coinsurance Clause: A clause providing that the insured shares in losses in the proportion that *his* insurance is less than a specified percentage of the *value* of the property insured." See *Dictionary of Insurance Terms* (Washington, D.C.: Insurance Department of the Chamber of Commerce of the United States, 1949), pp. 8 and 15. Emphasis supplied. The use of "actual cash value" in one definition and "value" in the other is not a significant distinction.

balanced with its expected indemnity payments, but the insured's losses are not fully restored. In contrast, under stated amount coinsurance requirements, rising values threaten the adequacy of the insurer's premium income, but losses up to the policy face are paid fully. The type of coinsurance requirement determines who primarily bears the adverse effects of underinsurance: the insurer through inadequate premium income or the insured through coinsurance penalties. This is true whether one, or more than one, policy can be applied toward the coinsurance requirement.

Clauses with Alternative Ratios

Depending on the circumstances of a loss, the coinsurance clause in an open stock burglary policy or a public and institutional property form can be either a policy to stated amount or policy to percentage of value coinsurance clause.

Open Stock Burglary Clause. This clause typically reads:

The company shall not be liable for a greater proportion of a loss of merchandise, exclusive of jewelry and of property held by the insured as a pledge or as collateral, than the limit of insurance stated in the declarations bears to (a) the *coinsurance percentage,* as stated in the declarations, *of the actual cash value* of all such merchandise contained within the premises at time of loss, or (b) the *coinsurance limit* stated in the declarations, *whichever is less.*[13]

If the coinsurance percentage of the value of covered property is not more than the stated amount of the coinsurance limit, the above clause is a policy to percentage of value coinsurance clause, under which losses are paid according to Equation 4–2. For larger inventories, the coinsurance limit (designated B) is the coinsurance requirement. The indemnity formula becomes:

$$I \leq \frac{F}{B} L, \qquad (4\text{–}3)$$

again subject to

---

[13] "Coinsurance" clause, Open Stock Burglary Policy, in *Study Kit for Students of Insurance—Casualty, Fire, Marine, Life* (Chicago: American Mutual Insurance Alliance), p. 122. Emphasis supplied.

$$I \leqq L \qquad\qquad (1\text{–}2)$$

and

$$I \leqq F. \qquad\qquad (1\text{–}3)$$

Equation 4–3 is Equation 4–1 with the coinsurance limit substituted for the conceptually equivalent agreed amount.

To illustrate, for an undertaker in Bucks County, Pennsylvania —for whom the coinsurance limit is $7500[14] and the coinsurance percentage is 60 percent[15]—the coinsurance limit is the coinsurance requirement only if his inventory (exclusive of jewelry and pledged property) exceeds $12,500 ($7500/0.6). A $3000 policy on $13,000 of covered inventory pays $2000 for a $5000 loss (3000/7500 of $5000). The $7500 coinsurance limit, less than 60 percent of $13,000, applies. The same policy would pay $2083.33 for a $5000 loss if the covered inventory were $12,000 (3000/7200 of $5000) because the coinsurance requirement is 60 percent of $12,000 (or $7200), less than the $7500 coinsurance limit. A policy at least equal to the coinsurance limit eliminates all coinsurance penalties, because such a policy at least equals the lesser of the coinsurance limit or any percentage (up to 100 percent) of any inventory.

The coinsurance limit is one standard of insurance to value[16] against open stock burglary, because underwriters reason that the value of the goods subject to one burglary is limited to the amount of the coinsurance limit by the portability of the goods, their unit value, and other factors, all of which are independent of the size of the inventory. In contrast, most physical damage perils—for which a percentage of value usually is the only measure of insurance to value—can consume virtually the whole property. Inventories less than the coinsurance limit also are subject to total burglary loss; for such inventories, a percentage of value also is insurance to value.[17]

---

[14] *Burglary Insurance Manual* (New York: National Bureau of Casualty Underwriters, 1958), p. 326.

[15] *Ibid.*, Pennsylvania Territorial Pages, p. 1.

[16] The amount of insurance assumed in the premium rate calculation.

[17] This paragraph is based on C. A. Kulp and John W. Hall, *Casualty Insurance*, 4th ed. (New York: The Ronald Press Co., 1968), pp. 629–633.

Public and Institutional Property Form Clause.   This coinsurance clause usually reads:

(A) This Company shall not be liable for a greater proportion of any loss, occurring after the inception date of this policy and prior to [expiration date of this clause] than the amount of *insurance under this policy* bears to $............

(B) If the expiration date set forth in the immediately preceding Paragraph (A) is not extended by endorsement, then in the event of loss occurring thereafter, this Company shall not be liable for a greater proportion of such loss than the amount of *insurance under this policy* bears to *90% of the actual cash value* of the property described herein at the time of loss.[18]

For a loss occurring before Paragraph A, as extended, expires, this clause is a policy to stated amount coinsurance clause. The insured is unlikely to incur a coinsurance penalty because, after appraisal, the insurer and insured have agreed on the coverage necessary for insurance to value. Losses after Paragraph A has expired are paid subject to a 90 percent policy to value clause. A coinsurance penalty is more likely here because Paragraph B becomes effective only after the insurer and insured have failed to agree on the amount of coverage needed under Paragraph A. The high 90 percent requirement in Paragraph B, subjecting the insured to coinsurance penalties even if he seeks full coverage but underestimates values by only 10 percent, presumably encourages the insured to agree with the insurer on appropriate coverage for an extension of Paragraph A.

CLAUSES WITH NUMERATORS EQUALING APPLICABLE INSURANCE

Contrast with Preceding Clauses

Insurance to percentage of value (or to stated amount) coinsurance clauses may give the insured more complete indemnity than do *policy* to percentage of value (or to stated amount) coin-

---

[18] Public and Institutional Property Form No. 1, Section II, Paragraphs (A) and (B), March, 1962. Emphasis supplied. The "90%" in Paragraph (B) is mandatory.

surance clauses. The apportionment of liability among insurers may differ according to whether one, or more than one, policy may be applied toward a coinsurance requirement.

Concurrent policies[19] share losses in the ratios of their face amounts, but no policy pays more than the least limit imposed by its face, its coinsurance provision, or any other restriction.[20] For example, two concurrent policies—with $5000 and $15,000 face amounts, neither subject to coinsurance—pay one-fourth and three-fourths, respectively, of losses not more than $20,000. If the $15,000 policy is subject to a $30,000 coinsurance requirement under a 60 percent *policy* to percentage of value clause on a $50,000 property, it is liable for no more than 15/30 of any loss. For a $20,000 loss, three-fourths of which is prorated to the $15,000 policy, this policy pays $10,000 (its limit of liability for the whole loss under its coinsurance clause). The one-fourth of the loss prorated to the $5000 policy exhausts its face, and the two policies together pay $15,000 for the $20,000 loss.

If the $15,000 policy had been subject to a 60 percent *insurance* to percentage of value clause (with both policies, totaling $20,000, applied to its $30,000 coinsurance requirement), the $15,000 policy would have been liable for up to 20/30 of the loss under its coinsurance requirement. The loss would have been apportioned between the policies as before, and the $5000 policy would have paid its face to meet its one-fourth share. Although the $15,000 policy would have been apportioned three-fourths of the loss, its liability, subject to coinsurance, would not have exceeded two-thirds of the loss, or $13,333.33. In all, the insured would have received $18,333.33 instead of $15,000. Substituting the so-called

---

[19] Concurrent policies are alike except for face amount, date, duration, insurer, deductibles, or coinsurance clauses. See *Guiding Principles— Casualty, Fidelity, Inland Marine—First Party Property Losses and Claims* (New York: Association of Casualty and Surety Companies *et al.,* November 1, 1963), p. 37. Nonconcurrent apportionments are discussed in Chapter 10 and Appendix 5.

[20] Prentiss B. Reed and Paul I. Thomas, *Adjustment of Property Losses,* 3rd ed. (New York: McGraw-Hill Book Co., Inc., 1969), p. 410. Restrictions other than the policy face, the loss, and coinsurance clauses are ignored in this study.

"coinsurance" clause for the so-called "average" clause here increases the insured's indemnity by raising the liability of the policy with the "coinsurance" clause, even though the policies are concurrent.[21]

Denominator Equaling Stated Amount

One of the rare examples of an insurance to stated amount coinsurance clause is the "Maintenance Clause" used by one perpetual fire insurer:

It is agreed and understood that at the time of a loss there shall not be less than \$_____ *concurrent insurance* on the Building, failing in which the Assured shall become a coinsurer to the amount of such deficiency.[22]

Since only by error would an insurer issue a policy for less than the (usually) full property value stated in the clause, other insurance normally would be pointless.

But, granted such an error, the formula for the idemnity paid by the gth policy containing an insurance to stated amount coinsurance clause, for a loss to which n other policies concurrent with the gth policy apply, is

$$I_g \leq \left(\frac{\sum_1^n F}{A_g} \right) L \tag{4-4}$$

---

[21] This example demonstrates that the statement of one source—that "the effect of the clause is the same whether called Coinsurance, Contribution, or Average"—need not be true. The source quoted is "Coinsurance, Contribution or Average Clause," *Rough Notes Monthly Policy, Form, and Manual Analyses* (Indianapolis, Ind.: The Rough Notes Co., Inc., August 1963), Fire: File 133.1, p. 1. Similar views are stated or implied in Laurence E. Falls, "Coinsurance," *Best's Insurance News, Fire and Casualty Edition*, vol. XLIX, no. 6 (October 1948), p. 26; Albert H. Mowbray and Ralph H. Blanchard, *Insurance, Its Theory and Practice in the United States*, 5th ed. (New York: McGraw-Hill Book Co., Inc., 1961), p. 83, n. 4; and E. J. Sloan, "The Average and 80% Clauses of Fire Insurance Policies," *Proceedings of the Insurance Institute of Hartford* (Hartford, Conn.: The Institute, 1908–1909), vol. I, p. 71.

[22] Material accompanying letter from Edwin C. Miller, Assistant Treasurer, Philadelphia Contributionship for the Insurance of Houses from Loss by Fire, August 6, 1965. Emphasis supplied.

subject to

$$I_g \leqq L \left(\frac{F_g}{\sum\limits_{1}^{n} F} \right) \qquad (1\text{-}2a)$$

and

$$I_g \leqq F_g. \qquad (1\text{-}3a)$$

Equation 1–2a recognizes the proration of losses among concurrent policies in the ratios of their face amounts.

Standing alone, a $200,000 policy with a $300,000 insurance to stated amount coinsurance clause pays only $40,000 for a $60,000 loss. But, if a $50,000 concurrent policy, not subject to coinsurance, also is liable for the loss, the coinsurance apportionment ratio in the $200,000 policy is raised to 250/300, giving this policy a liability of $50,000 for the whole loss if it stood alone. However, one-fifth (50/250) of the the loss is prorated to the $50,000 policy, which pays this $12,000 share. The $200,000 policy pays the remaining $48,000, its pro rata liability, which is less than its coinsurance clause liability.

Denominator Equaling Percentage of Value

The insurance to percentage of value coinsurance clause used in fire policies in the four states served by the South-Eastern Underwriters Association[23] is very similar to the following clause now in fire contracts used throughout the twenty Western Actuarial Bureau states:[24]

In consideration of the rate and/or form under which this policy is written, it is expressly stipulated and made a condition of this contract that the Insured shall at all times maintain *contributing insurance* on each item of property covered by this policy to the extent of at least the *percentage* specified on the first page of this policy *of the actual cash value* at the time of the loss, and that, failing to do so,

---

[23] Letter from R. L. Gatewood, Secretary, South-Eastern Underwriters Association, December 14, 1966. Table 27, p. 124, lists these states.
[24] Letter from Edwin N. Searl, General Manager, Western Actuarial Bureau, April 28, 1967. Table 27, p. 124, lists these states.

the Insured shall to the extent of such deficit bear his, her or their proportion of any loss.[25]

If c_g is the coinsurance percentage in the gth policy containing an insurance to percentage of value coinsurance clause, for a loss covered by n such concurrent policies, the gth policy will pay

$$I_g \leqq \left(\frac{\sum\limits_1^n F}{c_g V} \right) L \qquad (4\text{--}5)$$

subject to

$$I_g \leqq L \left(\frac{F_g}{\sum\limits_1^n F} \right) \qquad (1\text{--}2a)$$

and

$$I_g \leqq F_g. \qquad (1\text{--}3a)$$

The latter two constraints stipulate that no policy pays more than its share of the loss prorated by policy face or more than its own face.

The insured's greater flexibility in meeting coinsurance requirements in insurance to percentage of value, as opposed to policy to percentage of value, coinsurance clauses appears in the case of a $500,000 risk insured for $300,000 subject to an 80 percent coinsurance clause. If this clause is a *policy* to value clause, the insured must increase this policy by $100,000 in order to avoid coinsurance penalties. But with an *insurance* to value provision, if, for any reason, the insured is unable or unwilling to increase the face of one policy, he may buy another policy for $100,000 and be free of coinsurance penalties. The additional $100,000 policy may lack a coinsurance clause or may, for example, contain an insurance to percentage of value clause specifying up to 80 percent coverage. If both are subject to coinsurance, each of the policies would make up the other's coinsurance de-

---

[25] Form No. 38, captioned "Coinsurance Clause," Illinois Inspection and Rating Bureau, *Illinois Rule Book* (*Excluding Cook County*), (Chicago: The Bureau, loose-leaf, revised and supplemented periodically), p. 22, effective January 5, 1953. Emphasis supplied.

ficiency, share losses on a 75–25 basis, and, together, pay in full any loss up to $400,000.

A Clause with Alternative Ratios

The coinsurance clause which Iowa statute required until 1955[26] in all real property fire policies subject to coinsurance seems to be the only modern clause which could be either an insurance to stated amount or insurance to percentage of value coinsurance clause. The insurer and insured agreed, presumably before the policy was issued, on the type of coinsurance requirement. This superseded clause read:

In consideration of the acceptance by the insured of a reduction in premiums from the established rate of ...... per cent. to ...... per cent. it is hereby agreed that the insured shall maintain insurance during the life of this policy upon the property insured:
1. To the extent of .... dollars, or
2. To the extent of at least ...... per cent. of the actual cash value thereof at the time of the fire (whichever may be agreed upon) and, that failing to do so, the insured shall be a co-insurer to the extent of the deficit.[27]

In operation, this clause would be no different from those illustrated by Equations 4–4 and 4–5. But the Iowa clause allowed the insured and insurer more freedom than do most policy provisions prescribed by law.

CLAUSES WITH NUMERATORS EQUALING VALUE LAST REPORTED

The only coinsurance clauses with apportionment ratios in which the numerator is the value last reported are in provisional reporting form policies. As explained below, these policies, designed to insure fluctuating values, lack face amounts, the limit of

---

[26] In 1955, the mandatory wording was removed from the statute. See *Insurance Law Index Service,* ed. Leonard S. McCombs (Jenkintown, Pa.: McCombs & Co., Inc., supplemented monthly), "Iowa" section, p. 58.10.
[27] *Iowa Code,* 1948, section 515:11, as quoted in *Cyclopedia of Insurance in the United States,* ed. F. S. MacKay (Paterson, N.J.: The Index Publishing Co., 1965), p. 696.

coverage being based on the value last reported by the insured to the insurer. In order to encourage full reports of values, from which an adequate premium can be computed, these policies contain a coinsurance clause binding the insurer to pay no greater portion of any loss than the value last reported bears to the true value of covered property on the reporting date. Thus, the coinsurance requirement is 100 percent of protected values, whose fluctuations make a stated amount coinsurance requirement unworkable.

Mechanics of Provisional Reporting Form Policies[28]

Since policies with fixed face amounts are unsuited to properties (such as inventories) whose values change swiftly—the insured nearly always being forced to carry redundant or less than full coverage—periodic reporting forms have no face amounts. The insured reports regularly (usually monthly) the description and value of his covered property at each location and the amount and terms of specific insurance[29] on such property. The reporting form's limit of liability at each location is based on the excess of the reported values over the indicated specific insurance at that location, but is somewhat greater than this excess in order to insure fully any normal increase in values until the next report is due.[30] This limit of liability per location, together with a limit per loss, safeguards the insurer from unforeseeably large losses.

Premiums are based on reports of past values less specific insurance—even if reported values exceed limits of liability. The provisional premium paid when coverage begins is adjusted to reflect reported values. In order for the insurer's premium income to be adequate, the insured must give prompt reports which do not understate covered values or overstate specific insurance. A

---

[28] The material under this heading is taken from "Reporting Forms—General Principles," *The Fire, Casualty and Surety Bulletins* (Cincinnati, Ohio: The National Underwriter Company, loose-leaf, revised and supplemented periodically), Miscellaneous Fire, pp. Gd-1 through Gd-7, rearranged and reprinted at various dates between November 1949 and February 1962.

[29] In this context, specific insurance is coverage not written on a provisional reporting form (i.e., insurance with a fixed face amount).

[30] Locations acquired between reports also are covered up to certain limits.

frequent policy provision, reducing the insurer's limit of liability at any location to the values last reported (less specific insurance) at that location—without the additional coverage for normal increases of value given when reports are prompt—motivates insureds with rising values to report as required (usually within thirty days after the end of each month).[31] A coinsurance clause, usually called a "full reporting clause," discourages false reports.

Coinsurance in Provisional Reporting Form Policies

One of the most common full reporting clauses reads:

Liability under this policy shall not in any case exceed that proportion of loss (meaning the loss as provided in the Excess Clause at the location involved), which the *last reported value* filed prior to the loss, less the amount of specific insurance reported, if any, at the location where any loss occurs bears to the *total actual cash value* less the amount of specific insurance, if any, at that location *on the date for which report is made. . . .*[32]

The "loss as provided in the Excess Clause at the location involved" is the loss unpaid after specific insurance (to which the reporting form is excess) has exhausted its limit of liability.

The indemnity formula for a full reporting clause requires some new notation. Subscripts r and s distinguish the indemnity payments and policy faces of the reporting form and the specific policies, respectively. VLR denotes value last reported—the value of insured property at the location of the loss as last reported by the insured prior to the loss. V^* is the true value of the insured property at that location on the date for which the last report was made. The reporting form pays no more than

$$I_r \leq \left(\frac{(VLR) - F_s}{V^* - F_s}\right)(L - I_s). \qquad (4\text{-}6)$$

---

[31] The prospect of lower premiums presumably prompts insureds with falling values to report on time. Some policies suspend all coverage while tardy reports are outstanding or condition the return of excess provisional premium on timely filing. Special rules apply to tardiness of the first report.

[32] "Full Reporting Clause," Reporting Form "A" (M.L. 10), in *Sample Insurance Policies for Property and Liability Coverages* (New York: Insurance Information Institute), p. 86. Emphasis supplied. The omitted portion of the clause concerns newly acquired locations.

The sum of all indemnity payments must not exceed the loss, and no policy pays more than the least of its limits of liability.

As an example in which the reporting form's limits of liability per loss and per location play no part, assume an insured promptly but falsely reports values at one location as $120,000 when true values are $180,000. He correctly reports a $30,000 applicable specific policy. Assume that, for a $50,000 loss, the specific (primary) coverage has paid $20,000. The reporting form pays no greater portion of the $30,000 excess loss than the values which the reporting form insurer thought were covered by its policy at the reporting date are of the values actually insured by that policy at that time. The reporting form insurer thought it covered $90,000, or the false $120,000 value minus the true $30,000 specific policy. Actually, the reporting form protected $150,000, or the true $180,000 value less the true $30,000 specific policy. Thus the reporting form policy pays no more than 90/150 of $30,000, or $18,000. Together with the $20,000 from the specific policy, this payment leaves a $12,000 coinsurance penalty for the insured.

A full reporting clause invokes its 100 percent coinsurance requirement at the date for which the last report filed prior to the loss is made, rather than at the time of the loss or at the time of the last report filed prior to the insurer's payment of the loss.[33] Because of fluctuating values, the insurer does not expect the insured to match a fixed policy face to a percentage of value at time of loss. But the insured is expected to report true values regularly and to pay for full insurance on existing values. In return, the insurer pays fully any loss—up to the least of the policy's limits of liability—even though values may have increased since the last report.

SUMMARY

After explaining the various meanings of average and of average clause, this chapter describes the mechanics of coinsurance clauses, which can be classified by the numerators and denomina-

---

[33] For discussion of reports before and after loss, see *Commonwealth Insurance Company v. O. Henry Tent and Awning Company*, 287 Fed. (2d) 316 (1961).

tors of their coinsurance apportionment ratios. Numerators may equal the face of one policy, all applicable insurance, or—under provisional reporting form policies—values last reported prior to loss. Denominators (coinsurance requirements) may equal a stated sum or a percentage of value at time of loss (or at time of the last provisional reporting form report). All combinations of numerators and denominators are used except stated amounts with provisional reporting forms. Also, a few clauses provide that either a stated amount or a percentage of value is the coinsurance requirement, depending on the circumstances of a loss.

When the coinsurance requirement is a stated amount, usually set equal to the full appraised property value, coinsurance penalties are very unlikely because the policy face should equal the stated sum. With a percentage of value coinsurance requirement, coinsurance penalties are more likely because the insured must determine the changing property value to which the coinsurance requirement is applied. With a provisional reporting form policy, usually covering property with rapidly fluctuating value, the insured may avoid coinsurance penalties by promptly and accurately reporting full values and other insurance.

CHAPTER 5

Purposes of Coinsurance

PURPOSE

This chapter examines how coinsurance achieves the purposes which various writers have assigned to it. This study has noted at several points that coinsurance should balance each insured's pure premiums with his expected indemnity payments for coverage not exceeding his policy's coinsurance requirement. This balance is, in turn, a step toward other objectives, which have been described as (1) promoting equity among insureds; (2) safeguarding the adequacy of the insurer's premium income; (3) prompting reasonably full insurance for covered property; (4) establishing a more scientific premium rate structure; (5) fixing responsibility for maintaining insurance to value; and (6) improving the sales appeal of a policy. This chapter treats these objectives in the above order.

PROMOTING EQUITY AMONG INSUREDS

A very direct statement of the equity objective is the following:

The requirement of coinsurance is closely related to premium rates. The intent of the clause is to maintain equity between different policyholders, all paying the same rate for insurance.[1]

---

[1] Allen L. Mayerson, *Introduction to Insurance* (New York: The Macmillan Co., 1962), p. 224. Much the same thought is expressed in Frank Joseph Angell, *Insurance Principles and Practices* (New York: The Ronald

With a precise definition of equity among insureds, the effect of coinsurance on equity becomes clear. The Merritt Committee, in relating property insurance without coinsurance to flat assessment life insurance, provided a key to defining equity. The Committee noted that the same life insurance premium rate charged those aged thirty and those aged eighty includes a subsidy from the younger to the older which, if large, tends to drive away younger insureds. The premium rate once adequate for a balanced age group then becomes inadequate for those of advanced age and high mortality. The Committee drew this parallel:

> The principle is exactly the same in fire insurance. If a man who carries 80 per cent of insurance is charged the same rate as a man who carries only 30 per cent the effect is that the man who carries 80 per cent will be helping to pay for the hazard of him who carries only 30 per cent, and still more to the point that the tendency would be, under this unfair arrangement, for men to refuse to insure for the larger amount.[2]

In the Committee's view, life insurance premium rates are equitable if each class of insureds, grouped by age and condition of health, bears its own "hazard." This study adopts an analogous definition of equitable property insurance rates: Pure premium rates are equitable if each insured, grouped with others with like properties *insured to the same extent,* pays a periodic pure premium which is the same percentage of expected indemnity payments during the period for every other insured. For each insured, the ratio of expected indemnity payments to pure premiums is a constant, k. For the ith insured,

$$\frac{E(I)_i}{P_i} = k. \tag{5-1}$$

Press Co., 1959), p. 88; P. D. Betterley, *Buying Insurance, A Problem of Business Management* (New York: McGraw-Hill Book Co., Inc., 1936), p. 105; and Philip Gordis, *Property and Casualty Insurance, A Guidebook for Agents and Brokers,* 14th ed. (Indianapolis, Ind.: The Rough Notes Co., Inc., 1967), p. 48.

2 *Report of the Joint Committee of the Senate and Assembly of the State of New York, Appointed to Investigate Corrupt Practices in Connection with Legislation, and the Affairs of Insurance Companies, Other Than Those Doing Life Insurance Business,* Assembly Document No. 30 (Albany, N.Y., February 1, 1911), p. 86.

Equitable pure premium rates may be inadequate to pay losses ($k > 1$) or may be excessive ($k < 1$), but equity among insureds requires only that each insured be undercharged or overcharged in the same proportion relative to his expected indemnity payments. For pure premium rates to be just adequate for each insured, k equals one. Thus,

$$\frac{E(I)_i}{P_i} = 1 \qquad (5\text{-}2)$$

implies equity for all insureds and just adequate pure premium income for the entire insurance operation. Aggregate pure premium adequacy,

$$E(I) = P, \qquad (5\text{-}3)$$

follows from the summation of each insured's Equation 5–2.[3]

The equitable effects of coinsurance can be seen by comparing two essentially identical properties insured against sprinkler leakage subject to a 25 percent coinsurance clause at equal 25 percent coinsurance premium rates. The owner of Risk A is insured for exactly the stipulated percentage, but the owner of Risk B, insured for 10 percent of value, has paid only two-fifths (0.10/0.25) the premium paid by the owner of Risk A. Assume that equally severe losses occur to each property. If the losses are less than 25 percent of each property's value, Owner B, by the terms of his coinsurance clause, receives only two-fifths the full indemnity paid Owner A. If the loss equals or exceeds 25 percent of each property's value, each owner receives the face amount of his policy (the coinsurance clause no longer limiting indemnity), but Owner B again gets only two-fifths the sum paid Owner A. Regardless of the unpredictable occurrence of specific losses or

---

[3] These equity and adequacy conditions apply only to pure premiums—gross premiums less allowances for operating expenses, contingencies, and profit. Gross premium rate equity and adequacy can be defined by the same types of equations in which some factor is added (1) to $E(I)$ in order to account for each insured's fair share of expenses, etc., and (2) to P in order to account for each insured's expected service benefits, other than indemnity payments, from the insurer. Since expense allocation, adequate contingency reserves, and suitable profit margins are beyond the scope of this study, gross premium equity and adequacy are not defined precisely here.

of their size, each insured, paying the same premium rate for insurance on equally hazardous property covered for no more than the coinsurance requirement, has the same expected indemnity for each dollar of pure premium when coverage begins. In terms of *expected* values, each receives the same return per dollar of pure premium.

If some insured buys more coverage than the coinsurance clause requires, the pure premium rate he pays is inequitably high because rates should fall with larger policy faces (see Equation 2–4). Coinsurance does not increase indemnity paid to the overinsured; it only reduces indemnity to the underinsured. Therefore, policyholders insured to full value should have available a 100 percent coinsurance requirement at a premium rate lower than any other coinsurance rate.

Some writers have maintained that coinsurance achieves equity only if losses occur, actual indemnity, rather than expected indemnity, being the measure of equity. For example:

Since the coinsurance penalty, if any, applies only after a loss, it is by definition a less equitable device for distributing the cost of loss through insurance than any device that operates through the rate structure, since it hits only those who have been caught. The great majority of property owners who have not had losses but who have contributed just as surely to an undesirable underwriting situation have not contributed a penny.[4]

Coinsurance is not a perfect device for preventing the inequity which occurs when the individual policyholder's ratio of insurance to value does not bear inversely upon its premium rate. In the situation above, only 21 of the 1,000 insureds which had violated their coinsurance agreements were in any way penalized therefor. All the others enjoyed a premium rate much lower than that which should have attached to their 40 per cent ratios. In effect, the 21 unfortunates to whom fate brought losses bore the entire cost of the entire group's failure to meet its coinsurance agreement.[5]

---

[4] C. A. Kulp and John W. Hall, *Casualty Insurance*, 4th ed. (New York: The Ronald Press Co., 1968), p. 48.

[5] Donald L. MacDonald, *Corporate Risk Control* (New York: The Ronald Press Co., 1966), p. 87. Similar statements appear in Robert Riegel, "Coinsurance," *Journal of American Insurance*, vol. XXII, no. 6 (June, 1945), p. 20; Robert Riegel and H. J. Loman, *Insurance Principles and Practices*, rev. ed. (New York: Prentice-Hall, Inc., 1942), p. 370; and Robert Riegel and Jerome S. Miller, *Insurance Principles and Practices*, 5th ed. (Englewood Cliffs, N.J.: Prentice-Hall, Inc., 1966), p. 496.

The author disagrees with these views, because he believes that the insurer's product is protection—the availability or promise of indemnity—rather than actual indemnity, which depends on chance losses. The price paid for this protection before the protection is given must be based on expected indemnity, and the equity of the price should be judged by expected values in light of past experience.[6] Properly calculated rates for properly applied coinsurance requirements establish this prospective equity of equal protection for each pure premium dollar. The confusion of protection with actual indemnity, implicit in the statement that only those suffering losses are penalized by coinsurance, leads to much the same illogical position held by those who argue that only policyholders who suffer losses get their money's worth from their insurance.

The equity of coinsurance frequently has been likened to the equity of property taxation.[7] It is said that, just as the property tax should be assessed on the same percentage of each property's value, so the insurance premium rate should be paid on the same fraction of each insured's property. But, the analogy continues, the insurer, not having the sanctions which governments apply against taxpayers who understate taxable values, must reduce the indemnity payments to those who underinsure. This analogy has been criticized on the basis that sanctions are irrelevant and that coinsurance simply is a means of adjusting the price of protection to its cost.[8] The author believes it improper to compare

---

[6] When premiums are paid or adjusted after the protection period has passed, actual indemnity may influence the price of that protection to some extent.

[7] See W. J. Nichols, "The Coinsurance Clause," *The Fire Insurance Contract, Its History and Interpretation,* ed. The Insurance Society of New York (Indianapolis, Ind.: The Rough Notes Co., Inc., 1922), pp. 698–699; A. F. Dean, *The Philosophy of Fire Insurance,* ed. W. R. Townley (Chicago: Edward B. Hatch, 1925), vol. I, p. 126; S. S. Huebner and Kenneth Black, Jr., *Property Insurance,* 4th ed. (New York: Appleton-Century-Crofts, Inc., 1957), p. 130; and S. S. Huebner, Kenneth Black, Jr., and Robert S. Cline, *Property and Liability Insurance* (New York: Appleton-Century-Crofts, Inc., 1968), pp. 91–92.

[8] Ralph H. Blanchard, "Coinsurance," *Risk and Insurance and Other Papers* (Lincoln, Neb.: University of Nebraska Press, 1965), p. 143; and letter from Ralph H. Blanchard, Professor Emeritus of Insurance, Graduate School of Business, Columbia University, May 4, 1967.

the equity of coinsurance with that of the property tax because (1) fiscal equity, difficult to define, may differ from actuarial equity as defined above; and (2) neither the benefits which the taxpayer receives from services financed by property taxes nor the indemnity which each insured can expect under his policy are directly proportional to the value taxed or insured (partial losses being possible). At best, the taxation analogy greatly over-simplifies.

SAFEGUARDING THE ADEQUACY OF THE INSURER'S PREMIUM INCOME

With the same mechanism by which coinsurance can promote equity among insureds, it also can "protect the insurer,"[9] safe-guarding the adequacy of its aggregate pure premium income if many insureds buy less than the coverage presumed in the rate calculation and specified in the coinsurance requirement. For example, every insured who purchases only 10 percent sprinkler leakage coverage with the 25 percent coinsurance requirement and rate can expect to receive two-fifths the indemnity which the insurer predicted in setting the premium rate. With two-fifths the predicted premium from these underinsured policyholders, the insurer can just meet its liabilities, reduced by coinsurance penalties, to the underinsured. Losses at least equal to the coinsurance requirement bring payment of the face of all policies not exceeding that requirement. For policies larger than any coinsurance requirement, the premium rate theoretically is too high, and the insurer collects a theoretically excessive premium from these policies.

Occasionally, the adequacy objective of coinsurance has been slightly misstated. For example:

The purpose of a coinsurance, contribution, or average clause is to limit the liability of an insurer to the amount for which it would be

---

[9] Albert H. Mowbray, Ralph H. Blanchard, and C. Arthur Williams, Jr., *Insurance, Its Theory and Practice in the United States,* 6th ed. (New York: McGraw-Hill Book Co., Inc., 1969), p. 148.

liable if an adequate amount of insurance were carried on the property.[10]

Presumably, "an adequate amount of insurance" is the coinsurance requirement. The fault with this statement is that coinsurance seeks to limit the insurer's liability to *proportionately less* than it would have been if the coinsurance requirement had been met. For instance, if a coinsurance requirement is 90 percent of value, but the property is only 40 percent insured, coinsurance reduces the insurer's liability to four-ninths of what it would have been "if an adequate amount of insurance were carried."

Alternatively, it is correct that coinsurance limits the liability of each *unit of insurance* (usually $100) to what it would have been had the coinsurance requirement been met. For a property worth $10,000 (100 units of insurance) insured for $9000 under a 90 percent coinsurance requirement, each unit of insurance is liable for no more than one-ninetieth of any loss, up to the $100 value of that unit. If 40 units of coverage are purchased, the one-ninetieth of any loss paid by each unit results in a four-ninths payment of that loss, until the policy face is paid for losses of 90 percent of value or more. Without coinsurance, in this example a 40 percent property loss, instead of a 90 percent one, would exhaust the policy.

PROMPTING REASONABLY FULL INSURANCE

Views differ regarding the extent to which the purpose of coinsurance is to prompt policyholders to adequately insure. The four passages below view coinsurance as (1) compelling, (2) encouraging, (3) influencing, and (4) leaving the insured free to choose adequate coverage.

The object of the coinsurance clause is to *compel* the insured to take out insurance to the designated percentage of the value of his prop-

---

[10] Prentiss B. Reed, *Adjustment of Property Losses*, 2nd ed. (New York: McGraw-Hill Book Co., Inc., 1953), p. 202; and Prentiss B. Reed and Paul I. Thomas, *Adjustment of Property Losses*, 3rd ed. (New York: McGraw-Hill Book Co., Inc., 1969), pp. 401–402.

erty, usually either eighty or one hundred per cent, or else become his own insurer in the amount of the deficiency.[11]

The purpose of coinsurance is to *encourage* large amounts of insurance relative to the value of the property.[12]

The purpose of coinsurance is to *influence* the insured to buy an amount of insurance in relation to the value of the property.[13]

The company says to the property owner: "You may have as much or as little of our protection as you choose to pay for. If you insure for the full value of your property, you receive full protection; the smaller the proportion of value insured, the less the protection and indemnity."[14]

The author prefers the view expressed in the last passage. Coinsurance can be said to "compel" adequate insurance only for those few insureds who so fear coinsurance penalties that they feel they dare not underinsure. Coinsurance properly can be said to "encourage" or "influence" adequate protection only among insureds who understand it—seemingly a minority.

---

[11] George Richards, *Law of Insurance,* ed. Rowland H. Long, 4th ed. (New York: Baker, Voorhis & Co., 1932), p. 352. Emphasis supplied. Similar stress on compulsion can be found in "Note: Valuation and Measure of Recovery under Fire Insurance Policies," *Columbia Law Review,* vol. XLIX, no. 6 (June, 1949), p. 829; *Home Insurance Company v. Eisenson,* 181 Fed. (2d) 416 (1950); *Templeton v. Insurance Company of North America,* 201 S.W. (2d) 784 (1947); *Texas City Terminal Railway Company v. American Equitable Assurance Company of New York,* 130 F. Supp. 843 (1955); and *Harper v. Penn Mutual Fire Insurance Company,* 199 F. Supp. 663 (1961).

[12] C. Arthur Williams, Jr., and Richard M. Heins, *Risk Management and Insurance* (New York: McGraw-Hill Book Co., 1964), p. 196. Emphasis supplied. Similar views appear in James L. Athearn, *Risk and Insurance* (New York: Appleton-Century-Crofts, Inc., 1962), p. 280; John H. Magee and David L. Bickelhaupt, *General Insurance,* 7th ed. (Homewood, Ill.: Richard D. Irwin, Inc., 1964), p. 270. [A later edition of this book includes this elaborating statement: "While the coinsurance clause does not make mandatory the carrying of insurance up to a specified percentage of value, losses are adjusted as if insurance in such an amount were carried." David L. Bickelhaupt and John H. Magee, *General Insurance,* 8th ed. (Homewood, Ill.: Richard D. Irwin, Inc., 1970), p. 26.] Curtis M. Elliott, *Property and Casualty Insurance* (New York: National Association of Insurance Agents—McGraw-Hill Insurance Bookshelf, McGraw-Hill Book Co., Inc., 1960), p. 82.

[13] William H. Rodda, *Fire and Property Insurance* (Englewood Cliffs, N.J.: Prentice-Hall, Inc., 1956), p. 68, n. 2. Emphasis supplied.

[14] Charles J. Martin, *The Coinsurance Clause or Average Clause in Fire Insurance* (New York: Frank B. Jordan, General Insurance Broker), p. 5.

Two points about coinsurance and adequate coverage need emphasis. First, although determining adequacy of coverage is difficult, presumably insurance to the probable maximum loss (another imprecise term) is adequate. In this sense, for certain perils such as sprinkler leakage adequate coverage is much less than insurance to full value. Thus, much lower minimum coinsurance requirements should be available for sprinkler leakage coverage than for fire insurance, where full value is often subject to a single loss. Whether compelled, encouraged, influenced, or left free to choose, few insureds will accept a requirement that they insure beyond what the insurer states is the largest foreseeable loss.

Second, actuarial theory attaches no special significance to a particular percentage of insurance to value. In fact, a premium rate for 2 percent coinsurance is easier to compute properly than is an 80 percent coinsurance rate and requires fewer statistics.[15] Insurers are said to stress full coverage in order to maximize the social benefits of protection in the face of insureds' optimistic tendency to buy too little coverage and to blame insurers when losses are not paid fully[16] Granted the social benefits of insurance, it has been argued that consumers' freedom of choice demands that a full range of coinsurance requirements and rates be available so that insureds with different types of property and varying attitudes toward risk may purchase any desired amount of coverage at a price equal to the value of the protection.[17] The author, seeing little real conflict between these two views, believes that actuarially justified rate differentials would prompt adequate coverage if a full range of coinsurance requirements and rates were available. (Chapter 8 describes requirements and rates now offered.)

---

[15] The proper computation requires the precise distribution of losses up to the coinsurance requirement but only the total percentage of losses which are anywhere above the coinsurance requirement (see Equation 2–3).

[16] Interview with John B. Davis, Assistant Vice President, Insurance Company of North America, January 17, 1967.

[17] *Report of the Co-Insurance Committee of the Board of Fire Underwriters of the Pacific on Percentage Co-Insurance and the Relative Rates Chargeable Therefor, Also on the Cost of Conflagration Hazard of Large Cities* (San Francisco, 1905), p. 4.

ESTABLISHING A MORE SCIENTIFIC
PREMIUM RATE STRUCTURE

As the following excerpts indicate, some authors see a more scientific premium rate structure as the goal of coinsurance.

But essentially it [the coinsurance clause] is designed to place the . . . insurance contract on manufacturing and mercantile properties upon such a basis that its proper cost or rate can be determined, and thus it is a part of the rate-making system.[18]

The purpose of Co-insurance is to develop a proper basis of exposure. Without such a basis it is difficult to promulgate adequate but not excessive rates.[19]

The purpose of including an insurance to value requirement in the replacement cost extension [of the Homeowners policy] is to provide a proper basis for making replacement cost benefits available.[20]

The making of scientific rates seems to be inseparable from the goals of premium rate equity and adequacy and not to be a separate purpose of coinsurance. A proper rating basis is not an end in itself but is a tool for constructing a rate structure with desirable characteristics such as equity, adequacy, and reasonableness.

FIXING RESPONSIBILITY FOR MAINTAINING
INSURANCE TO VALUE

If its policies lack a percentage of value coinsurance requirement, an insurer with many underinsured risks is likely to collect premium insufficient to meet its liabilities for losses and its opera-

---

[18] F. E. Wolfe, *Principles of Property Insurance* (New York: Thomas Y. Crowell Co., 1930), p. 135.

[19] Letter from James P. White, Superintendent, Property-Personal Lines Department, St. Paul Fire and Marine Insurance Company, October 20, 1966.

[20] Letter from Frank J. Caso, Manager, Personal Lines Division, Multi-Line Insurance Rating Bureau, November 18, 1966.

ting costs.[21] Two statements of the purpose of coinsurance (expressed before agreed amount endorsements or provisional reporting form policies gained wide use) indicate that coinsurance makes the insured responsible for maintaining insurance to value:

The very purpose of the coinsurance clause is to place upon the insured the responsibility for ascertaining the value of his property, and for keeping it properly insured; and it goes without saying that, having assumed this responsibility, he must live up to it or he will be caught at a disadvantage.[22]

It is impossible for the company or its agent, or even the owner himself, to closely estimate the value of property, and even if it could be estimated, values are constantly fluctuating. The only way to adjust the matter to ensure equity to all concerned must be through a mutual agreement that if the property is not insured for a stipulated portion of its value at the time of the fire, the assured shall be a coinsurer for the deficit.[23]

Either the insurer or the insured must see that each property is covered to just the assumed fraction of value if losses up to the policy face can be paid in full from the insurer's pure premium income without discrimination among insureds. Hence, fixing responsibility for maintaining insurance to value is closely linked with the equity and adequacy objectives of coinsurance. But this responsibility can be shared between the insurer and the insured (under an agreed amount endorsement or provisional reporting form) or be borne exclusively by the insured (under any percentage of value coinsurance clause). The financial consequences of underinsurance may be felt by the insurer (through inadequate premiums) or by the insured (through coinsurance penalties). The various types of coinsurance clauses define which party incurs these consequences and, thus, who should take care to maintain insurance to value.

---

[21] In practice, the de facto waiver of coinsurance requirements for small losses, explained in Chapter 10, may lead to premium inadequacy.

[22] *Report of the Joint Committee of the Senate and Assembly of the State of New York . . . , op. cit.,* p. 90. Losses seldom being certain, "may be caught" seems more accurate.

[23] Dean, *op. cit.,* pp. 125–126.

IMPROVING SALES APPEAL OF POLICY

Because lower price can be a competitive advantage and be-cause a coinsurance requirement lowers the premium rate, an insurer can use coinsurance to improve the sales appeal of a policy. In the words of one author:

The purpose of such a [coinsurance] clause is to give a lower rate to the insured who carries a higher amount of insurance to value.[24]

An insurer's competitive price advantage is strengthened when it can use coinsurance clauses in policies which other insurers sell at flat (no coinsurance) rates. For this to be feasible, the rate manual must permit the coverage to be sold with or without coinsurance, and the insured must be made aware of the impor-tance of meeting his coinsurance requirement. Without this awareness, coinsurance may become a competitive disadvantage in the wake of a loss. The larger average policy face sold at a lower premium rate with coinsurance tends to reduce adminis-trative and selling costs (including percentage commissions) per $100 of insurance sold. The need for increased coverage to meet rising coinsurance requirements during inflation provides an effec-tive entree for "repeat" sales.[25]

SUMMARY

By balancing pure premiums with expected indemnity pay-ments, coinsurance can (1) promote equity among insureds; (2) safeguard the adequacy of the insurer's premium income; (3) prompt reasonably adequate insurance: (4) establish a more scientific premium rate structure; (5) fix responsibility for main-

---

[24] John Adam, Jr., "Underwriting in Fire Insurance," *Property and Lia-bility Insurance Handbook,* ed. John D. Long and Davis W. Gregg (Home-wood, Ill.: Richard D. Irwin, Inc., 1965), pp. 201–202.

[25] This paragraph is based on an interview with Putnam Schroeder, Re-search Specialist, Insurance Company of North America, September 20, 1966.

taining insurance to value; and (6) improve a policy's competitive sales appeal.

Most of these goals are linked closely to pure premium rate equity and adequacy. Pure premium rates are equitable and just adequate if, for the ith insured,

$$\frac{E(I)_i}{P_i} = 1. \tag{5-2}$$

CHAPTER 6

Loss-Severity Distributions

PURPOSE

This chapter explores characteristics of, and gives data on, distributions of losses by dollar amount (dollar loss-severity distributions) and by percentage of value (percentage loss-severity distributions). Dollar loss-severity distributions are needed to compute proper pure premium rates for agreed amount endorsements; proper rates for percentage coinsurance clauses must be based on percentage loss-severity distributions. The fire loss data presented here—fire being the only peril for which usable loss-severity statistics are available—are used in the coinsurance rate models in Chapter 7.

CHARACTERISTICS OF LOSS-SEVERITY DISTRIBUTIONS

Loss-severity distributions are conditional[1] probability distributions of losses by dollar size or percentage of value.

Conditional Probability Distributions

Let $s(L)$ represent the percentage of all losses from a given peril that are of size L (either in dollars or as a fraction of value).

---

[1] Conditioned on the occurrence of some loss greater than zero.

Then $s(L)$ is the conditional probability of a loss of L. If no loss can be greater than V (property value), then

$$\int_0^V s(L)dL = 1, \qquad (6\text{--}1)$$

since the distribution accounts for all possible losses.[2] Equation 6–1 is a generalized loss-severity function.

If N risks are insured, and, of these, M suffers a loss greater than zero during a policy period, M/N is the probability (f) of some loss during that period. The unconditional probability[3] of a loss of L—denoted as $p(L)$—is

$$p(L) = (M/N)s(L) = fs(L). \qquad (6\text{--}2)$$

Since few risks suffer a loss during a policy period, the integral of the *unconditional* probabilities from *more than zero* to V is much less than one, but over the range *zero* to V, including "zero loss,"

$$\int_0^V p(L)dL = 1. \qquad (6\text{--}3)$$

The fact that both the conditional probabilities of losses greater than zero and the unconditional probabilities of all losses—including "zero loss"—form complete probability distributions simplifies premium rate computation.

Dollar Size or Percentage of Value

Loss-severity distributions can relate the conditional probability of a loss greater than zero either to the dollar size of that loss or to the fraction of full value which that loss represents, but not to both factors. This is a simplistic view of loss severity.

---

[2] A probability distribution is defined as a function including all possible outcomes and specifying probabilities which total one. See Taro Yamane, *Mathematics for Economists* (Englewood Cliffs, N.J.: Prentice-Hall, Inc., 1962), p. 403.

[3] An unconditional probability of a loss is a joint probability equal to the product of the probability of a nonzero loss and the conditional probability of a loss of that given size. See John Neter and William Wasserman, *Fundamental Statistics for Business and Economics*, 2d ed. (Boston: Allyn & Bacon, Inc., 1961), p. 291.

Presumably, smaller properties suffer a greater proportion of total, or high percentage of value, losses than do larger properties, but no statistics seem to be available on this point. Also, the probability of a $100,000 direct loss is zero for a $50,000 property but greater than zero for a $200,000 one. To some extent, the low relative frequency of, for example, $500,000 losses is caused by the relative scarcity of $500,000 structures.

But, for one practical and one theoretical reason, a loss-severity distribution must deal only with dollar or percentage size of loss. Practically, statistics on the before-loss value of damaged properties are not sufficient to permit the data to be stratified to obtain percentage loss-severity figures for properties in different size classes. Theoretically, in order to use these distributions for computing coinsurance rates, the actuary must know the size distribution of losses up to the coinsurance requirement and the percentage of losses equal to or above the coinsurance requirement. Coinsurance requirements may be either dollar amounts (not always fixed percentages of value[4]) or percentages of value (regardless of property value). Hence, a loss-severity distribution useful for computing coinsurance rates must be expressed in the same terms as the coinsurance requirement,[5] either dollars or percentages of value, but not both.

SOME LOSS-SEVERITY DISTRIBUTIONS

A Dollar Fire Loss-Severity Distribution

The most complete recent statistics on dollar size of fire losses (except those to dwellings) come from a census of 132,081 fires doing at least $250 damage which occurred during 1961 and 1962

---

[4] Interview with John B. Davis, Assistant Vice President, Insurance Company of North America, December 22, 1966.

[5] A. W. Whitney, "The Co-Insurance Clause," paper read before the Fire Underwriters' Association of the Pacific meeting in San Francisco, January 13, 1904, p. 5; and *Report of the Co-Insurance Committee to the Board of Fire Underwriters of the Pacific on Percentage Co-Insurance and the Relative Rates Chargeable Therefor, Also on the Cost of Conflagration Hazard of Large Cities* (San Francisco, 1905), p. 15.

made available to the author by a reliable confidential source and presented in Table 4. Column 1 of this table gives the classes of

TABLE 4. A dollar loss-severity distribution

(1) Size of Loss (in $10,000 units) $X_1 \leq L < X_2$		(2) Number of Losses	(3) Percentage of Number of Losses	(4) Arithmetic Mean Loss	(5) Percentage of Losses $\geq X_1$
X_1	X_2				
0.025	0.5	102,003	77.2276	$ 1,340	100.0000
0.5	1.0	13,292	10.0635	7,027	22.7724
1.0	2.5	10,157	7.6900	15,317	12.7089
2.5	5.0	3,841	2.9081	34,749	5.0189
5.0	10.0	1,817	1.3757	68,869	2.1108
10.0	25.0	753	0.5701	149,175	0.7352
25.0	50.0	167	0.1264	342,503	0.1651
50.0	100.0	35	0.0265	652,743	0.0386
100.0		16	0.0121	1,884,127	0.0121
Totals and overall mean		132,081	100.0000%	$ 6,563	. . .

Source: Confidential.

loss size in $10,000 units from the original data. Columns 2 and 3 indicate the number and percentage of fires in each class. Column 4 lists the arithmetic mean loss in each class. For example, fires of at least $5,000 but less than $10,000 averaged $7,027. Column 5 contains the percentage of losses equal to or greater than the lower bound (X_1) of each class. For example, because losses less than $250 were excluded, 100 percent of the losses are $250 or more; 22.77 percent are at least $5000. About one-hundredth of 1 percent of all losses are at least $1,000,000.

With an IBM 7040 computer, a function was fitted to the percentages in Column 5, with the size of loss in $10,000 units as the independent variable (x) and the percentage of losses equal to or greater than each X_1 as the dependent variable (y). For 22.77 percent of losses equal to or greater than $5,000, $y = 22.77$ and $x = 0.5$. Equations of the forms

$$y = x/a$$

$$y = a + bx + cx^2$$

$$y = a + b(\ln x)$$

and

$$\ln y = a + b(\ln x)$$

yielded fits (as measured by sums of squared deviations of predicted from actual y values) inferior to that of the equation

$$\ln y = 2.5972 - 0.9909(\ln x) - 0.1226(\ln x)^2. \quad (6\text{-}4)$$

The symbol $\ln y$ represents the logarithm of y to the base e (approximately equaling 2.71828) rather than the logarithm to the base 10 (written $\log y$).[6] In order to meet the restrictions of the computer program, \$250 (or 0.025) was rounded to \$300 (or 0.03). In Table 5, the percentages of losses equal to or greater

TABLE 5. Comparison of actual with predicted percentages of fire losses at least equaling various dollar amounts

Loss at Least Equal to x (in \$10,000 units)	Actual Percentage	Predicted Percentage
.03[a]	100.0	96.0
.50	22.8	25.2
1.00	12.7	13.4
2.50	5.02	4.88
5.00	2.11	1.98
10.00	0.74	0.71
25.00	0.17	0.15
50.00	0.04	0.04
100.00	0.01	0.01

[a] Rounded from 0.025 to fit computer program.
Source: Table 4, Equation 6–4, and *Standard Mathematical Tables*, ed. Robert C. Weast, Samuel M. Selby, and Charles D. Hodgman, 12th ed. (Cleveland, Ohio: The Chemical Rubber Publishing Co., 1959), pp. 171–178.

than the class lower bounds, as predicted in Equation 6–4, are compared with the actual percentages.

Percentage Fire Loss-Severity Distributions

Very little is known about distributions of fire losses as percentages of sound value before loss[7] because of (1) the difficulty

---

[6] Yamane, *op. cit.*, p. 62.
[7] Robert Riegel and Jerome S. Miller, *Insurance Principles and Practices*, 5th ed. (Englewood Cliffs, N.J.: Prentice-Hall, Inc., 1966), p. 496, n. 8.

of obtaining accurate property values just prior to loss;[8] (2) the greater priority given to fire rate-making problems which are more pressing than the problem of accounting precisely for insurance to value;[9] and (3) the technical barriers to assembling data on a per loss, rather than a per policy, basis.[10]

Many writers have estimated that the preponderance of fire losses are small fractions of value and that from 4 to 6 percent of losses are total.[11] Without statistical evidence or any indication of the types of properties to which these estimates refer, evaluation of them is difficult. Other writers have presented complete percentage distributions of fire losses but have not specified the source of the underlying loss experience.[12] These distributions are said to be definitely "*j*-shaped,"[13] but Figure 1 shows that this description is ambiguous, not indicating whether a total loss is the least likely loss (as in Distribution A) or whether losses

---

[8] Robert E. Schultz and Edward C. Bardwell, *Property Insurance* (New York: Rinehart & Co., 1959), p. 68.

[9] Interview with L. H. Longley-Cook, retired Vice President and Actuary, Insurance Company of North America, September 20, 1966. He mentioned, for example, more exact classification of properties by factors affecting loss *frequency* in order to collect an *adequate* premium from each class of properties.

[10] Letter from G. M. Lynch, then National Manager, Education, General Adjustment Bureau, Inc., September 29, 1966.

[11] See, for example, "Attention to Co-Insurance on Small Losses Is Vital," *Loss Research*, vol. VIII, no. 3 (April 1951), p. 3; William N. Bament, "Co-Insurance," address to the Insurance Society of New York, March 30, 1920, p. 1; Avard L. Bishop, "The Co-Insurance Clause," *Journal of American Insurance*, vol. VI, no. 3 (March 1929), p. 5; "Further Descriptions of Co-Insurance Clause," *The Eastern Underwriter*, vol. XXIII, no. 43 (October 13, 1922), p. 19; Allen L. Mayerson, *Introduction to Insurance* (New York: The Macmillan Co., 1962), p. 224; Robert Riegel and H. J. Loman, *Insurance Principles and Practices*, rev. ed. (New York: Prentice-Hall, Inc., 1942), p. 368; Schultz and Bardwell, *op. cit.*, p. 68; and F. E. Wolfe, *Principles of Property Insurance* (New York: Thomas Y. Crowell Co., 1930), p. 142.

[12] W. H. A. Elink-Schuurman, "Über die Prinzipien einer Feuerschadenstatistik," *Reports, Memoirs and Proceedings of the Sixth International Congress of Actuaries*, vol. II (1909), pp. 279–280; Francis C. Moore, *Fire Insurance and How to Build* (New York: The Baker & Taylor Co., 1903), p. 580; Herbert Wilmerding, *Graded Co-Insurance* (Philadelphia: no publisher indicated, November, 1902), p. 4; and J. W. Wingo, *Co-Insurance—When Your Client Asks "Why?"* (Hartford, Conn.: Hartford Fire Insurance Company, 1965), p. 4.

[13] Riegel and Miller, *op. cit.*, p. 496, n. 8.

Figure 1. Two plausible "j-shaped" percentage loss-severity distributions

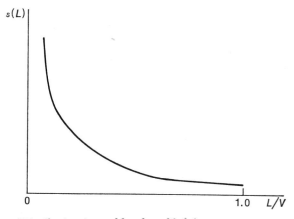

(Distribution A: total loss least likely)

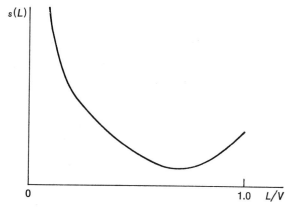

(Distribution B: concentrations of minor and severe losses)

tend to cluster at low and high percentages of value (as in Distribution B). One study suggests that the percentage distribution of rural fire losses is "*u*-shaped," most fires causing either slight or nearly total damage.[14] Apparently, the only percentage fire

---

[14] Paul Johansen, "On Fire Insurance of Rural Buildings," *Transactions of the XVth International Congress of Actuaries,* vol. II (1957), p. 211.

loss-severity distributions for which the source of the basic data is known come from A. W. Whitney's work, Ruth E. Salzmann's study, and the detailed records of the Oregon Fire Marshal.

The Whitney Distributions. A. W. Whitney, while a University of California mathematics professor, presented four percentage fire loss-severity distributions in 1904 and eight more in 1905.

His four 1904 distributions covered fire losses to (1) dwellings (of unspecified construction), (2) contents of dwellings, (3) brick buildings, and (4) contents of brick buildings. In introducing his distribution for dwelling structures, Whitney said:

I now propose to make the following assumptions. I will suppose that 50,000 dwellings, each of value $10,000, are insured for $4,000 for one year, that the fire-record shows that during the year 1,000 of these are more or less damaged by fire and that the fire-loss is distributed as follows: 751 suffer damages less than $1,000, say on the average $500 (in reality less than $500) . . . but let me exhibit this in a table.[15]

This table is reproduced as Table 6.

Whitney then gave the source for all his 1904 distributions, saying:

I may say that while this column of *N*s as well as other values that I shall give later is based on statistics from the Reports of the San Francisco Underwriters' Fire Patrol, no practical conclusions should be founded upon them for the reason that these Reports give only value of *insurance*, not value of *property*. The necessity of assuming a relation between amount of insurance carried and property-value has introduced an element of uncertainty, and this table therefore cannot be depended upon as more than a very rough approximation to the truth.[16]

Whitney's 1904 distribution of dwelling fire losses is stressed here because this one distribution has been repeated frequently by writers who differ as to its source and significance.[17]

---

[15] Whitney, *op. cit.*, p. 5.

[16] *Ibid.*, p. 6. Emphasis in the original. When insurance is less than full value, ratios of loss to *insurance* inflate the severity of each loss and overstate the frequency of total losses *to the property*.

[17] See "Insurance Facts for Policyholders: Coinsurance," *Insurance Bulletin Number Six* (Washington, D.C.: Insurance Department of the Cham-

TABLE 6. The Whitney 1904 percentage fire loss-severity distribution for dwellings

Tenths of Insurance	N	Loss			Average Loss
		Between $	0 and $ 1,000		$ 500 (in reality less) *
1	751	"	1,000 "	2,000	1,500
2	107	"	2,000 "	3,000	2,500
3	47	"	3,000 "	4,000	3,500
4	30	"	4,000 "	5,000	4,500
5	20	"	5,000 "	6,000	5,500
6	16	"	6,000 "	7,000	6,500
7	12	"	7,000 "	8,000	7,500
8	9	"	8,000 "	9,000	8,500
9	5	"	9,000 "	$10,000	9,500
10	3	$9,000			
Total 1,000					

* Whitney used this phrase in his table.
Source: A. W. Whitney, "The Co-Insurance Clause," paper read before the Fire Underwriters' Association of the Pacific, January 13, 1904, p. 5.

The *N* values for all four of Whitney's 1904 distributions are
given in Table 7, with the classes of loss size captioned as in

TABLE 7. The Whitney 1904 distributions of percentage fire loss for
dwellings, contents of dwellings, brick buildings, and contents
of brick buildings

		Number of Fires		
Tenths of Insurance	*Dwellings*	*Dwelling Contents*	*Brick Buildings*	*Brick Contents*
1	751	491	925	575
2	107	186	55	140
3	47	98	12	95
4	30	59	4	60
5	20	42	2	50
6	16	35	1	35
7	12	28	1	25
8	9	24	0	15
9	5	21	0	5
10	3	16	0	0
Totals	1,000	1,000	1,000	1,000

Source: A. W. Whitney, "The Co-Insurance Clause," paper read before the Fire
Underwriters' Association of the Pacific, January 13, 1904, pp. 5, 8, and 9.

Whitney's tables. The 1,000 fires presumed in each distribution
are more than Whitney studied, and Whitney acknowledged that
the assumption that the arithmetic mean loss in each class
equaled the class midpoint was a distortion.

Dissatisfied with this distortion of average losses and seeking

ber of Commerce of the United States, October 1961), p. 2; Laurence E.
Falls, "Coinsurance," *Best's Insurance News, Fire and Casualty Edition*,
vol. XLIX, no. 6 (October 1948), p. 26, reprinted in H. Wayne Snider, ed.,
Readings in Property and Casualty Insurance (Homewood, Ill.: Richard D.
Irwin, Inc., 1959), p. 210; S. S. Huebner and Kenneth Black, Jr., *Property
Insurance*, 4th ed. (New York: Appleton-Century-Crofts, Inc., 1957), p.
128; and S. S. Huebner, Kenneth Black, Jr., and Robert S. Cline, *Property
and Liability Insurance* (New York: Appleton-Century-Crofts, Inc., 1968),
p. 90. All these sources say that the Whitney dwelling distribution is a distribution of losses as percentages of value, not as percentages of insurance.
The Chamber of Commerce and Falls attribute the distribution to Whitney
but say that it is hypothetical, as do Riegel and Miller, *op. cit.*, p. 496, n. 8.
Huebner and Black state that Whitney received his data from the "San
Francisco Fire Patrol," not the San Francisco Underwriters' Fire Patrol,
although Huebner, Black, and Cline correct this error. None of these writers
who refer to Whitney's 1904 dwelling distribution state that it was meant
to apply to dwellings only.

figures on losses as fractions of property values, Whitney turned to insurers' statistics for eight distributions published in a 1905 committee report which he authored. Whitney studied the loss and "sound value" statistics reported by the loss adjusters of about ninety insurers on 5,642 fire losses in urban San Francisco during the five years 1899–1903, excluding all conflagration losses.[18] From these records, he constructed distributions for eight property classes: frame business buildings; brick business buildings; dwellings (construction unspecified); "special hazards, frame" (not further defined); and the contents of each of these four classes. The number of losses comprising each distribution was not specified, although each presumed 10,000 losses.

For reasons he did not give, Whitney published the arithmetic mean loss in each category of loss size only for the distribution for frame business buildings. This distribution, of which the Merritt Committee later published an approximation without giving credit to Whitney,[19] is shown in Table 8, using Whitney's ambiguous[20] captions for the categories of loss size.

All of Whitney's 1905 distributions appear, as Whitney gave them, in Table 9. These figures seem to support the conclusions that (1) frame structures suffer a larger proportion of severe losses than do brick; (2) contents losses tend to be more severe than losses to structures; and (3) total losses are not the least likely losses. A slightly *u*-shaped distribution for most of Whitney's classes of properties also is suggested by the positions of the arithmetic mean losses in the lowest and highest loss category in Table 8. In the 0 to 10 percent category, a concentration of very small losses pulls the arithmetic mean for this category

---

[18] *Report of the Co-Insurance Committee . . . , op. cit.*, pp. 5 and 37.

[19] *Report of the Joint Committee of the Senate and Assembly of the State of New York, Appointed to Investigate Corrupt Practices in Connection with Legislation, and the Affairs of Insurance Companies, Other Than Those Doing Life Insurance Business,* Assembly Document No. 30 (Albany, N.Y., February 1, 1911), p. 83. See also Albert Mowbray and Ralph H. Blanchard, *Insurance, Its Theory and Practice in the United States,* 5th ed. (New York: McGraw-Hill Book Co., Inc., 1961), pp. 85–86. The Merritt Committee did not claim to have originated this distribution.

[20] From the captions, it is not clear in what class losses of exactly 10, 20, 30, etc., percent of value belong.

TABLE 8. The Whitney 1905 distribution of percentage fire loss for frame business buildings

Size of Loss					Number	Arithmetic Mean Loss
Between	0/10	and	1/10	of value	8,293	1.8%
"	1/10	"	2/10 "	"	576	14.2
"	2/10	"	3/10 "	"	326	24.5
"	3/10	"	4/10 "	"	215	34.7
"	4/10	"	5/10 "	"	139	44.8
"	5/10	"	6/10 "	"	97	54.9
"	6/10	"	7/10 "	"	69	65.0
"	7/10	"	8/10 "	"	49	75.0
"	8/10	"	9/10 "	"	42	85.0
"	9/10	"	10/10 "	"	194	99.5
Total					10,000	

Source: *Report of the Co-Insurance Committee to the Board of Fire Underwriters of the Pacific on Percentage Co-Insurance and the Relative Rates Chargeable Therefor, Also on the Cost of Conflagration Hazard of Large Cities* (San Francisco, 1905), pp. 20 and 31.

below 5 percent. In the 90 to 100 percent category, a cluster of total, or very severe, losses pulls the arithmetic mean loss for the category above 95 percent.[21]

The Salzmann Distributions. Ruth E. Salzmann has published four distributions of fire losses to dwelling structures, expressing the losses as percentages of face amounts of Homeowners insurance based on the experience of the Insurance Company of North America for the 1960 incurred year, valued as of May 31, 1961. The dwellings are cross-classified by construction (frame or brick) and by public fire protection (protected or unprotected). Table 10 presents the absolute number of losses in each category of each distribution (and percentages computed by the present author), disaggregated by the present author into mutually exclusive categories from their published cumulative "equal to or less than" form.

---

[21] David Durand, "A Simple Method for Estimating the Size Distribution of a Given Aggregate Income," *The Review of Economic Statistics,* vol. XXV, no. 4 (November 1943), p. 228, shows how clusters of observations at one extreme of a total distribution pull the arithmetic means of classes within that distribution toward the cluster and away from the class midpoints.

TABLE 9. The Whitney 1905 percentage fire loss distributions for various classes of property

Ratio of Loss to Value	Frame Business Buildings	Contents of Frame Business Buildings	Brick Business Buildings	Contents of Brick Business Buildings	Dwellings	Contents of Dwellings	Special Hazards (Frame)	Contents of Special Hazards (Frame)
0/10 and 1/10	8,293	7,172	9,370	6,724	8,627	8,360	5,413	4,264
1/10 " 2/10	576	915	337	965	502	658	791	806
2/10 " 3/10	326	425	144	580	201	284	539	668
3/10 " 4/10	215	310	85	429	130	178	431	553
4/10 " 5/10	139	221	42	324	93	114	360	507
5/10 " 6/10	97	180	16	260	73	85	309	507
6/10 " 7/10	69	147	4	214	60	64	273	530
7/10 " 8/10	49	123	2	183	53	57	237	553
8/10 " 9/10	42	98	0	167	48	68	209	599
9/10 " 10/10	194	409	0	154	213	132	1,438	1,013
Totals	10,000	10,000	10,000	10,000	10,000	10,000	10,000	10,000

Source: Report of the Co-Insurance Committee to the Board of Fire Underwriters of the Pacific on Percentage Co-Insurance and the Relative Rates Chargeable Therefor, Also on the Cost of Conflagration Hazard of Large Cities (San Francisco, 1905), p. 31.

TABLE 10. The Salzmann percentage fire loss-severity distributions

Loss as Percentage of Insurance $X_1 < L/F \leq X_2$		Class of Dwelling							
		Frame Protected		Brick Protected		Frame Unprotected		Brick Unprotected	
X_1	X_2	No.	%*	No.	%*	No.	%*	No.	%*
0.0	0.1	546	11.2	210	14.7	169	12.7	54	14.3
0.1	0.2	611	12.6	188	13.1	214	16.1	66	17.5
0.2	0.3	502	10.3	163	11.4	164	12.3	35	9.3
0.3	0.4	382	7.9	109	7.6	115	8.6	36	9.5
0.4	0.5	297	6.1	92	6.4	71	5.3	27	7.1
0.5	0.6	272	5.6	78	5.4	78	5.9	19	5.0
0.6	0.7	223	4.6	76	5.3	56	4.2	11	2.9
0.7	0.8	170	3.5	48	3.4	35	2.6	9	2.4
0.8	0.9	148	3.0	34	2.4	35	2.6	15	4.0
0.9	1	159	3.3	49	3.4	31	2.3	8	2.1
1	2	671	13.8	196	13.7	127	9.5	43	11.4
2	3	275	5.7	64	4.5	75	5.6	21	5.6
3	4	132	2.7	23	1.6	33	2.5	5	1.3
4	5	86	1.8	14	1.0	14	1.1	2	0.5
5	6	46	0.9	9	0.6	7	0.5	2	0.5
6	7	34	0.7	8	0.6	13	1.0	3	0.8
7	8	31	0.6	9	0.6	2	0.2	0	0
8	9	20	0.4	3	0.2	1	0.1	2	0.5
9	10	31	0.6	8	0.6	14	1.1	4	1.1
10	20	94	1.9	19	1.3	18	1.4	4	1.1
20	30	37	0.8	6	0.4	8	0.6	4	1.1
30	40	27	0.6	5	0.3	7	0.5	2	0.5
40	50	16	0.3	4	0.3	7	0.5	1	0.3
50	60	8	0.2	6	0.4	4	0.3	1	0.3
60	70	10	0.2	3	0.2	2	0.2	0	0
70	80	9	0.2	3	0.2	5	0.4	0	0
80	90	6	0.1	1	0.1	3	0.2	1	0.3
90	100	19	0.4	4	0.3	25	1.9	3	0.8
Totals ...		4,862	100.0	1,432	100.0	1,333	100.0	378	100.0

* Percentages, rounded to nearest one-tenth percent, may not add to 100.0 percent.
  Source: Ruth E. Salzmann, "Rating by Layer of Insurance," *Proceedings of the Casualty Actuarial Society*, vol. L (1963), pp. 23–26.

Like the 1904 Whitney distributions, the Salzmann distributions overstate the severity of each loss by relating it to insurance rather than to full property value. If it was true in 1960, as it was reported to be true in 1964, that the average Homeowners policy was 70.8 percent of the replacement value of the dwelling structure,[22] losses of 70.8 percent or more of value can be expected to appear as total losses in the Salzmann distribution, and the average 10 percent loss to insurance in Salzmann's data was a 7 percent loss of value.

Because of this inflation of losses, the concentration of small losses in Salzmann's results is noteworthy. In the least concentrated class, frame-protected dwellings, about 68 percent of the losses were no more than 1 percent of the insurance, and 95 percent no more than 10 percent of the insurance. For frame-unprotected dwellings, the corresponding percentages were 73 and 94 percent. These results challenge the justification for many underwriters' refusal to give coinsurance credit for fire coverage of frame-unprotected buildings on the traditional, but apparently invalid, assumption[23] that all fire losses for this class are total.[24]

The Oregon Distributions.   From insurers' reports, the Office of the Oregon Fire Marshal records on index cards the location, type of property damaged, amount of insurance under all fire policies, sound property value just prior to loss, and the indemnity payment for each Oregon fire loss reported to insurers. The author examined the cards for all 2,860 fires to "frame-protected" properties other than dwellings during 1964 and 1965, the only years for which these cards were available.[25] As explained on page 21, the author believes that loss and sound

---

[22] "Adequate Insurance to Value Would Have Put Homeowners in the Black," *The National Underwriter,* vol. LXVIII, no. 95 (November 6, 1964), p. 1.

[23] Writers who have endorsed this assumption are cited in footnote 11.

[24] Interview with Ruth E. Salzmann, then Actuary, Treaty Reinsurance Department, Life Insurance Company of North America, May 4, 1967.

[25] In these years, 24,692 fires were reported to the fire marshal, of which 19,062 dwelling fires and 2127 vehicle fires were excluded from this study because coinsurance generally is not used in policies against dwelling and vehicle losses. Losses to brick-protected and frame- and brick-unprotected properties numbered 643, too few for reliable distributions for each of these classes. See Office of the Oregon State Fire Marshal, *Annual Statistical Reports for the Calendar Years 1964 and 1965* (Salem, Ore.: State printing, 1965 and 1966), p. 20 and p. 21, respectively. A property is "protected" if it has Class 9 or better public fire protection. Letter from Norbert J. Lecher, Statistician, Office of the Oregon State Fire Marshal, September 9, 1966.

value statistics from adjusters' reports, which may distort "true" values, are more relevant to an insurer's operations than "true" values would be because insurers pay most losses on the basis of adjusters' reports. If insurers improve their procedures for estimating pre-loss sound values of damaged properties, these Oregon data may have less significance.

The Oregon data, while seemingly the best available, have at least two weaknesses. First, the number of losses is too small to produce reliable results for such diverse properties. Second, the "frame-protected" class contains a great variety of dissimilar properties: contents of trailer homes (and of all other properties in this class), machinery in metal products plants, church structures, and oil risks, to take extreme examples. But separating these properties into more homogeneous construction and protection classes virtually would have destroyed any credibility these figures may have. This study will have served a useful purpose if it establishes the need for better data on the distribution of fire and other losses as percentages of value.

Three distributions have been constructed from these Oregon losses: one for losses to properties with before-loss sound values not exceeding $10,000, one for losses to larger properties, and one for losses to all properties regardless of sound value. The separation of large from small properties permits a crude estimate of the effect of property size on the distribution of losses as percentages of value. These three distributions are detailed in Tables 11 through 13. Unlike any other distributions the author has seen, the Oregon distributions distinguish between total losses and partial losses above 90 percent of value. Blank spaces within columns indicate changes in the width of the class intervals for size of loss. For comparison with the Whitney 1905 distributions, Table 14 summarizes the Oregon distribution for all sound values.

A comparison of Tables 11 and 12 suggests that losses to small properties are less concentrated at small percentages of value than are losses to large properties. For properties valued over $10,000, 22.1 percent of losses do not exceed one one-thousandth (0.1 percent) of value; for smaller properties, the corresponding figure is about six-tenths of 1 percent. Losses not more than 1 per-

TABLE 11. Percentage fire loss-severity distribution of 1118 losses during 1964 and 1965 to Oregon properties with sound values not exceeding $10,000

Loss as Percentage of Sound Value $X_1 < L/V \leq X_2$		Number of Losses	Arithmetic Mean Loss	% of Number of Losses
X_1	X_2			
0	0.01	0	0 %	0.000
0.01	0.02	0	0	0.000
0.02	0.03	1	0.02200	0.089
0.03	0.04	0	0	0.000
0.04	0.05	0	0	0.000
0.05	0.06	0	0	0.000
0.06	0.07	1	0.07000	0.089
0.07	0.08	1	0.07368	0.089
0.08	0.09	1	0.08571	0.089
0.09	0.1	3	0.09777	0.268
0.1	0.2	21	0.16724	1.878
0.2	0.3	18	0.26293	1.610
0.3	0.4	33	0.35475	2.952
0.4	0.5	19	0.47045	1.699
0.5	0.6	30	0.58864	2.683
0.6	0.7	27	0.65254	2.415
0.7	0.8	20	0.76027	1.789
0.8	0.9	16	0.85234	1.431
0.9	1	32	0.96635	2.862
1	2	159	1.47633	14.222
2	3	89	2.51236	7.961
3	4	47	3.46312	4.204
4	5	41	4.47704	3.667
5	6	33	5.51104	2.952
6	7	23	6.51174	2.057
7	8	14	7.64025	1.252
8	9	17	8.66384	1.521
9	10	20	9.60938	1.789
10	20	75	14.62943	6.708
20	30	37	25.07774	3.309
30	40	33	34.24266	2.952
40	50	26	45.86380	2.326
50	60	26	54.58132	2.326
60	70	22	64.33499	1.968
70	80	15	75.51198	1.342
80	90	16	85.56791	1.431
$90 < L/V < 100$		19	95.49306	1.699
Equal to 100*		183	100.00000	16.369
Totals		1,118		100.000%†

* If the last two classes were combined into a class "greater than 90 percent, not greater than 100 percent," this combined class would contain 202 losses, 18.068 percent of the total number of losses, with an average ratio of loss to sound value of 99.57608 percent.

† Corrected for error due to rounding.

Source: Calculated from data in the files of the Office of the Fire Marshal, State of Oregon.

TABLE 12. Percentage fire loss-severity distribution of 1742 losses during 1964 and 1965 to Oregon properties with sound values exceeding $10,000

Loss as Percentage of Sound Value $X_1 < L/V \leq X_2$		Number of Losses	Arithmetic Mean Loss	% of Number of Losses
X_1	X_2			
0	0.01	52	0.00613%	2.985
0.01	0.02	58	0.01503	3.330
0.02	0.03	59	0.02484	3.387
0.03	0.04	52	0.03567	2.985
0.04	0.05	39	0.04434	2.239
0.05	0.06	39	0.05455	2.239
0.06	0.07	36	0.06534	2.067
0.07	0.08	35	0.07503	2.009
0.08	0.09	28	0.08426	1.607
0.09	0.1	26	0.09490	1.493
0.1	0.2	197	0.14486	11.309
0.2	0.3	124	0.24489	7.118
0.3	0.4	87	0.34935	4.994
0.4	0.5	67	0.45482	3.846
0.5	0.6	46	0.54834	2.641
0.6	0.7	41	0.65089	2.354
0.7	0.8	47	0.74012	2.698
0.8	0.9	38	0.85350	2.181
0.9	1	23	0.95423	1.320
1	2	145	1.43641	8.324
2	3	56	2.43966	3.215
3	4	49	3.51186	2.813
4	5	27	4.53122	1.550
5	6	18	5.51080	1.033
6	7	14	6.32915	0.804
7	8	14	7.54090	0.804
8	9	14	8.52423	0.804
9	10	7	9.51329	0.402
10	20	76	14.20888	4.363
20	30	32	24.04491	1.837
30	40	16	34.99545	0.918
40	50	19	45.05497	1.091
50	60	17	55.29000	0.976
60	70	22	64.85147	1.263
70	80	24	75.58988	1.378
80	90	18	83.41304	1.033
$90 < L/V < 100$		26	95.72280	1.493
Equal to 100*		54	100.00000	3.100
Totals		1,742		100.000%†

* If the last two classes were combined into a class "greater than 90 percent, not greater than 100 percent," this combined class would contain 80 losses, 4.592 percent of the total number of losses, with an average ratio of loss to sound value of 98.60991 percent.

† Corrected for error due to rounding.

Source: Calculated from data in the files of the Office of the Fire Marshal, State of Oregon.

TABLE 13. Percentage fire loss-severity distribution of 2860 losses during 1964 and 1965 to Oregon properties for all sound values

(1) Loss as Percentage of Sound Value $X_1 < L/V \leq X_2$		(2) Number of Losses	(3) Arithmetic Mean Loss	(4) % of Number of Losses
X_1	X_2			
0	0.01	52	0.00613%	1.818
0.01	0.02	58	0.01503	2.028
0.02	0.03	60	0.02479	2.098
0.03	0.04	52	0.03567	1.818
0.04	0.05	39	0.04434	1.364
0.05	0.06	39	0.05455	1.364
0.06	0.07	37	0.06547	1.294
0.07	0.08	36	0.07499	1.259
0.08	0.09	29	0.08431	1.014
0.09	0.1	29	0.09520	1.014
0.1	0.2	218	0.14702	7.622
0.2	0.3	142	0.24718	4.965
0.3	0.4	120	0.35084	4.196
0.4	0.5	86	0.45827	3.007
0.5	0.6	76	0.56431	2.657
0.6	0.7	68	0.65155	2.378
0.7	0.8	67	0.74613	2.343
0.8	0.9	54	0.85316	1.888
0.9	1	55	0.96128	1.923
1	2	304	1.45730	10.629
2	3	145	2.48428	5.070
3	4	96	3.48800	3.357
4	5	68	4.49856	2.378
5	6	51	5.51100	1.783
6	7	37	6.44265	1.294
7	8	28	7.59058	0.979
8	9	31	8.60079	1.084
9	10	27	9.58447	0.944
10	20	151	14.41775	5.280
20	30	69	24.59875	2.413
30	40	49	34.48847	1.713
40	50	45	45.52229	1.573
50	60	43	54.86150	1.504
60	70	44	64.59323	1.538
70	80	39	75.55991	1.364
80	90	34	84.42709	1.189
$90 < L/V < 100$		45	95.62580	1.573
Equal to 100*		237	100.00000	8.287
Totals		2,860		100.00%†

* If the last two classes were combined into a class "greater than 90 percent, not greater than 100 percent," this combined class would contain 282 losses, 9.860 percent of the total number of losses, with an average ratio of loss to sound value of 99.30199 percent.
† Corrected for error due to rounding.
Source: Calculated from data in the files of the Office of the Fire Marshal, State of Oregon.

TABLE 14. Summary of percentage fire loss-severity distribution of 2860 losses during 1964 and 1965 to Oregon properties for all sound values

Loss as Percentage of Sound Value $X_1 < L/V \leq X_2$		Number of Losses	Arithmetic Mean Loss	% of Number of Losses
X_1	X_2			
0	10	2,104	1.47570%	73.566
10	20	151	14.41776	5.280
20	30	69	24.59875	2.413
30	40	49	34.48847	1.713
40	50	45	45.52229	1.573
50	60	43	54.86150	1.504
60	70	44	64.59323	1.538
70	80	39	75.55991	1.364
80	90	34	84.42709	1.189
90	100	282	99.30199	9.860
Totals		2,860		100.000%*

* Corrected for error due to rounding.
Source: Table 13.

cent of value comprise 60.6 percent of losses to larger properties, 19.9 percent of losses to smaller ones. For losses not exceeding 10 percent of value, the percentages are 80.2 and 59.6 percent, respectively. These differences seem good evidence that the probability of a loss of a given size is inversely related to its dollar size as well as to the fraction of full property value lost. A given dollar loss is a higher percentage of the value of a smaller property than of a larger one. These differences between small and large properties are important because, if small properties suffer a greater proportion of total or severe losses than do large properties, the *percentage* premium rate credit for a given percentage of coinsurance in a fire policy on a small property should be less than the credit for the same coinsurance percentage on a large property. However, for no peril included in this study do coinsurance rate schedules, examined in Chapter 8, distinguish large from small properties.

The separate category for total losses clarifies the shape of the upper tails of percentage fire loss-severity distributions. It appears that all sizes of *partial* losses above 80 percent of value are about equally rare, but that *total* losses are relatively frequent —16 percent of all losses for small properties, 3 percent for large properties, and 8 percent overall. In Tables 11 through 13, the arithmetic means of the classes containing *partial* losses over 90 percent of value are not pulled significantly above the class mid-points by *partial* losses concentrated near full value. For the types of properties studied, this evidence suggests neither a continuous, smooth *j*- nor *u*-shaped distribution, but a downward sloping, flat-bottomed curve with an upward discontinuity at 100 percent of value, as shown in Figure 2.

Figure 2. Percentage fire loss-severity distribution suggested by Oregon data.

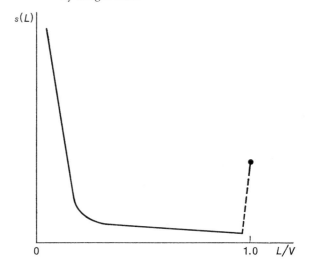

The summary distribution of all Oregon fire losses to frame-protected properties (Table 14) bears striking resemblance to Whitney's 1905 distributions for frame buildings and their contents, Table 8 and Table 9. All three distributions are practically level for losses between 20 and 90 percent of value. The 73.6 percent of losses not more than 10 percent of value in the Oregon distribution, which combines losses to structures and contents, is lower than the corresponding percentage in Whitney's distribution of building losses (82.9 percent) but higher than the corresponding percentage for his contents losses (71.7 percent). In the Whitney frame business building distribution, losses not exceeding 10 percent of value average 1.8 percent of value; in the Oregon distribution, these losses average 1.5 percent of value. Losses above 90 percent of value (including total losses) average 99.5 and 99.3 percent of value in the Whitney and Oregon distributions, respectively. The percentage of losses above 90 percent of value in the Oregon distribution (9.9 percent of all losses), higher than in either of the Whitney distributions (2.0 percent for frame business buildings, 4.1 percent for their contents), may indicate that urban buildings in San Francisco at the turn of the twentieth century had better construction or fire protection than do some frame-protected structures in present day Oregon. The similarities among these distributions are consistent with the premise that percentage fire loss-severity distributions are stable over time and can be verified by more extensive research.

The percentage distribution of losses to all Oregon properties, Column 4 of Table 13, was converted into a cumulative "more than" ogive, analogous to that for the dollar fire loss-severity distribution in Column 5 of Table 4. With a computer, functions of the forms shown on page 79 were fitted to this ogive, with the best results achieved by the equation

$$\ln y = 6.1221 - 0.0516(\ln x) - 0.1035(\ln x)^2. \qquad (6\text{--}5)$$

The dependent variable y is the conditional probability of a loss greater than x, given some nonzero loss, and x is the fraction of value damaged. The y values are multiplied by 1000 and the x values by 100, so that, if the conditional probability of a loss above 90 percent of value is 0.09860, y is 98.60, and x is 90.00. Table 15 compares the predictions of Equation 6–5 with the actual points on the ogive.

SUMMARY

This chapter explores the characteristics, and gives some examples, of dollar and percentage fire loss-severity distributions.

A loss-severity distribution relates the conditional probability, given some loss greater than zero, of a loss of a particular size to

TABLE 15. Comparison of actual with predicted percentages of Oregon fire losses exceeding certain percentages of value

Loss above X Percent of Value X	Actual Percentage	Predicted Percentage
0.01	98.2	150.0*
0.02	96.2	125.2*
0.03	94.1	113.0*
0.04	92.2	105.0*
0.05	90.9	98.9
0.06	89.5	94.3
0.07	88.2	90.7
0.08	87.0	87.6
0.09	85.9	85.0
0.10	84.9	82.6
0.20	77.3	69.1
0.30	72.3	62.2
0.40	68.1	57.8
0.50	65.1	54.5
0.60	62.5	52.0
0.70	60.1	49.9
0.80	57.8	48.3
0.90	55.9	46.8
1.0	54.0	45.6
2.0	43.3	38.1
3.0	38.3	34.3
4.0	34.9	31.9
5.0	32.5	30.1
6.0	30.7	28.7
7.0	29.4	27.6
8.0	28.5	26.6
9.0	27.4	25.8
10.0	26.4	25.1
20.0	21.2	21.0
30.0	18.7	18.9
40.0	17.0	17.6
50.0	15.5	16.6
60.0	14.0	15.8
70.0	12.4	15.2
80.0	11.0	14.7
90.0	9.9	14.2
100.0	0.0	....†

* Not a possible value.
† Beyond capacity of computer.
Source: Table 13, Equation 6–5, and *Standard Mathematical Tables*, eds. Robert C. Weast, Samuel M. Selby, and Charles D. Hodgman, 12th ed. (Cleveland, Ohio: The Chemical Rubber Publishing Co., 1959), pp. 171–178.

the size of that loss, expressed as either a dollar amount or a percentage of value. The unconditional probabilities of losses (including "zero loss") and the conditional probabilities of losses greater than zero both form complete probability distributions, essential for computing proper coinsurance rates. A more sophisticated distribution, relating the conditional probabilities of losses to both the dollar amount of damage and the percentage of value lost, could not be used unless coinsurance requirements combined (probably not in an additive sense) dollar sums and percentages of value.

A dollar fire loss-severity distribution of 132,000 fires to all properties except dwellings is presented. The Salzmann distribution of Homeowners dwelling fire losses as percentages of insurance casts doubt on the validity of the common underwriting assumption that frame-unprotected structures suffer only total losses from fire. The Whitney 1905 percentage fire loss-severity distributions for frame business buildings and their contents are similar to the present author's distribution of 2,680 Oregon fire losses to frame-protected properties (buildings and contents combined). The Oregon statistics suggest that (1) small properties tend to suffer a greater proportion of total or severe losses than do large properties; and (2) while severe *partial* losses are rare, total losses are relatively common (approximately 8 percent of all losses). Instead of a *j*- or *u*-shaped percentage loss-severity distribution, these results suggest, at least for some types of properties, a distribution which declines quickly, has a wide, flat bottom, and has an upward discontinuity at 100 percent of value.

CHAPTER 7

Coinsurance Rates in Theory

PURPOSE

This chapter demonstrates how coinsurance requirements should be computed for both agreed (or stated) amount clauses and percentage coinsurance requirements. The first section gives the required basic data and assumptions; the second presents the pure premium rate models; and the third outlines the implications of the models. Modified for administrative expenses, these implications guide the analysis of actual coinsurance rates in Chapter 8.

BASIC DATA AND ASSUMPTIONS

Basic Data

The three parameters, or determinants, of a pure premium coinsurance rate are (1) the frequency of loss, (2) the distribution of losses by size, and (3) the coinsurance requirement.

Loss Frequency. Loss frequency can be determined by the experience of a large number of essentially identical risks. If 2000 losses occur in a group of 100,000 risks during a policy period (usually one year), loss frequency (designated by f) is 0.02, even though one risk may have suffered more than one of these losses.

If this relative frequency is accurate, pure premiums based on the assumption of no more than one loss per period to any property can be adequate to pay the aggregate losses of the group. Because (as Appendix 3 shows) loss frequency affects only the rate level and not the rate relativities (ratios between coinsurance rates), the generality of the rate models is not reduced by assuming a 0.02 relative frequency of some loss to a property in a policy period.

Loss-Severity Distribution.   A loss-severity distribution, which sets the relativities between pure premium coinsurance rates, gives the percentage of losses in a given size category. These categories may be ranges of dollar amounts or percentages of insurable value. If 3.5 percent of losses to class A properties fall into size class 1, then $s_1 = 0.035$. If f_A is 0.02, then the unconditional probability of a class 1 loss to one class A property is $f_A s_1$, or $(0.02)(0.035)$, or 0.0007.[1] If \$1000 (or 0.1 of insurable value, V) is the arithmetic mean loss in class 1 (designated L_1), \$0.70 (or $0.00007V$) is the expected value of class 1 losses to one class A property. In symbols, this expected value is $f_A s_1 L_1$.

Stated amount coinsurance rates are based on the distribution of fire losses by dollar size in Table 4. Percentage coinsurance rates are based on the distribution of Oregon fire losses by percentages of value from Table 13. The data from these tables are reproduced in the tables showing the rate calculations, pages 105 and 106.

Coinsurance Requirements.   From the categories of loss size by dollar amount, without interpolation or extrapolation of the statistics, rates can be computed for stated amounts of \$5000, \$10,000, \$25,000, \$50,000, \$100,000, \$250,000, \$500,000 and \$1,-000,000 (see page 109). The distribution in Table 4 includes losses over \$1,000,000, but the number of losses below any figure larger than \$1,000,000 cannot be determined from the open class "\$1,-

---

[1] The chance of a class 1 loss to a class A property is a joint probability, the product of (1) the probability of a loss of whatever size to a class A property and (2) the probability, given some class A loss, that the loss will be of class 1 size. See John Neter and William Wasserman, *Fundamental Statistics for Business and Economics*, 2nd ed. (Boston: Allyn & Bacon, Inc., 1961), p. 291, for a discussion of joint probabilities.

000,000 and over." For computing coinsurance rates, the number
or proportion of losses below the coinsurance requirement must
be known.

Rates are calculated for percentage coinsurance requirements
of 1, 5, 10, 20, 30, 40, 50, 60, 70, 80, 90, and 100 percent (see
page 110).

Assumptions

Rates Equitable and Just Adequate. The basic equation of
the rate models rests on the assumption that each insured's expected value of indemnity payments in a policy period equals
his pure premium. This equation expresses the "adequate, reasonable, and not unfairly discriminatory" standard of rate regulation.

Insured Properties Homogeneous. For all properties in the
class for which rates are computed, relative frequencies of some
loss (fs) and loss size distributions (s values) are the same. The
model procedures for one class can be applied to all others.

Rate Determinants Known and Stable. Loss frequency and
severity are known and are free of dynamic influences, such as
technology, but specific losses cannot be predicted. Also, the
volume of losses not reported to insurers—a factor which varies
with economic conditions and bears on premium equity and
adequacy[2]—is stable.

Losses Precisely Adjusted. The value of each insured property
is presumed exactly determinable, and, for each loss, any coinsurance penalties are properly assessed. Thus, no valuation or loss
adjustment difficulties, treated throughout Chapter 10, disrupt the
application of coinsurance.

No Other Insurance. The assumption that the insurance for
which the rate is calculated is the only coverage applicable to
each insured property eliminates unpredictable elements in the

---

[2] Lars-G. Benchert and Ingvar Sternberg, "An Attempt to Find an Expression for the Distribution of Fire Damage Amount," *Proceedings of the
XVth International Congress of Actuaries,* vol. II (1957), p. 289.

expected value of indemnity payments due to proration of liability among insurers.

Interest Ignored. The models ignore interest on pure premiums collected (usually at the beginning of the policy period) before they are disbursed as loss payments (at mid-period, on the average). An ideal model would take account of interest, but doing so gains little precision for annual policies and introduces complications not essential to an understanding of coinsurance.

No More than One Loss per Period. The assumption that no policy incurs more than one loss per policy period avoids double counting of losses in the following models, which derive pure premium rates for an individual policy on the basis of its expected experience rather than aggregate pure premiums for a group of policies on the basis of the experience of the group. While the individual policy and aggregate class methods are equivalent, the individual method is simpler and more direct than the aggregate one.

Multiple losses do occur to one property in a single policy period, and they must be taken into account by either method. If the aggregate method were used, the sum of all losses to all properties in the class (including multiple losses to one property) would be compared with the total insurance assumed to be written on all properties in the class. In the individual method, multiple losses to one property enter through the factor of loss frequency. Loss frequency can be estimated by a study, over many policy periods, of the number of losses to many properties. Some of these losses are multiple losses to one property in one policy period. All of these losses determine the relative frequency of loss assumed for one property during one policy period. Since multiple losses in a single policy period raise the assumed relative frequency of one loss during one policy period, proper weight is given to multiple losses to one property under the individual policy method. If, in the computation of rates under this method, more than one loss to one property in one period were permitted, multiple losses would be given double weight, overall loss frequency would be inflated, and redundant aggregate premiums for the insurer would result.

CALCULATION OF PURE PREMIUM
COINSURANCE RATES

Pure premium coinsurance rates are computed on the assumption of a policy face equal to the coinsurance requirement.[3] As explained in Chapters 2 and 5, the coinsurance mechanism balances pure premiums and expected indemnity payments if the policy face is equal to or less than that assumed.[4] The general pure premium rate as previously shown in Equation 2–3 is

$$R = f \left(\frac{\int_0^F Ls(L)dL + F\left[1 - \int_0^F s(L)dL\right]}{F} \right)$$

where f is the probability of some loss, and s is the probability, given some loss, of a loss of a particular size.

Stated Amount Rates

Since, under an agreed amount clause, the policy face generally equals the full property value determined by an insurance agent and an insured,[5] losses exceeding the policy face can be presumed impossible. Hence, the rate equation for each $100 of an agreed amount of insurance, A, is

$$R = f \left(\frac{\int_0^F Ls(L)dL}{A/100} \right). \tag{7–1}$$

---

[3] A. W. Whitney, "The Actuarial Theory of Fire Insurance Rates as Depending upon the Ratio of Insurance to Sound Value Hence a Determination of the Rates for Use with a Coinsurance Clause," *Reports, Memoirs, and Proceedings of the Sixth International Congress of Actuaries,* vol. II (Vienna, 1909), p. 397.

[4] But not if more than assumed. Since proper pure premium rates vary inversely with coinsurance requirements, the rate for a given requirement is too high for the insured with coverage exceeding it. Therefore, equity to all insureds demands that a coinsurance rate for full coverage be available.

[5] Interview with John B. Davis, Assistant Vice President, Insurance Company of North America, December 22, 1966.

Equation 7–1 is Equation 2–3 simplified, because the second, bracketed, element in the numerator of Equation 2–3 is not needed for losses above the policy face. Table 16 gives the data

TABLE 16. Loss data for stated amount coinsurance rates

(1) Stated Amount (A_n)	(2) Conditional Probability of Losses $s(L_n)$ $(A_{n-1} < L_n \leq A_n)$	(3) Unconditional Probability of Losses $fs(L_n)$ (2% of Col. 2)*	(4) Arithmetic Mean Loss
$ 5,000........	0.772276	0.01544552	$ 1,340
10,000.........	0.100635	0.00201270	7,027
25,000.........	0.076900	0.00153800	15,317
50,000.........	0.029081	0.00058162	34,749
100,000.........	0.013756	0.00027512	68,868
250,000.........	0.005701	0.00011402	149,175
500,000.........	0.001265	0.00002530	342,503
1,000,000.........	0.000265	0.00000530	652,743
Totals............	0.999879†	0.01999758†	

* Assumed probability of some loss, *f*, is 0.02.
† Fails to total 1.00 (or 0.02) because losses above $1,000,000 are excluded.
Source: Table 4.

for arithmetically calculating stated amount pure premium coinsurance rates. Column 1 of this table lists the agreed amounts. Column 2 gives the conditional probabilities (*s* values) of losses not exceeding the particular agreed amount, but more than the next smaller agreed amount. Thus, the *s* value for a loss above $5000, but not above $10,000, is about 0.1006, i.e., approximately 10 percent of all losses are in this category. Column 3 shows the unconditional probability of these losses ($f \times s$), 2 percent of the conditional probability. Column 4 contains the arithmetic mean of losses above the preceding agreed amount, but not greater than the agreed amount in the same row. For example, losses above $5000, but not above $10,000, average $7027. Therefore, the expected value of losses in this category is $14.1432429, or $0.100635 \times 0.02 \times \$7027$.

The pure premium rate for $5000 of coverage is

$$R_{5000} = \frac{(0.01544552 \times 1340)}{50} = \frac{20.69699680}{50}$$

$$= \$0.41394 \text{ per } \$100. \tag{7-1a}$$

The rate for $10,000 is

$$R_{10,000} = \frac{(0.01544552 \times 1340) + (0.00201270 \times 7027)}{100}$$

$$= \frac{20.69699680 + 14.14324290}{100}$$

$$= \$0.34840 \text{ per } \$100. \qquad (7\text{--}1b)$$

Computation of other agreed amount rates, shown in Table 17, is an extension of this process.

TABLE 17. Pure premium coinsurance rates for various stated amounts

Stated Amount	Rate per $100 per Policy Period
$ 5,000	$0.41394
10,000	0.34840
25,000	0.23359
50,000	0.15722
100,000	0.09756
250,000	0.04583
500,000	0.02465
$1,000,000	$0.01578

Source: Computed from Table 16.

Agreed (or stated) amount coinsurance rates decline as policy size increases, even though each property is assumed fully insured. Thus, coinsurance rates for percentage coinsurance requirements are faulty because they give the same percentage credit for 100 percent coinsurance regardless of the size of the property insured. In contrast, rates for percentage coinsurance requirements are not affected by policy size but fall as insurance approaches the full property value (see Table 19). This contrast is due to the fact that stated amount coinsurance rates presuppose that only the dollar size of a loss determines its s value, while percentage coinsurance rates presume that the size distribution of losses depends entirely on the fraction of value destroyed. Neither presumption is correct. However, one of the parameters of any coinsurance rate is the proportion of losses equal to or less than the assumed policy face (coinsurance requirement). The size of losses must be expressed in the same terms (i.e., dollar amounts or percentages of value) as the assumed policy face.

Only if coinsurance requirements were to reflect both dollar amounts and percentages of value would a loss distribution taking account of both dollars and fractions of value be useful. A simple additive combination of percentage and stated amount coinsurance requirements is theoretically questionable. A slightly better means of accounting for both dollar and percentage loss-severity is to impose alternative dollar amount or percentage coinsurance requirements, as in open stock burglary insurance. But the most direct method of accounting for both dollar amounts and percentages of loss would be to devise percentage coinsurance credits for properties in different size classes.

The low frequency of large dollar amounts of loss is caused to some degree by the relative scarcity of properties with values over, say, $100,000. Also, the distribution excludes losses under $250, causing some understatement of rates, especially for the lower face amounts.

If a policy should be less than its agreed amount, coinsurance reduces every indemnity payment proportionately. An insured with three-fourths the required coverage pays three-fourths the premium contemplated by the insurer, and three-fourths of each loss is paid, up to the policy face, which is three-fourths of that assumed. Consequently, the balance between expected indemnity and premiums for each insured maintains the equity and adequacy of the premium rate. Since the agreed amount equals full value, fair treatment of the insured who exceeds his coinsurance requirement in order to get full protection is no problem, because it is assumed that no one insures for more than the full value.

Percentage Coinsurance Rates

With a percentage of value coinsurance clause, an insured may choose any available coinsurance percentage (c). From the current insurable value of his property (V), he can determine the present dollar amount of the coinsurance requirement ($C = cV$). Since the pure premium coinsurance rate relativities are determined by the distribution of losses as percentages of value, V can be any amount, such as the $100,000 assumed here. Because the assumed policy face equals C, the rate equation, from Equation 2–3, becomes

$$R = f \left(\frac{\int_0^c Ls(L)dL + F\left[1 - \int_0^c s(L)dL\right]}{F/100} \right). \quad (7\text{–}2)$$

Table 18 gives the Oregon data on fire loss severity in a form suited for calculating percentage coinsurance rates. Column 1 lists the coinsurance percentages. Column 2 gives the percentages of losses (s values) greater than the preceding coinsurance percentage but not greater than the one in the same row. For example, 21.43356 percent of the losses are greater than 1 percent, but not greater than 5 percent, of value. Column 3 contains the s values times the assumed loss frequency of 0.02, or the unconditional probabilities of losses. Column 4 gives the arithmetic mean loss as a fraction of value for each of the intervals between coinsurance requirements—for example, 2.3556 percent of value for losses above 1, but not above 5, percent of value. Column 5 gives the unconditional probabilities ($f \times s$) of losses greater than each coinsurance requirement—losses for which any policy equal to or less than the coinsurance requirement pays its face. For instance, 0.006503498, or 0.02 minus the sum of the unconditional probabilities of smaller losses, is the unconditional probability of a loss exceeding 5 percent of value.

Applied to a $100,000 risk, Equation 7–2 indicates a pure premium rate per $100 for 1 percent coinsurance ($1000) of

$$\frac{(0.009209790)(306.40) + (0.010790210)(1000.00)}{10} = \$1.36121.$$

$$(7\text{–}2a)$$

For 5 percent ($5000) coverage,

$$\frac{0.009209290)(306.40) + (0.004286712)(2355.60) +}{50}$$

$$\frac{(0.006503498)(5000.00)}{50} = \$0.90874. \quad (7\text{–}2b)$$

TABLE 18. Loss data for calculation of percentage coinsurance requirements

(1) c_n	(2) Conditional Probability of Losses $s(L_n)$ $(C_{n-1} < L_n \leq C_n)$	(3) Unconditional Probability of Losses $fs(L_n)$ (2% of Col. 2) *	(4) Arithmetic Mean Loss (L_n/V)	(5) Unconditional Probability of Losses Greater than C_n $[fs(L) > C_n]$
1%	0.4604895	0.009209790	0.003064	0.010790210
5	0.2143356	0.004286712	0.023556	0.006503498
10	0.0608392	0.001216784	0.072263	0.005286714
20	0.0527972	0.001055944	0.144178	0.004230770
30	0.0241259	0.000482518	0.245988	0.003748252
40	0.0171329	0.000342658	0.344885	0.003405594
50	0.1573430	0.000314686	0.455223	0.003090908
60	0.0150350	0.000300700	0.548615	0.002790208
70	0.0153846	0.000307692	0.645932	0.002482516
80	0.0136364	0.000272728	0.755599	0.002209788
90	0.0118881	0.000237762	0.844271	0.001972028
100%	0.0986014	0.001972028	0.993020	0.000000000

* Assumed probability of some loss, f, is 0.02.
Source: Table 13.

Rates for other coinsurance percentages are computed analogously. These rates and the rate relativities (to the 80 percent coinsurance rate) are given in Table 19.[6]

TABLE 19. Pure premium coinsurance rates for various percentage coinsurance requirements

Coinsurance Requirement	Pure Premium Rate per $100	Pure Premium Rate as Percentage of 80% Rate
1%	1.36121	351.95
5	0.90874	234.96
10	0.75272	194.62
20	0.61122	158.04
30	0.53982	139.57
40	0.49385	127.69
50	0.46038	119.03
60	0.43259	111.85
70	0.40827	105.56
80	0.38676	100.00
90	0.36687	94.86
100%	0.34852	90.11

Source: Computed from Table 18.

For the insured with a coinsurance deficiency, pure premiums and indemnity payments remain balanced. For example, if F/C equals 3/5, the insured receives three-fifths of any loss which is less than the coinsurance requirement, while insureds meeting the requirement are fully paid. For losses at least equal to the coinsurance requirement, the deficient policy, like those just meeting the requirement, pays its face, but this is only three-fifths the face paid by the other policies. The insured with three-fifths the assumed coverage pays three-fifths the assumed premium and can expect to receive three-fifths the indemnity paid to those meeting the requirement, regardless of the size of losses. Thus, equity among insureds applies to *expected* values. The occur-

---

[6] For a reversal of the procedure in this section, that is, for computation of the distribution of losses by size, given percentage coinsurance rate relativities, an assumed level of rates, and arithmetic mean losses between coinsurance requirements, see Appendix 5.

rence or size of any loss has no bearing on equity, although some authors have maintained otherwise.[7]

If less than 100 percent coinsurance is available, however, an insured seeking complete protection may exceed the coinsurance requirement, perhaps buying 100 percent coverage at the 80 percent coinsurance rate. Since, as the policy face rises, rates should fall by the following factor (previously shown in Equation 2–4)

$$\frac{\text{expected value of losses less than policy face}}{\text{policy face squared}}$$

and since coinsurance does not raise indemnity payments, the 80 percent rate is inequitable for this insured, creating redundant premiums. Therefore, coinsurance requirements, whether they be stated amounts or percentages of value, should be available at distinct premium rates for the largest amount of coverage desired by a substantial number of insureds.

Rate of Premium Rate Change

Equation 2–4 shows that, if losses less than the policy face are possible, pure premium rates should fall as the assumed policy face (coinsurance requirement) increases. A further set of relationships, first noted in 1904,[8] ties the rate of decrease in the pure premium rate to the shape of the distribution of losses as percentages of value. These relationships are: (1) if small losses

---

[7] See C. A. Kulp and John W. Hall, *Casualty Insurance*, 4th ed. (New York: The Ronald Press Co., 1968), p. 48; Donald L. MacDonald, *Corporate Risk Control* (New York: The Ronald Press Co., 1966), p. 87; W. J. Nichols, "The Coinsurance Clause," *The Fire Insurance Contract, Its History and Interpretation*, compiled and edited by the Insurance Society of New York (Indianapolis, Ind.: The Rough Notes Co., Inc., 1922), p. 700; Robert Riegel, "Coinsurance," *Journal of American Insurance*, vol. XXII, no. 6 (June 1945), p. 20; Robert Riegel and H. J. Loman, *Insurance Principles and Practices*, rev. ed. (New York: Prentice-Hall, Inc., 1942), p. 370; and Robert Riegel and Jerome S. Miller, *Insurance Principles and Practices*, 5th ed. (Englewood Cliffs, N.J.: Prentice-Hall, Inc., 1966), p. 496.

[8] A. W. Whitney, "The Co-Insurance Clause," paper read before the Fire Underwriters' Association of the Pacific, January 13, 1904, pp. 7–11; and A. W. Whitney, "The Conflagration Hazard and Coinsurance," *Proceedings of the Thirteenth Annual Meeting of the Fire Underwriters' Association of the Pacific* (San Francisco, 1906), p. 77.

outnumber large ones, rates decrease at a decreasing rate; (2) if large losses outnumber small ones, rates decrease at an increasing rate; and (3) if losses of all sizes are equally numerous, rates decrease at a constant rate. Mathematically, these relationships imply that the second derivative of the pure premium rate with respect to the policy face in Equation 2–3 (the first derivative being the negative of the fraction in the text, page 111) is negative in case 1, positive in case 2, and zero in case 3.

By way of numerical illustration, assume five percentage coinsurance requirements of 20, 40, 60, 80, and 100 percent. Assume three distributions of losses as percentages of value, as are shown in Tables 20, 21, and 22. Column 1 in each table gives the coinsurance percentages for which rates are desired. Each Column 2 presents a distribution of losses as percentages of value, expressed in dollars on the basis of a $10,000 property value. Each Column 3 gives the percentage of losses in each size class of losses. For example, in Table 20, where small losses predominate, 25 percent of losses exceed 20, but not 40, percent of value. Each Column 4 gives the arithmetic mean loss in each loss size category—for example, $8500 for losses greater than 80, but not greater than 100, percent of value, in Table 21, where large losses predominate. The placement of class mean losses is not crucial except, in the distribution where losses of all sizes are equally probable (Table 22), mean losses must equal class midpoints. Pure premium rates per $100, with an assumed 0.02 relative frequency of some loss, are shown in each Column 5, opposite the corresponding coinsurance percentage. For example, in Table 21, the 20 percent coinsurance rate is $1.9750, and the 100 percent rate is $1.3400. Each Column 6 gives the decrease in each coinsurance rate from the preceding rate. For example, the difference between the 40 and 60 percent rates in Table 20 is $0.2125. Since the intervals between all coinsurance percentages are equal, it can be seen that coinsurance rates decrease by decreasing amounts in Table 20 (small losses predominating), by increasing amounts in Table 21 (large losses predominating), and by a constant amount in Table 22 (all sizes of loss equally likely).

For the perils selected for this study, small losses predominate

TABLE 20. Percentage coinsurance rate changes—small losses predominating

(1) Coinsurance Percentage	(2) Size of Loss $X_1 < L \leq X_2$		(3) Percentage of Losses	(4) Arithmetic Mean Loss	(5) Coinsurance Rate per $100*	(6) Decrease in Rate
	X_1	X_2				
20	$ 0	$ 2,000	45	$ 500	$1.3250	$.....
40	2,000	4,000	25	3,000	1.0875	0.2375
60	4,000	6,000	15	5,000	0.8750	0.2125
80	6,000	8,000	10	7,000	0.7062	0.1618
100	8,000	10,000	5	9,500	0.5800	0.1262

* Based on 0.02 probability of some loss.
Source: Computed from hypothetical data.

TABLE 21. Percentage coinsurance rate changes—large losses predominating

(1) Coinsurance Percentage	(2) Size of Loss $X_1 < L \leq X_2$		(3) Percentage of Losses	(4) Arithmetic Mean Loss	(5) Coinsurance Rate per $100*	(6) Decrease in Rate
	X_1	X_2				
20	$ 0	$ 2,000	5	$1,500	$1.9750	$.....
40	2,000	4,000	10	3,000	1.8875	0.0875
60	4,000	6,000	15	5,000	1.7750	0.1125
80	6,000	8,000	25	7,000	1.6188	0.1562
100	8,000	10,000	45	8,500	1.3400	0.2788

* Based on 0.02 probability of some loss.
Source: Computed from hypothetical data.

TABLE 22. Percentage coinsurance rate changes—losses of all sizes equally probable

(1) Coinsurance Percentage	(2) Size of Loss $X_1 < L \leqq X_2$ X_1	X_2	(3) Percentage of Losses	(4) Arithmetic Mean Loss	(5) Coinsurance Rate per $100*	(6) Decrease in Rate
20	$ 0	$ 2,000	20	$1,000	$1.8000	$......
40	2,000	4,000	20	3,000	1.6000	0.2000
60	4,000	6,000	20	5,000	1.4000	0.2000
80	6,000	8,000	20	7,000	1.2000	0.2000
100	8,000	10,000	20	9,000	1.0000	0.2000

* Based on 0.02 probability of some loss.
Source: Computed from hypothetical data.

Therefore, pure premium rates for insurance of these perils should decrease at decreasing rates for increasing coinsurance requirements.

Adjustments for Expense Allowances

Gross premium coinsurance rates are pure premium rates plus allowances for operating expenses, contingency reserves, and profit. Before the conclusion that gross coinsurance rates should fall at decreasing rates is adopted, the effect of these allowances (or loadings) must be studied.

Loadings can vary with pure premium volume, amount of insurance, or number of policies in different ways for different insurers. Rating formulas generally assume that all loadings vary as a constant percentage of pure premium.[9] In actual fact, for an average property insurer, about 10 percent of gross premium represents expenses "not allocable by premium volume."[10]

Whether loadings are wholly variable with pure premiums (and, therefore, are a constant percentage of the pure premium rate) or are partially fixed in amount (and, therefore, are a decreasing percentage of the premium rate for larger policies), loadings have little effect on the decreasing rate of decline in coinsurance rates. If loadings are a constant percentage of pure premium rates, gross rates are a constant multiple of pure rates, and the gross rates retain the relativities of the pure rates. Alternatively, if some loadings are fixed per policy, the average of this fixed cost falls at a decreasing rate along the path of a rectangular hyperbola as the policy face increases.[11] In either case, as long as losses which are small percentages of value predominate, pure and gross coinsurance rates should decrease by decreasing amounts for equal increments in coinsurance requirements.

---

[9] C. Arthur Williams, Jr., and Richard M. Heins, *Risk Management and Insurance* (New York: McGraw-Hill Book Co., 1964), p. 197, n. 8.

[10] C. Arthur Williams, Jr., *Price Discrimination in Property and Liability Insurance,* University of Minnesota Studies in Economics and Business, no. 19 (Minneapolis: University of Minnesota Press, 1959), p. 17.

[11] William S. Vickrey, *Microstatics* (New York: Harcourt, Brace & World, Inc., 1964), p. 168, shows that the average of costs which are fixed per unit of output (here $100 of insurance) is described by a rectangular hyperbola.

IMPLICATIONS OF THE MODELS

The implications of these models for gross premium coinsurance rates—for agreed amount clauses and for percentage coinsurance requirements—are that (1) a full range of coinsurance requirements and credits should be available; (2) no premium "reversals"[12] should exist; and (3) coinsurance rates should decrease at a declining rate with added coverage. The third point has been examined above, pages 112–15; the first two require some explanation.

Full Range of Requirements and Credits

For each policy face, there is only one gross or pure premium rate which is equitable and just adequate for a given insured. Coinsurance maintains rate adequacy and equity for face amounts equal to or lower than that assumed in the rate computation but it does not maintain equity for higher face amounts. Hence, a full range of coinsurance requirements, as finely graduated as practical, each with a separate rate, should be available. For insureds wishing full coverage, only a 100 percent coinsurance rate is proper. In theory, even the smallest policy should contain a coinsurance clause to balance expected indemnity with pure premiums.

No Reversals

A reversal occurs if the percentage decrease in the gross premium rate is greater than the percentage increase in the policy face, resulting in negative marginal revenue for the insurer and implying negative marginal cost for the unit of insurance where the reversal occurs. With bands of coinsurance rates, each rate

---

[12] A premium reversal occurs when a premium rate reduction is so great that the cost of more insurance is less than the cost of less insurance. Letter from R. Williams, Executive Secretary, Pacific Fire Rating Bureau, December 8, 1966.

applicable over an interval between coinsurance requirements, reversals are inevitable at the boundaries between bands. But reversals should not occur between the corresponding upper or lower boundaries of two rate bands.

For example, if an insured with a $100,000 building insures it for 79 percent of value at a 70 percent coinsurance rate which is 110 percent of the 80 percent rate (of, say, $1.00), his insurance will cost $869. He could have purchased 80 percent coverage at the 80 percent rate for $69 less. Therefore, by crossing the boundary between bands of rates, this insured has created an inevitable reversal. However, for 80 percent coverage, in contrast to 70 percent coverage, each at the associated coinsurance rate, there is no reversal in these rates, because 80 percent coverage costs $30 more than 70 percent coverage.

In contrast, a decrease between the 70 and 80 percent rates of more than about 14 percent, or $(80 - 70)/70$, would have created a reversal between the coinsurance rates. If the 80 percent rate, at $1.00, had been 80 percent of the 70 percent rate, 70 percent coverage for the $100,000 risk would have cost $875, and 80 percent coverage $800. This last illustration is the type of reversal which all schedules of coinsurance rates should avoid.

SUMMARY

This chapter presents data and assumptions for calculating agreed amount and percentage of value pure premium coinsurance rates, gives models for computing rates, and points out implications of the models.

The essential information is (1) a probability of some loss; (2) a size distribution of losses (either dollar amounts or percentages of value, corresponding to the form of coinsurance requirement); and (3) the coinsurance requirement. Ratios among coinsurance rates (coinsurance rate relativities) are independent of loss frequency. The necessary assumptions are (1) equality of expected indemnity and pure premiums; (2) homogeneous risks in credible numbers; (3) knowledge and stability of the parameters—loss frequency, loss severity, and assumed amount of insurance; (4)

precise adjustment of losses; (5) no other insurance; (6) zero time value of money (a convenience); and (7) a limit of one loss per policy per period (unnecessary if the rate is computed for a class rather than for an individual policy).

The pure premium coinsurance rates follow mathematically from the equality of pure premiums and expected indemnity payments.

The rate models imply that (1) a full range of coinsurance requirements, as finely graduated as is practical, should be available at separate premium rates; (2) premium reversals should not occur except, inevitably, at borders between bands of premium rates; and (3) pure and gross premium coinsurance rates should decrease at a declining rate with increasing coinsurance requirements, given that small losses predominate.

CHAPTER 8

Coinsurance Rates in Practice

PURPOSE

This chapter describes and analyzes current[1] schedules of percentage of value coinsurance rates for sprinkler leakage, water damage, earthquake, fire, and extended coverage endorsement insurance. Coinsurance rates for agreed amount endorsements are negotiated between insurers and individual insureds, are not published,[2] and, therefore, cannot be described in detail. But lower rates generally are offered for larger agreed amounts,[3] as is theoretically proper (see page 106).

All schedules of coinsurance rates described below are analyzed as a group at the conclusion of this chapter. The schedules are examined as to the extent to which they (1) offer a full range of coinsurance requirements, each with a distinct rate; (2) contain no reversals except at boundaries between coinsurance rates; (3) stipulate rates decreasing at a declining rate;

---

[1] Schedules of percentage of value coinsurance credits in the rate manuals for the various states are constantly changing in detail, and major changes occur occasionally. The schedules described in this chapter were in force as of the early summer of 1970, but they may not be applicable at any other date.

[2] Interview with John B. Davis, Assistant Vice President, Insurance Company of North America, January 17, 1967.

[3] Interview with Edward B. Black, Secretary—Underwriting, Insurance Company of North America, January 17, 1967.

(4) use a format which encourages insureds to select and fulfill a high coinsurance requirement; and (5) establish different rate *relativities* on the basis of factors apparently influencing the shapes of loss size distributions.

The heavy and widely conceded[4] reliance on judgment in setting coinsurance rates suggests that coinsurance rate relativities of separate rating organizations are likely to differ and that the mathematical precision assumed in the models of Chapter 7 probably is not achieved.

DESCRIPTION OF PERCENTAGE COINSURANCE RATE SCHEDULES

Sprinkler Leakage Coinsurance Credits

Table 23 gives the set of sprinkler leakage coinsurance credits[5] recommended by the Fire Insurance Research and Actuarial Association and promulgated by the local fire rating bureaus in all states.[6] For example, if a certain flat (no coinsurance) rate is $1.00 per $100, the 50 percent coinsurance rate is $0.15.

These rates apply to both specific and blanket sprinkler leakage coverage. The only restriction on coinsurance in blanket

---

[4] *Proceedings of the National Association of Insurance Commissioners,* vol. I (1965), pp. 208–209; L. H. Longley-Cook, "Problems of Fire Insurance Rate Making," *Proceedings of the Casualty Actuarial Society,* vol. XXXVIII, part I (November 1951), p. 102; Letter from George W. Clarke, General Manager, Washington (State) Surveying and Rating Bureau, October 19, 1966; letter from W. E. Ferris, Manager, Inspection and Rating, New Hampshire Board of Underwriters, September 15, 1966; letter from R. L. Gatewood, Secretary, South-Eastern Underwriters Association, December 14, 1966; letter from H. Reed Mullikin, Executive Manager, Middle Department Association of Fire Underwriters, December 21, 1966; letter from A. C. Richter, Manager, Rating Division, State of Minnesota Insurance Division, November 15, 1966; letter from Edwin N. Searl, Manager, Western Actuarial Bureau, April 28, 1967; and letter from R. Williams, Executive Secretary, Pacific Fire Rating Bureau, December 8, 1966.

[5] A coinsurance credit is the difference between a flat rate and a coinsurance rate.

[6] Interview with P. R. Bechtolt, Manager, Fire Insurance Research and Actuarial Association, January 31, 1967.

TABLE 23. Uniform schedule of sprinkler
leakage coinsurance credits

Coinsurance Percentage	*Reduction of Flat Rate*
10	60%
25	80
50	85
80 or 90	90
100	91%

Source: Georgia Inspection and Rating Bureau,
Georgia Rule Book (Atlanta: The Bureau, loose-leaf,
revised and supplemented periodically), p. 126F,
effective May 15, 1963.

policies is that coverage without coinsurance is forbidden. For specific coverage without coinsurance, the minimum policy is $25,000.

Water Damage Coinsurance Credits

A uniform schedule of water damage coinsurance rates, recommended by the Fire Insurance Research and Actuarial Association, has been promulgated by local bureaus in all states.[7] Table 24 gives these coinsurance rate credits and minimum requirements.

Earthquake Coinsurance Credits

Due to relatively great seismic activity around the Pacific rim, the earthquake rating system in Arizona, California, Idaho, Montana, Nevada, Oregon, Utah, and Washington differs from the one system used in the rest of the United States.[8] The Pacific system originated in the Pacific Fire Rating Bureau; the non-Pacific (or national) system is recommended by the Fire Insurance Research and Actuarial Association.[9]

---

[7] Interview with P. R. Bechtolt, Manager, Fire Insurance Research and Actuarial Association, January 31, 1967.

[8] Mark R. Greene, "Allied Lines Insurance," *Property and Liability Insurance Handbook*, ed. John D. Long and Davis W. Gregg (Homewood, Ill.: Richard D. Irwin, Inc., 1965), pp. 105–106.

[9] Interview with P. R. Bechtolt, Manager, Fire Insurance Research and Actuarial Association, January 31, 1967.

TABLE 24. Uniform schedule of water
damage coinsurance credits
and minimum requirements

Credits

Coinsurance Percentage	Reduction of Flat Rate
1	5.0%
2½	15.0
5	35.0
7½	50.0
10	60.0
15	71.0
20	76.5
25	80.0
50	86.0
80 or higher	90.0%

Minimum Requirements*

Property Value	Minimum Coinsurance Percentage
Under $ 50,000	25
$ 50,000 but under $ 75,000	20
75,000 but under 100,000	15
100,000 but under 250,000	10

* Additional restrictions: (1) minimum policy on property valued at $250,000 or more is $25,000; (2) policy issued at flat rate must be for at least $25,000; (3) minimum requirements apply to each item of insurance; and (4) blanket coverage must be subject to at least 10 percent coinsurance.

Source: *Manual of Rates, Rules and Clauses for Water Damage Insurance* (New York: Fire Insurance Research and Actuarial Association, 1963), pp. 4–5.

Non-Pacific States. Coinsurance credits for specific earthquake coverage outside the Pacific area are given in Table 25. The coinsurance requirements and credits for specific insurance apply to blanket coverage of one building and its contents. For blanket coverage of more property, three alternatives exist: (1) the 100 percent coinsurance rate; (2) the 90 percent clause at the 80 percent rate; or (3) any or no coinsurance clause, at the same coinsurance or flat rate charged for specific insurance, subject to a pro rata distribution clause. With a pro rata distribution clause, any loss is paid as if the blanket policy had been a specific one for the pro rata coverage.

TABLE 25. Schedule of earthquake coinsurance credits in non-Pacific states

Coinsurance Percentage	Percentage of 80% Coinsurance Rate
None (flat rate)	500
50	140
80	100
90	95
100	90

Source: *Manual of Rates, Rules and Clauses for Earthquake and Volcanic Eruption Insurance*, Revision No. 2—1957 (New York: Fire Insurance Research and Actuarial Association, 1950), p. 2.

Pacific States. The eight Pacific states named above follow the schedule of coinsurance credits in Table 26 for specific earthquake coverage. The Pacific system makes no provision

TABLE 26. Schedule of earthquake coinsurance credits in Pacific states

Coinsurance Percentage	Percentage of 70% Coinsurance Rate
None (flat rate)	Not permitted
40	140
50	125
60	110
70	100
80	95
90	90
100	85

Source: *Tariff Rules*, loose-leaf, revised and supplemented periodically (San Francisco: Pacific Fire Rating Bureau), Earthquake section, p. 23M.

for blanket earthquake or volcanic eruption insurance when these are the only perils covered. All earthquake insurance must be subject to coinsurance.

Fire Coinsurance Credits

Before 1875, localized systems of fire insurance rates followed many diverse patterns. Between 1875 and 1900, A. F. Dean, F. C. Moore, and others each developed fire rating schedules.[10] Many of the schedules now used in the states served by various fire insurance rating advisory organizations and unaffiliated state fire insurance rating bureaus are based on the work of Dean, Moore, and others. The states served by these advisory organizations and state bureaus are listed in Table 27.

TABLE 27. States served by various insurance rating or advisory organizations and by individual state fire insurance rating bureaus

Western Actuarial Bureau	*South-Eastern Underwriters Association*
Arkansas	Alabama
Colorado	Florida
Illinois	Georgia
Indiana	South Carolina
Iowa	
Kansas	*New England Insurance Rating Association*
Kentucky	Connecticut
Michigan	Massachusetts
Minnesota	Maine
Missouri	Rhode Island
Nebraska	Vermont
New Mexico	
North Dakota	*Middle Department Association of Fire Underwriters*
Ohio	Delaware
Oklahoma	Pennsylvania
South Dakota	
Tennessee	*State Bureaus*
West Virginia	District of Columbia
Wisconsin	Hawaii
Wyoming	Idaho
Pacific Fire Rating Bureau	Louisiana
Alaska	Maryland
Arizona	Mississippi
California	New Hampshire
Montana	New Jersey
Nevada	New York
Oregon	North Carolina
Utah	Texas*
	Virginia
	Washington

* Rates in Texas are established by a state regulatory board rather than by an advisory bureau serving insurers.

Source: Files of the Fire Insurance Research and Actuarial Association.

---

[10] Kent H. Parker, "Ratemaking in Fire Insurance," *Property and Liability Insurance Handbook*, ed. John D. Long and Davis W. Gregg (Homewood, Ill.: Richard D. Irwin, Inc., 1965), pp. 169–172.

While probably no two states use the same set of fire insurance rates, all states served by an advisory organization follow essentially that organization's system of fire coinsurance requirements and credits. However, the rating bureau of each state is free to modify the advisory organization's recommended requirements and credits, and the bureaus in many states do so. Therefore, the description of a coinsurance rate schedule of one state served by an advisory rating organization probably is not wholly accurate for another state served by that same advisory organization.

On the advice of one familiar with these systems,[11] the author has studied seven representative states: Illinois (Western Actuarial Bureau); California (Pacific Fire Rating Bureau); Georgia (South-Eastern Underwriters Association); Massachusetts (New England Insurance Rating Association); Pennsylvania (Middle Department Association of Fire Underwriters); New York State (unaffiliated); and Washington State (unaffiliated). The principal features of most schedules appear in this sample of seven. Nearly all schedules of fire coinsurance rates are more detailed than those for the perils previously discussed, presumably because the basic fire rating schedules give greater attention to the characteristics of risks in order to separate them into rating classes.

Western Actuarial Bureau Credits.[12] Table 28 gives Illinois fire coinsurance credits for properties outside Cook County (Chicago area). This table applies only to specific insurance on unsprinklered properties.

Blanket fire insurance on any Illinois property must be subject to at least 80 percent coinsurance (90 percent for sprinklered risks). If the insured files a sworn statement of values, an average rate (arithmetic mean weighted by property values) is computed. Otherwise, the highest premium rate for any item

---

[11] Interview with P. R. Bechtolt, Manager, Fire Insurance Research and Actuarial Association, January 31, 1967.

[12] This section is based on Illinois Inspection and Rating Bureau, *Illinois Rule Book* (Chicago: The Bureau, loose-leaf, revised and supplemented periodically), pp. 45–48 and 157–159, all effective May 15, 1967.

TABLE 28. Schedule of Illinois fire coinsurance credits (excluding Cook County)

Class of Construction and Protection	Reduction of Flate Rate for											
	50% Clause		60% Clause		70% Clause		80% Clause		90% Clause		100% Clause	
	Bldg.	Conts.	Bldg.	Conts.	Bldg.	Conts.	Bldg.	Conts.	Bldg.	Conts.	Bldg.	Conts.
Fire-resistive												
Protected[a]	56%	NC^c	62%	NC	66½%	45%	70%	50%	73%	55%	75%	58%
Unprotected[b]	45	NC	50	NC	55	35	60	40	64	45	66	48
Incombustible												
Protected	45	NC	50	50%	55	55	60	60	64	64	66	66
Unprotected	NC	NC	NC	NC	45	45	50	50	55	55	58	58
Masonry[d]	NC	NC	NC	NC	20	NC	25	15	30	20	35	25
Frame	NC	NC	NC	NC	NC	NC	10	10	15	15	20	20
Live and rolling stock	NC	NC	NC	NC	NC	24	NC	30	NC	35	NC	38
Lumber yards	NC	NC	NC	NC	NC	NC	10	10	15	15	20	20
Incombustible contents in masonry												
Protected	NC	NC	NC	NC	NC	34	NC	40	NC	45	NC	48
Incombustible contents in frame buildings												
Protected	NC	NC	NC	NC	NC	20	NC	25	NC	30	NC	35
Unprotected	NC	NC	NC	NC	NC	15	NC	20	NC	25	NC	30

[a] Protected: located in area with Class 8 or better public fire protection.
[b] Unprotected: located in area with Class 9 or 10 public fire protection.
[c] NC—no credit.
[d] Protected only; no coinsurance credit for unprotected risks of this construction.
Source: Illinois Inspection and Rating Bureau, *Illinois Rule Book* (Chicago: The Bureau, loose-leaf, revised and supplemented periodically), pp. 45–48, effective May 15, 1967.

of blanketed property is charged for all blanketed properties. All blanket fire policies subject to 80 percent coinsurance must contain a pro rata distribution clause. Different coinsurance credits apply, depending on whether the blanketed properties are sprinklered and whether sworn values have been filed. With values of unsprinklered properties on file, the average rate is used for 80 percent coinsurance, and the 80 percent specific coinsurance credit is applied to the average rate for 90 percent coinsurance. For 100 percent coinsurance an additional credit of 5 percent off the average rate is allowed. If no values are filed on unsprinklered properties, for 80 percent coinsurance the flat rate for the most hazardous property is charged for all blanketed properties, and for 90 or 100 percent coinsurance the 90 or 100 percent rate credit for the most hazardous property is applied to the rate for all properties. With sprinklered properties, the filing of values entitles the insured with 90 percent coinsurance to the credit for 80 percent specific coverage applied to the average rate, and to the 90 percent specific credit from the average rate for 100 percent coinsurance. If no values are filed on sprinklered properties, the 80 percent specific rate for the most hazardous property is charged on all properties for 90 percent coinsurance, and the highest 90 percent specific rate is charged for 100 percent coinsurance.

Pacific Fire Rating Bureau Credits.[13] Following the format of the California schedule, Table 29 gives an example of fire coinsurance credits for specific insurance on unsprinklered risks in Pacific Fire Rating Bureau states.

A brief separate table for all sprinklered properties indicates that the published 70 percent rate is reduced 5 percent for 80 percent coinsurance, 10 percent for 90 percent coinsurance, and 15 percent for 100 percent coinsurance. If the 70 percent rate does not exceed $1.00, the flat rate is $0.50 more than seven-tenths of the 70 percent rate. If the 70 percent rate ex-

---

[13] This section is based on Pacific Fire Rating Bureau, *Tariff Rules* (San Francisco: The Bureau, loose-leaf, revised and supplemented periodically), p. 2E, effective June 1, 1969, and p. 5, effective July 1, 1969.

TABLE 29. Schedule of California fire coinsurance credits for unsprinklered risks

Public Fire Protection Class	Coinsurance Percentage	Reduction of Published* Rate					
		Fire-Resistive		Joisted Masonry		Frame	
		Bldgs.	Conts.	Bldgs.	Conts.	Bldgs.	Conts.
1–4	100%	70%	40%	54%	40%	30%	30%
	90	67	35	50	35	25	25
	80	64	30	45	30	20	20
	70	59	25	40	24	10	10
	60	53	15	35	15	NC†	NC
5–6	100	65	35	50	35	20	20
	90	62	30	45	30	15	15
	80	60	25	40	25	10	10
	70	55	20	35	20	5	5
	60	49	10	25	10	NC	NC
7	100	63	30	45	30	15	15
	90	60	25	40	25	10	10
	80	56	20	35	20	5	5
	70	50	15	30	15	NC	NC
	60	45	5	20	5	NC	NC
8	100	61	25	40	25	15	15
	90	58	20	35	20	10	10
	80	54	15	30	15	5	5
	70	48	10	25	10	NC	NC
	60	40	5	20	5	NC	NC
9	100	61	NC	25	NC	10	NC
	90	58	NC	20	NC	5	NC
	80	54	NC	15	NC	NC	NC
	70	48	NC	10	NC	NC	NC
	60	40	NC	NC	NC	NC	NC
10	100	61	NC	20	NC	NC	NC
	90	58	NC	15	NC	NC	NC
	80	54	NC	10	NC	NC	NC
	70	48	NC	5	NC	NC	NC
	60	40	NC	NC	NC	NC	NC

* For fire-resistive buildings, the published rate is the 50 percent coinsurance rate. For all other risks, the published rate is the flat rate. For fire-resistive risks, the flat rate is 155.4 percent of the 50 percent coinsurance rate.

† NC—no credit.

Source: Pacific Fire Rating Bureau, *Tariff Rules* (San Francisco: The Bureau, looseleaf, revised and supplemented periodically), p. 2E, effective June 1, 1969, and letter from R. Williams, Executive Secretary, Pacific Fire Rating Bureau, December 1, 1966.

ceeds $1.00, the flat rate is $0.20 higher than the 70 percent rate.[14]

Blanket fire insurance on all eligible properties subject to less than 90 percent coinsurance must include a pro rata distribution clause. Otherwise, blanket insurance is available subject to any (or no) coinsurance requirement at the same coinsurance (or flat) rate as specific coverage.

South-Eastern Underwriters Association Credits.[15] Table 30 gives specific coinsurance credits in Georgia, one of the states served by the South-Eastern Underwriters Association. This schedule classifies risks by occupancy as well as by protection and construction. In a list accompanying this schedule, each occupancy is assigned a letter, A through M. This letter designates a particular table in the schedule of coinsurance credits. The assigned letter is an index of the occupancy's hazard, an A occupancy being less hazardous than a B occupancy, and so forth. Table D is reserved for all sprinklered properties of any occupancy. Georgia's rules for coinsurance in blanket fire policies are identical to California's.

New England Insurance Rating Association Credits.[16] Massachusetts and other New England Insurance Rating Association states present fire coinsurance credits in sentence rather than tabular form. For specific insurance on eligible properties, the published 80 percent coinsurance rate is reduced 5 and 10 percent for 90 and 100 percent coinsurance, respectively. The minimum coinsurance requirement for blanket coverage is 90

---

[14] Thus, if a 70 percent rate is $0.60, the flat rate is $0.92 (70 percent of $0.60 plus $0.50). For a 70 percent rate of $1.20, the flat rate is $1.20 plus $0.20, or $1.40.

[15] This section is based on material with letter from R. L. Gatewood, Secretary, South-Eastern Underwriters Association, December 14, 1966; and Georgia Inspection and Rating Bureau, *Georgia Rule Book* (Atlanta: The Bureau, loose-leaf, revised and supplemented periodically), pp. 49–74, effective various dates September, 1957 through December, 1969.

[16] This section is based on New England Insurance Rating Association, *Manual of Rules and Clauses* (Boston: Recording & Statistical Corp., loose-leaf, revised and supplemented periodically), p. 25, effective November 18, 1966, and p. 47, effective August 31, 1964, and letter from Robert H. Stocker, Jr., Executive Manager, New England Insurance Rating Association, June 1, 1967.

TABLE 30. Schedule of Georgia fire coinsurance credits

| Table No. | Construction and Protection Class | Change in Published Rate | | | | |
		None (*Flat Rate*)	75% Clause	80% Clause	90% Clause	100% Clause
A	Fire-resistive wherever located	+300%	NP*	R†	−10%	−18%
	Incombustible Classes 1–8					
	Buildings	+300	R	−20%	−25	−30
	Classes 9 & 10	+300	R	NC	− 5	−10
	Masonry or frame Classes 1–4					
	Buildings	+100	R	−20	−25	−30
	Contents	+100	R	−15	−20	−25
	Classes 5–8					
	Buildings	NC‡	R	−20	−25	−30
	Contents	NC	R	−15	−20	−25
	Classes 9 & 10	NC	R	NC	NC	NC
B	Fire-resistive or noncombustible wherever located	+300	NC	R	− 5	−10
	Incombustible wherever located	+300	NC	R	− 5	−10
	Masonry or frame					
	Classes 1–8	+100	NC	R	− 5	−10
	Classes 9 & 10	+100	NC	R	NC	NC
C	Fire-resistive, noncombustible, or incombustible (Apply Table B)					
	Masonry or frame					
	Classes 1–4	+100	R	NC	− 5	−10
	Classes 5–8	NC	R	NC	− 5	−10
	Classes 9 & 10	NC	R	NC	NC	NC
D	Sprinklered properties wherever located					
	Buildings	NP	NP	R	− 5	−10
	Contents—baled cotton	NP	NP	NP	NP	R
	Contents—other	NP	NP	R	− 5	−10
E	Fire-resistive, noncumbustible, or incombustible (Apply Table B)					

TABLE 30. (*Continued*)

Table No.	Construction and Protection Class	None (*Flat Rate*)	75% Clause	80% Clause	90% Clause	100% Clause
			Change in Published Rate			
	Masonry or frame					
	Classes 1–4	+100	NC	R	– 5	–10
	Classes 5–8	NC	NC	R	– 5	–10
	Classes 9 & 10	NC	NC	NC	NC	NC
F	Fire-resistive, noncombustible, or incombustible (Apply Table B)					
	Masonry or frame					
	Classes 1–8	+100%	NC	R	– 5%	–10%
	Classes 9 & 10	NC	NC	R	NC	NC
G	Fire-resistive, noncombustible, or incombustible Buildings only (Apply Table B)					
	Masonry or frame wherever located Buildings only	+100	NC	R	– 5	–10
H	All construction wherever located	+300	NC	R	– 5	–10
I	Fire-resistive, noncombustible, or incombustible (Apply Table B)					
	Masonry or frame wherever located	+100	NC	R	– 5	–10
J	All construction					
	Classes 1–8	NP	NP	R	– 5	–10
	Classes 9 & 10	NP	NP	R	NC	NC
K	All construction wherever located	NP	NP	R	NC	NC
L	All construction wherever located	NP	NP	NP	NP	R
M	All construction (Apply Table F)					

° NP—not permitted at any rate.
† R—published rate.
‡ NC—no credit or no charge.
  Source: Georgia Inspection and Rating Bureau, *Georgia Rule Book* (Atlanta: The Bureau, loose-leaf, revised and supplemented periodically), p. 51, effective December 15, 1969, p. 52, effective June 15, 1959, and p. 53, effective November 2, 1959.

percent, for which the 80 percent specific coinsurance rate is charged, with 5 percent credit for 100 percent coinsurance. For undisclosed reasons, the Association's rules do not allow pro rata distribution in blanket policies.

Only specific insurance can be written flat, the rate being ten-sevenths of the 80 percent rate (twice the 80 percent rate for fire-resistive or sprinklered properties). Any property can be insured against fire subject to any coinsurance requirement if no rate credit is given, and, on request, the Association allows coinsurance credits, differing from those published, as it deems appropriate.

Middle Department Association of Fire Underwriters Credits.[17] For specific coverage of all eligible Pennsylvania and Delaware properties, the published 80 percent coinsurance rate is reduced 5 and 10 percent for 90 and 100 percent coinsurance, respectively. For some properties, the 90 percent rate is published, and 100 percent coinsurance (with a 5 percent credit) is the only other alternative to the flat rate. Blanket coverage must be subject to at least 90 percent coinsurance, for which the 80 percent specific rate is charged, with a 5 percent credit for 100 percent coinsurance. Blanket policies without coinsurance are forbidden, even with a pro rata distribution clause.

Flat rates are derived by dollar charges, which vary with construction. For full fire-resistive construction, the flat rate is $0.75 higher than the published rate. Some other flat rate charges are: for buildings fire-resistive except for roofs, $0.65; for buildings of incombustible material, $0.40; for brick, stone, or concrete buildings, $0.30; and, for frame structures, $0.20. Insurance on sprinklered properties must be subject to coinsurance.

New York State Credits.[18] The New York Fire Insurance Rating Organization allows 5 percent credit from the published 80

---

[17] This section is based on Middle Department Association of Fire Underwriters, *Rule Book* (Philadelphia, Pa.: The Association, loose-leaf, revised and supplemented periodically), pp. 1–05, effective November 19, 1958, 1–16, effective August 3, 1959, and 1–17, dated February, 1968).

[18] This section is based on New York Fire Insurance Rating Organization, *General Rules* (New York: The Organization, loose-leaf, revised and supple-

percent rate for 90 percent coinsurance and 10 percent credit for 100 percent coinsurance for specific fire coverage on non-dwelling properties unless otherwise provided. For specific fire coverage on some properties, coinsurance requirements as low as 50 percent are permitted. In these cases, if the published premium rate assumes 80 percent coinsurance, that rate must be increased 14.2 percent for 70 percent coinsurance, 33.3 percent for 60 percent coinsurance, and 60.0 percent for 50 percent coinsurance. If the published rate assumes 90 percent coinsurance, the percentage point increases are 12.4 for 80 percent coinsurance, 28.6 for 70 percent coinsurance, 50.0 for 60 percent coinsurance, and 80.0 for 50 percent coinsurance. Blanket insurance must be subject to at least 90 percent coinsurance, for which the 80 percent rate is payable, with a 5 percent credit for 100 percent coinsurance. These rules apply to sprinklered and unsprinklered risks.

Specific insurance without coinsurance is permitted on all properties except those (1) rated as sprinklered, fire-resistive, or electrical or (2) located in the boroughs of New York City or in the surrounding five-county suburban area. Dollar charges are added to 80 percent rates to arrive at flat rates (some of which are shown in Table 31), the charges differing only with grades of fire protection (in contrast to Middle Department flat rate charges, based only on construction).

A higher flat rate for a protected risk than for an unprotected one, when the 80 percent rates are the same for both risks, produces a larger percentage coinsurance credit from the flat rate in protected areas than in unprotected ones. For example, the $0.05 80 percent rate is a 90 percent credit from the $0.50 protected flat rate and an 80 percent credit from the $0.25 unprotected flat rate. If fires in protected areas tend to do less damage than those in unprotected ones, New York is correct in giving a larger percentage credit for 80 percent coinsurance in protected areas than in unprotected ones or, conversely, in imposing a larger surcharge for no coinsurance

mented periodically), p. 4, effective December 31, 1960, p. 14, effective May 3, 1965, p. 20a, effective January 1, 1969, and p. 3a of Dwelling Rules section, effective May 16, 1965.

TABLE 31. Selected rates from New York Flat Rate
Table

80% Coinsurance Rate	Flat Rate Unprotected Area	Flat Rate Protected Area*
$0.05..............	$0.25	$0.50
0.10..............	0.30	0.53
0.20..............	0.40	0.57
0.50..............	0.70	0.85
0.75..............	0.94	1.12
0.80..............	0.99	1.18
1.00..............	1.19	1.43
1.25..............	1.43	1.80
1.50..............	1.68	2.12
1.75..............	1.92	2.45
2.00..............	2.17	2.73
2.25..............	2.41	3.02
2.50..............	2.66	3.29
3.00..............	3.15	3.79
5.00..............	5.11	5.32

* Protected area: area with a National Board of Fire
Underwriters (now American Insurance Association) public fire protection rating of Class 8 or better.
Source: New York Fire Insurance Rating Organization,
General Rules (New York: The Organization, loose-leaf, revised and supplemented periodically), p. 14, effective May
3, 1965, and p. 15, effective December 31, 1960.

in a protected area than in an unprotected one. If coverage is
not subject to coinsurance, insurance to a given percentage of
value provides full indemnity for a greater proportion of fires
in protected areas than the same amount of coverage does in
unprotected ones, if fires in unprotected areas are more severe.

Only New York State provides coinsurance credits on dwelling (at least 80 percent coinsurance being mandatory on New
York City homes). For dwellings outside the New York City
area, a separate table of 80 percent coinsurance and flat rates
classifies dwellings as to whether they (1) are located in a
protected or unprotected area; (2) are of frame, masonry, or
fire-resistive construction; and (3) house no more than two, or
more than two, families. Credits are greater for buildings than
for contents. In general, credits are greater for homes with
better protection, more fire-resistive construction, and fewer
occupants. Fire-resistive dwellings and their contents cannot

be insured flat, but frame and masonry homes and their contents in areas with Class 9 or 10 public fire protection (i.e., so-called unprotected classes) can only be insured flat.

Washington State Credits.[19] The Washington schedule of fire coinsurance credits does not distinguish risks by protection, occupancy, construction, or the presence of sprinklers, nor does it differentiate buildings from contents. For all eligible properties, if the published 80 percent coinsurance rate does not exceed $1.00, alternatives to the published rate are: for 70 percent coinsurance, a 5 percent increase; for 90 percent coinsurance, a 5 percent decrease; for 100 percent coinsurance, a 10 percent decrease; and for no coinsurance, $0.30 added to nine-tenths of the 80 percent rate. If the 80 percent rate exceeds $1.00 the alternatives are: for 70 percent coinsurance, a $0.05 increase; for 90 percent coinsurance, a $0.05 decrease; for 100 percent coinsurance, a $0.10 decrease; and for no coinsurance, a $0.20 increase. For instance, if an 80 percent rate is $0.60, the corresponding 70 percent rate is $0.63, the 90 percent rate is $0.57, the 100 percent rate is $0.54, and the flat rate is $0.84 ($0.30 plus 90 percent of $0.60). For an 80 percent rate of $1.20, the 70 percent rate is $1.25, the 90 percent rate is $1.15, the 100 percent rate is $1.10, and the flat rate is $1.40.

Although blanket and specific credits are the same, blanket insurance must contain a 90 or 100 percent coinsurance clause or a pro rata distribution clause. Policies on sprinklered risks require at least 90 percent coinsurance.

Extended Coverage Coinsurance Credits

One insuring agreement for all the extended coverage perils —windstorm, hail, explosion, riot, riot attending a strike, civil commotion, damage from aircraft or vehicles, and smoke—

---

[19] This section is based on a letter from George W. Clarke, General Manager, Washington (State) Surveying and Rating Bureau, October 19, 1966; and Washington (State) Surveying and Rating Bureau, *General Rules* (Seattle, Wash.: The Bureau, loose-leaf, revised and supplemented periodically), p. 9, effective December 1, 1965, p. 11, effective February 15, 1964, and Appendix A, pp. 1–5, effective August 15, 1962.

generally can be obtained only in an endorsement to a fire policy in an amount equaling the fire coverage.[20] Because the extended coverage endorsement, lacking its own coinsurance clause, relies on the coinsurance requirement of the fire policy, the basic approach to coinsurance is the same in both coverages in any given jurisdiction. The description here is limited to extended coverage coinsurance credits in the same regions and states whose fire coinsurance credits have been described.

In Massachusetts (and all New England Insurance Rating Association states), Pennsylvania, Delaware, and New York, the published 80 percent extended coverage rate is used with specific fire policies subject to 80 percent coinsurance (or 90 percent coinsurance, if this is the minimum allowed). Ninety or 100 percent coinsurance in the fire policy brings a 5 or 10 percent reduction in the extended coverage rate (5 percent for 100 percent coinsurance when the fire policy coinsurance minimum is 90 percent). Except in New York, flat extended coverage rates are derived in the same way as flat fire rates. New York flat extended coverage rates usually are twice the 80 percent rates. Rules for coinsurance in blanket extended coverage endorsements and blanket fire policies are identical.[21]

In Washington State and Pacific Fire Rating Bureau states except Montana, alternatives to the published 80 percent extended coverage rates are: for 70 percent coinsurance in a

---

[20] Albert H. Mowbray and Ralph H. Blanchard, *Insurance, Its Theory and Practice in the United States,* 5th ed. (New York: McGraw-Hill Book Co., Inc., 1961), p. 112. Policies against any one of the extended coverage perils often are obtainable, however. In special cases, a separate policy, giving only extended coverage protection, is said to be available. See Robert Riegel and Jerome S. Miller, *Insurance Principles and Practices,* 5th ed. (Englewood Cliffs, N.J.: Prentice-Hall, Inc., 1966), p. 489.

[21] See New England Insurance Rating Association, *Manual of Rates, Rules and Forms for Extended Coverage, Vandalism and Malicious Mischief, Special Extended Coverage, Builders' Risk Special Extended Coverage, Windstorm and Hail—Massachusetts* (Boston: Recording & Statistical Corp., loose-leaf, revised and supplemented periodically), p. 2, effective May 28, 1965, and Middle Department Association of Fire Underwriters, *op. cit.,* p. 3–01, effective July 1, 1960; and New York Fire Insurance Rating Organization, *Rules for Extended Coverage Endorsement* (New York: The Organization, loose-leaf, revised and supplemented periodically), pp. 3 and 12-d, both effective June 30, 1969.

blanket or specific fire policy, a 5 percent increase; for 90 percent coinsurance, a 5 percent decrease; and for 100 percent coinsurance, a 10 percent decrease. Flat extended coverage rates, used when fire policies specify less than 70 percent coinsurance, are: for fire-resistive or all-steel properties, 400 percent of the published rate on structures and 200 percent on contents; for other properties, 200 percent of the published rate on both structures and contents.[22]

Without distinguishing specific from blanket insurance, schedules of extended coverage coinsurance rates in Western Actuarial Bureau states differentiate among builders' risks, other buildings, and dwellings. The "other buildings" class is divided into fire- or wind-resistive structures and ordinary buildings. While adhering to this classification system, each Western Actuarial Bureau state promulgates different rates for each class.[23] For example, for Illinois fire- or wind-resistive "other buildings" outside Cook County, the extended coverage rate is $0.18 per $100 with a fire policy subject to 80 or 90 percent coinsurance and $0.20 with other fire policies. For "other buildings" of ordinary construction, the rates are $0.125 with fire policies subject to 80 or 90 percent coinsurance and $0.36 with other fire policies.[24]

The South-Eastern Underwriters Association published coinsurance rates (based on 80 percent coinsurance in the fire policy) are reduced 5 or 10 percent for 90 and 100 percent coinsurance in any specific policy. If the fire and extended coverage policy blankets real property at two or more locations, the only extended coverage credit is 5 percent for 100 percent

---

[22] Material with letter from R. Williams, Executive Secretary, Pacific Fire Rating Bureau, December 8, 1966.

[23] See, for example, Mountain States Inspection Bureau, *Colorado Rule Book* (Denver, Colo.: The Bureau, loose-leaf, revised and supplemented periodically), p. 52, effective September 14, 1964; and Mountain States Inspection Bureau, *New Mexico Rule Book* (Denver, Colo.: The Bureau, loose-leaf, revised and supplemented periodically), p. 55, effective July 21, 1964.

[24] Illinois Inspection and Rating Bureau, *op. cit.,* p. 31a, effective September 12, 1966.

coinsurance. For floating fire and extended coverage policies,[25] the published extended coverage rate applies regardless of coinsurance. Extended coverage subject to less than 80 percent coinsurance is not allowed.[26]

ANALYSIS OF PERCENTAGE COINSURANCE RATE SCHEDULES

This section explores the extent to which the schedules described above (1) offer a wide range of coinsurance percentages at separate rates; (2) avoid reversals; (3) provide rates decreasing at a declining rate; (4) are in a format encouraging insurance to 100 percent of value; and (5) establish different coinsurance rate *relativities* on the basis of factors which seem to affect the distribution of losses as percentages of value. Chapters 2 and 7 indicate that an ideal schedule of coinsurance credits should meet these five criteria.

Range of Coinsurance Percentages

Ideally, the minimum coinsurance percentage should be low, a 100 percent coinsurance credit should be offered, and the intervals between coinsurance percentages should be narrow (perhaps no more than 10 percentage points).

The sprinkler leakage schedule meets these criteria well, except that the absence of coinsurance percentages between the 25, 50, and 80 percent requirements may cause some unfair treatment of insureds with 40 or 70 percent coverage.

Low water damage coinsurance percentages are available nominally, but their use is restricted by the $25,000 policy minimum. Also, it is difficult to justify theoretically the same rate for any coinsurance requirement of 80 percent or more. If losses above 80 percent of value are thought impossible, the

---

[25] Floating insurance covers movable property anywhere within a specified region.

[26] Georgia Inspection and Rating Bureau, *Extended Coverage Manual* (Atlanta: The Bureau, loose-leaf, revised and supplemented periodically), p. 11, effective July 16, 1962.

total premium for 100 percent coverage should equal that for 80 percent instead of being 25 percent (10/8) higher.

The Pacific set of earthquake credits seems preferable to the non-Pacific one because (1) by barring flat insurance, the Pacific schedule eliminates price discrimination through flat rates (but note that this prohibition restricts consumer choice); and (2) only in the Pacific area is credit given for 60 and 70 percent coinsurance.

Minimum fire coinsurance percentages are relatively high (80 percent throughout most of the East, generally no lower than 50 percent elsewhere), but the intervals between requirements are narrow. Additional credit is given for 100 percent coinsurance with specific insurance in all states. The range and graduation of extended coverage coinsurance percentages generally parallel those of fire insurance.

Blanket coverage typically carries fewer coinsurance options than does specific coverage. With 100 percent coinsurance, the insured must buy the same amount of coverage in order to avoid coinsurance penalties under either blanket or specific policies on the same property. Thus, 100 percent blanket and specific coinsurance rates should be equal. Blanket coverage to less than full value with a pro rata distribution clause is equivalent to specific insurance and should carry the same coinsurance credit. But if blanket coverage for less than full value is not subject to pro rata distribution, the insured may receive full protection at all locations (barring simultaneous losses) with less than full aggregate coverage. Hence, the premium *rate* for 90 percent or less blanket coverage without pro rata distribution should be higher than the rate for the same percentage of specific coverage.

Only the non-Pacific schedule of earthquake coinsurance credits fully meets these criteria for coinsurance in blanket coverage. The other schedules are subject to two criticisms. On the one hand, most schedules of coinsurance credits included in this study limit the freedom of choice of the insured who wishes blanket coverage by failing to authorize less than 80 percent coinsurance in a blanket policy even though the blanket coverage is subject to pro rata distribution and is, therefore, equivalent to specific coverage. On the other hand, the blanket insured is favored over the buyer of specific insurance in South-Eastern Underwriters Association, Pacific Fire Rating Bureau, and (for unsprinklered properties) the Western Actuarial Bureau by the fact that 90 percent blanket insurance *without pro rata distribution* receive the same co-insurance credit as 90 percent specific coverage. The inconsistencies brought out by these two criticisms would be eliminated if coinsurance rate schedules reflected the fact that any amount of blanket insurance should carry the same premium rate as the same amount of specific insurance on a given property if either (1) both are subject to 100 percent coinsurance *or* (2) the blanket policy has a pro rata distribution clause attached to it.

Reversals

Except as the bands of coinsurance rates make a reversal inevitable for the insured who just meets a higher coinsurance requirement by increasing his coverage from, say, 79 to 80 percent of value, no schedule of coinsurance credits included in this study contains a reversal (where the cost of more insurance is lower than the cost of less) between two adjacent rates, both subject to coinsurance.

Where the minimum coinsurance percentage is high, an insured desiring little coverage may save money by buying unwanted insurance just to qualify for the coinsurance credit. For example, in the non-Pacific earthquake schedule, the 50 percent minimum coinsurance percentage carries a rate which is 140 percent of the 80 percent rate, while the flat rate is 500 percent of the 80 percent rate. If the flat rate on a $100,000 risk is $1.00 per $100, the 50 percent coinsurance rate is $0.28. An insured wanting $15,000 flat coverage would pay $150, $10.00 more than the cost of $50,000 coverage with 50 percent coinsurance. The insured with $15,000 flat coverage must be overcharged by this schedule—otherwise the $35,000 of insurance between $15,000 and $50,000 has a negative $10.00 marginal cost.

As another illustration, under the South-Eastern Underwriters Association fire schedule, where the flat rate is often 400 percent of the 75 percent rate, the insured finds that 75 percent coverage costs about the same as 19 percent coverage. The extra 56 percent coverage is free.

Rate of Rate Decrease

Since losses of small percentages of value predominate for the perils selected for this study, gross premium coinsurance rates should decrease at a declining rate as the coinsurance percentage rises (see pages 111–15). This pattern is followed consistently only in the sprinkler leakage, water damage, and Western Actuarial Bureau specific fire coinsurance rates. All other examined schedules contain rates decreasing at a constant rate—such as a 5 percent credit for an additional 10 percent of coinsurance—at least between some coinsurance percentages. The constant rate of decrease has the advantage of simplicity but is theoretically dubious.

Rate Schedule Format

If insurance to 100 percent, or at least to a high fraction, of value is deemed desirable, coinsurance credits should be presented to insureds in the format which most strongly encourages acceptance of, and compliance with, a high coinsurance requirement. The rate reductions for high coinsurance percentages are best emphasized when coinsurance credits are expressed as percentages of a relatively low base, such as the rate for a high coinsurance requirement. The flat rate can be made to appear a forbiddingly high multiple of a coinsurance rate when the 80 or higher percentage rate is published. This is the format of the Pacific and non-Pacific earthquake credits and of the South-Eastern Underwriters Association fire credits. With the mathematically equivalent alternative—publication of the flat rate, with all coinsurance rates as percentage reductions—the differences among the flat and coinsurance rates do not seem as great as when a coinsurance rate is published, because the flat rate is a larger base on which to express the rate relativities. For example, if the 80 percent rate is $0.25 and the flat rate is $1.00, the 80 percent rate is a 75 percent reduction of the flat rate, but the flat rate is 400 percent of the 80 percent rate. Nonetheless, the published sprinkler leakage, water damage, and Western Actuarial Bureau fire rates are flat rates.

When coinsurance and flat rate relativities are published in sentence rather than in tabular form, the average insured may be unlikely to grasp the significance of rate reductions with coinsurance because comparison of flat with coinsurance rates may be more difficult.

To remind insureds of their savings by accepting coinsurance, perhaps more coinsurance clauses should begin: "In return for a rate reduction from ____(flat rate)____ to ____(coinsurance rate)____ per $100 of insurance, the insured agrees. . . ."

Differentiation by Loss-Severity Characteristics

As shown in Appendix 3, the distribution of losses as percentages of value is the only determinant of relativities among percentage coinsurance rates. A schedule expressing coinsurance and flat rates as percentage credits and charges from some published rate establishes rate relativities which theoretically imply the same distribution of losses as percentages of value for all properties subject to that schedule. One schedule for both frame and brick buildings is proper only if the percentage loss-severity distribution is the same for both types of buildings. Whenever the same set of coinsurance credits applies to properties with different characteristics, the implication is that these characteristics do not influence the distribution of losses by size.

Thus, all schedules of credits for percentage coinsurance requirements questionably assume that loss severity relative to value is independent of property size. When coinsurance relativities are constant, regardless of the level of the published rate, loss severity also is implicitly independent of loss frequency (the only determinant of pure premium rate levels). Expense loadings aside, only increased loss frequency can raise the general level of all coinsurance rates. Appendix 3 shows that, if the frequency of all sizes of loss doubles, all pure premium coinsurance rates double, but their relativities remain constant. These relativities are determined only by the percentage loss-severity distribution. Thus, a schedule of coinsurance credits stipulating the same percentage credits (i.e., the same rate relativities) from $1.00 and $2.00 flat rates implies that a property carrying the $1.00 flat rate can expect losses which follow the same percentage loss-severity distribution as do expected losses to a property charged the $2.00 flat rate.

The coinsurance rate schedules included in this study show little consistency in identifying factors assumed to affect loss severity. The sprinkler leakage, water damage, and Pacific and non-Pacific earthquake coinsurance credits, applicable to all eligible properties, disputably assume that the shape of the percentage loss-severity distribution is not affected by the damageability of the particular property insured. Only the New England and Middle Department advisory organizations recommend fire coinsurance credits which take no account of construction or protection. The South-Eastern Underwriters Association is alone in distinguishing among occupancies for fire coinsurance credits. However, the factors which bear importantly on the size distribution of losses cannot be determined without better statistics than now exist.

When—as for Pacific Fire Rating Bureau sprinklered fire risks, some New York and Middle Department fire risks, and the more hazardous Washington State fire risks—the differentials among coinsurance rates are constant dollar amounts rather than constant percentages, coinsurance rate relativities vary with the published rate. If the flat rate is $0.80 above the 80 percent rate, with $0.10 and $0.15 credits for 90 and 100 percent coinsurance, a $0.50 80 percent rate implies that the flat rate ($1.30) is 260 percent of the 80 percent rate, and that the 90 ($0.40) and 100 ($0.35) percent rates are 80 and 70 percent, respectively, of the 80 percent rate. Theoretically, these relativities imply a greater concentration of smaller percentage losses than for the risk charged the 80 percent rate of $1.00. For the $1.00 80 percent rate, the flat rate is 180 percent, the 90 percent rate is 90 percent, and the 100 percent rate is 85 percent of the 80 percent rate. When a coinsurance rate becomes a greater percentage of the flat rate as the coinsurance and flat rates both increase by equal dollar amounts, the implication is that a growing proportion of the total expected value of all losses is composed of losses which equal or exceed that particular coinsurance requirement. Thus, the constant dollar differences among flat and coinsurance rates are consistent with the assumption that, as increasing loss frequency raises the general rate level, losses tend to be more severe. Sufficient data are not available to assess the assumption of interdependence between loss frequency and severity, but the author believes that some interdependence is more plausible than total independence.

The constant percentage differentials (producing constant relativities regardless of the flat rate) suggest that loss frequency and severity are independent. J. K. Woolley, author of the Washington State system of constant dollar differentials, expressed this contrast between constant percentage and constant dollar coinsurance credits:

Certainly if schedule rating is as sound as it appears to be from the experience of over a quarter of a century, it seems obvious that as the schedule rate increases the possibility of total loss increases. [The] General Basic Schedule [used in Washington State] recognizes this. . . . An actual reversal of the percentage credit plan results in a sliding rather than a fixed differential between flat and coinsurance rates which increases the percentage credit as the conditions are improved and as the rate, based upon an assumed uniform percentage of insurance to value, decreases. In other words, as a building or the contents of a building become less hazardous, as indicated by the reduced schedule rate, the value of the coinsurance principle proportionately increases.[27]

---

[27] J. K. Woolley, *The Principles and Mechanics of Fire Insurance Rating as Incorporated in General Basic Schedule* [Seattle: Washington (State) Surveying and Rating Bureau, 1937], pp. 3–4.

Woolley's approach assumes that *any* factor raising loss frequency increases loss severity. Only better statistics can prove him right or wrong.

Other schedules may indirectly follow Woolley's system of giving less credit for a given coinsurance percentage as more frequent losses raise rate levels. In these schedules, credits for, say, frame-unprotected risks are less than for brick-protected ones for any given coinsurance percentage. Frame-unprotected rates generally are higher than brick-protected ones. Thus, by means of construction and protection classes, these schedules correlate rate levels and coinsurance credits to some extent, but, within classes, these schedules assume that loss frequency and severity are independent.

SUMMARY

This chapter describes and analyzes schedules of percentage of value coinsurance rates used nationally for sprinkler leakage, water damage, and earthquake insurance and for fire and extended coverage insurance in seven representative regions and states.

A well-constructed schedule of coinsurance credits should (1) offer different credits for a wide range of coinsurance requirements, including full coverage, with narrow intervals between requirements; (2) avoid reversals; (3) stipulate coinsurance rates declining at a decreasing rate for larger coinsurance requirements; (4) adhere to a format encouraging insurance to an adequate percent of value; and (5) establish different coinsurance rate relativities for property characteristics significantly affecting the size distribution of losses.

None of the schedules precisely meets the first and third criteria; some fulfill the fourth; all meet the second. Compliance with the fifth requires more research into factors bearing on percentage loss severity. It appears that property size and loss frequency—ignored in most schedules of percentage coinsurance credits—should be recognized as probably influencing percentage loss severity.

CHAPTER 9

Coinsurance and Underwriting

PURPOSE

The purpose of this chapter is to examine the decisions which an insurer's underwriter must make with respect to co-insurance.

The function of underwriting may be defined as "the selection and classification of risks and the setting of standards that limit coverage."[1] Coinsurance is one of the limits of coverage, the proper use of which is at least partially within the underwriter's control. The principal coinsurance underwriting decisions, in the order they will be discussed, are:

1. Whether a particular policy should be subject to any coinsurance requirement.
2. If so, whether it should be expressed as a percentage of insurable value, as a stated amount, or as a requirement of periodic reports of values.
3. If a percentage of value requirement is desirable, how much latitude should the insured be given in selecting the percentage.

---

[1] Herbert S. Denenberg, *et al., Risk and Insurance* (Englewood Cliffs, N.J.: Prentice-Hall, Inc., 1964), p. 446.

In daily practice, the underwriter usually adheres to a state rating bureau rule book which indicates when and how coinsurance is to be used. For a given type of property, the rule book states whether a coinsurance clause or an agreed amount endorsement is mandatory, permitted, or forbidden. If a schedule of coinsurance requirements and rates is presented in the rule book, the underwriter, with the consent of the insured, must choose one of these requirements or accept the risk at flat rates. The rule book may be silent about coinsurance, but the state legislature may have decreed that coinsurance is required or prohibited on the type of property under consideration. Thus, the underwriter may have no coinsurance decisions to make, since the rule book or statute already may have made them.

In a broader sense, the rule book provisions are underwriting decisions made at some past time—decisions considered sufficiently important to be made rules. These rules are important in "the setting of standards that limit coverage." Further, it can be assumed that the directives in the state rule book are, in a large part, guides posted by experts to promote the proper use of coinsurance. These rules presumably have been promulgated in the interests of insurers and insureds, covering matters which otherwise would be within the discretion of the individual underwriter. In short, the rules which preclude individual underwriting decisions represent universalized underwriting decisions of the past.

The effect of coinsurance statutes is discussed in Chapter 11.

USE OF COINSURANCE

A basic underwriting rule is that a coinsurance requirement should be used whenever a significant number of losses less than the face amount of insurance is expected. The only exceptions are where a practicable alternative is available or where a coinsurance requirement is not feasible.[2] In the types of in-

---

[2] Interview with John B. Davis, Assistant Vice President, Insurance Company of North America, January 17, 1967; and letter from James P. White, Superintendent, Property-Personal Lines Department, St. Paul Fire and Marine Insurance Company, October 20, 1966.

surance selected for this study, the predominance of partial losses in most situations requires the use of some device to take account of small losses. Therefore, the decision of when to impose some coinsurance requirement is best resolved by enumerating the exceptional situations where coinsurance is (1) unnecessary, (2) less advantageous than a feasible alternative, or (3) impractical.

Unnecessary Situations

Coinsurance is not used where all losses to the property are assumed to be at least as great as the face amount of insurance. Only if all losses are of this size is coinsurance unnecessary in theory, because the loss-severity distribution no longer plays a part in rate making. The author has found only two situations in which underwriters of the types of insurance included in this study assume that only total losses to property occur. The first concerns fire insurance on unprotected properties; the second, coverage of fragile or artistic objects.

Properties usually considered unprotected against fire are those located in areas given a public fire protection rating of Class 9 or 10 by the American Insurance Association (formerly the National Board of Fire Underwriters). If a fire breaks out in such a property, underwriters are said to reason, the property will be totally destroyed.[3] Underwriters are correct in reasoning that, if all losses are total, no rate credit should be given for any coinsurance requirement, so the coinsurance clause can be eliminated in this case. But it appears that, at least for unprotected frame dwellings, lack of public fire protection does not imply that all fire losses will be total. Salzmann's study of Homeowners experience for unprotected frame dwellings suggests that over 73 percent of all fires in these risks are extinguished before doing damage amounting to more than 10 percent of the insur-

---

[3] John R. Blades, "Coinsurance," *Best's Insurance News, Fire and Casualty Edition*, vol. XLII, no. 2 (June 1941), p. 38. Blades makes no exceptions for fire-resistive properties.

ance.[4] In practice, coinsurance credits generally are not given in a fire policy on an unprotected frame structure.[5] There are jurisdictions, however, in which a coinsurance requirement of 80 percent is stipulated for fire coverage of such buildings, but no rate credit is given for the clause.[6] Neither the writer nor the person who informed him of this practice can see the logic of this seemingly inequitable procedure.

In many states where fire policies are written without coinsurance because the property is in an unprotected area, the extended coverage endorsement also lacks a coinsurance provision. The absence of a coinsurance requirement for extended coverage is due to the fact that this coverage is given in an endorsement which does not itself contain a coinsurance clause.[7] Selling extended coverage not subject to coinsurance on properties "unprotected" from fire can be justified only on the dubious assumption that all losses caused by extended coverage perils will be at least as great as the face of the fire policy.

The second instance in which underwriters dispense with coinsurance on the premise that all losses will be at least as great as the amount of insurance involves fragile articles and some objects of art.[8] Mirrors, ornamental glassware, statuary, and small paintings are examples. It is said that the artistic and economic value of these properties, if not their physical existence, can be assumed totally destroyed if the insured peril strikes them.[9] But since many such pieces are insured on a scheduled or appraised value basis, the insurer usually knows the relationship of insurance to value for this type of exposure without relying on a coinsurance requirement.

---

[4] Ruth E. Salzmann, "Rating by Layer of Insurance," *Proceedings of the Casualty Actuarial Society*, vol. L (1963), p. 23.

[5] Interview with C. Neville Wight, former Assistant Executive Manager, Middle Department Association of Fire Underwriters, September 22, 1966.

[6] Interview with John B. Davis, Assistant Vice President, Insurance Company of North America, December 22, 1966.

[7] Letter from W. H. Ferris, Manager, Inspection and Rating, New Hampshire Board of Underwriters, September 15, 1966.

[8] Interview with C. Neville Wight, former Assistant Executive Manager, Middle Department Association of Fire Underwriters, September 22, 1966.

[9] Robert Riegel and Jerome S. Miller, *Insurance Principles and Practices,* 5th ed. (Englewood Cliffs, N.J.: Prentice-Hall, Inc., 1966), p. 679.

Advantageous Alternatives to Coinsurance

One authority has voiced the wish that coinsurance requirements may one day be eliminated.[10] Without coinsurance and
coinsurance penalties, insureds would be spared much disap-
pointment, and insurers could provide more complete protection. The only reason coinsurance endures, this scholar asserts,
is that, in most cases, there is no practicable alternative means
of marketing insurance at adequate, reasonable, and equitable
premium rates.

Although there are many means other than coinsurance by
which an insurer can promote insurance to an assumed percentage of value (see Chapter 2), few are as effective or as con-
venient for the insurer as a coinsurance requirement. Three
alternatives to coinsurance can be effective in limited situations:
(1) scheduling each item of property insured; (2) appraisal of
the insured property; and (3) gradation of premium rates by
face amount or percentage of value insured. It has been claimed
that these alternatives should be used when feasible because
coinsurance penalties are eliminated,[11] the alternatives are more
understandable,[12] and loss settlement is simplified.[13]

Scheduling of Insured Items.[14]   When each insured property
is listed in the policy opposite a specified amount of insurance,
the underwriter can determine if the requested amount of coverage is adequate for that property. Properties typically insured
under a schedule—cameras, fine arts, furs, musical instruments,
silverware, stamps and coins, and valuable papers[15]—usually

---

[10] Letter from P. G. Buffinton, Vice President, State Farm Fire and
Casualty Insurance Company, October 21, 1966.

[11] S. S. Huebner, Kenneth Black, Jr., and Robert S. Cline, *Property and
Liability Insurance* (New York: Appleton-Century-Crofts, Inc., 1968), p. 96.

[12] F. E. Wolfe, *Principles of Property Insurance* (New York: Thomas Y.
Crowell Co., 1930), p. 141.

[13] Edward A. Ketcham and Murray Ketcham-Kirk, *Essentials of the Fire
Insurance Business* (Madison, Wis., 1922), pp. 370–371.

[14] Material under this heading is based on an interview with John B.
Davis, Assistant Vice President, Insurance Company of North America,
January 17, 1967.

[15] Robert F. Degener, "Inland Marine Insurance—Floaters," *Property
and Liability Insurance Handbook,* ed. John D. Long and Davis W. Gregg

have high, yet imprecise unit value. Agreement on the value before loss simplifies loss adjustment.

Appraisal of Insured Property.[16]   Large buildings are frequently appraised by the insurer when a policy is written or renewed. The insurer's appraisal expense is justified by the larger premium earned under the policy. Appraisal is particularly necessary for so-called "jumbo" risks, which are always insured for the full appraised value determined annually. Premiums are adjusted to reflect actual values and hazards. Use of percentage coinsurance in a policy blanketing many buildings of a "jumbo" risk is made impractical by the high cost of determining the coinsurance requirement after each loss.

For properties not qualifying as "jumbo" risks, underwriters usually see three disadvantages of insurers' appraisals as a means of securing insurance to value. First, the premium income from the average policy does not support the expense of periodic appraisal. Second, in practice, the insurer is bound by the last appraisal and may be forced to make an overly generous settlement of a partial loss rather than go to court to assert the legally correct point that the insurer's appraisal is only an estimate, a service to the insured, and is not binding on the insurer. Third, appraising each insured property before loss, rather than only properties which suffer losses, is likely to spawn a great number of unnecessary disputes among insurers, outside appraisers, and insureds. Almost all appraisals give rise to some disputes. It has been said in rebuttal to this third disadvantage, however, that the valuation of a standing building is much less subject to question than the appraisal of the former value of a pile of ashes.[17] In Delaware, Tennessee, and Vermont, the insured has a statutory right to demand, or the insurer a statutory duty to provide, an appraisal of

---

(Homewood, Ill.: Richard D. Irwin, Inc., 1965), p. 392; and Robert I. Mehr and Bob A. Hedges, *Risk Management in the Business Enterprise* (Homewood, Ill.: Richard D. Irwin, Inc., 1963), p. 468.

[16] Material under this heading is based on an interview with Edward B. Black, Secretary—Underwriting, Insurance Company of North America, January 17, 1967.

[17] John D. C. Roane, then President, National Association of Independent Insurance Adjusters, "Appraisals and Underinsurance," address to a meeting of Maryland insurance agents, Ocean City, Maryland, June, 1952.

real property insured against fire when the policy is written or renewed (see pages 197–98).

Gradation of Premium Rates. The third alternative to coinsurance is the gradation of premium rates. Rates may be graded according to the amount of insurance purchased or the relationship between the policy face and the insurable value of the property.

Although gradation of rates by absolute amounts of coverage is widely used for burglary and robbery insurance,[18] this system is not common with insurance against fire or the allied perils selected for this study. Such gradation assumes the same type of loss-severity distribution as do stated amount coinsurance requirements: the probability of loss is a function of the dollar size of loss. The difference between rates graded by policy size and stated amount coinsurance requirements is that, under the graded rate system, the insured may purchase coverage for less than full value, while stated amount coinsurance requirements assume full coverage.

Gradation of rates according to the percentage of value insured (where no coinsurance clause protects the insurer against changes in value) involves two questionable assumptions. First, the underwriter must be assumed to know the insurable value of the property when the policy is written or renewed. This assumption can be realized only if the insurer appraises each insured property periodically or if the insured's statement of value can be taken as honest and accurate. The second assumption is that the relationship of insurance to insurable value at the beginning of the policy period, the relationship on which the premium rate is based, is not upset by any change in value during the policy term. Since neither of these assumptions seems supportable, it is unlikely that the advantages claimed for graded rates—absence of "compulsion" in coinsurance requirements and fuller understanding by the insured[19]—can be achieved on a wide scale.[20]

---

[18] Charles N. Kaplan, "Burglary, Theft and Robbery Insurance Rates," *Examination of Insurance Companies* (New York: New York State Insurance Department, 1955), vol. V, pp. 112–114.

[19] Huebner, Black, and Cline, *op. cit.*, p. 96.

[20] Albert H. Mowbray and Ralph H. Blanchard, *Insurance, Its Theory and Practice in the United States,* 5th ed. (New York: McGraw-Hill Book Co., Inc., 1961), p. 88.

Not Used When Impractical

The third broad reason that underwriters often refuse to use a coinsurance requirement, no matter how theoretically desirable the requirement may be, is that they think it impractical because (1) the property is extremely obsolete or heavily depreciated; (2) the property has little value; or (3) the insured does not understand coinsurance.

Property Obsolete or Depreciated.[21] The proper concept of insurable value for an economically obsolete or heavily depreciated property is difficult to define. Both obsolescence and depreciation distort actual cash value and replacement cost, so that complying with a percentage of value coinsurance requirement could force the insured to carry unreasonably large, or permit him to buy unduly small, amounts of insurance.

For example, the replacement cost of an obsolete United States brewery, erected according to the German plan of solid stone or brick walls at least four feet thick, is very high and probably exceeds the use value of the property. Furthermore, extensive damage would likely be repaired with modern, less expensive materials. The owner of this brewery should not be required to insure the building against fire for a high percentage of its replacement cost. Neither would actual cash value—replacement cost minus depreciation—be an appropriate standard for a coinsurance requirement because the slight depreciation of solid stone structures means that the actual cash value is almost equal to the replacement cost.

In contrast, the actual cash value of a frame warehouse built in the 1890's in an urban area close to transportation facilities has great use value, even though its actual cash value may have depreciated to virtually zero. However, repairs to this building would have to be made with new materials of greater value than

---

[21] Material under this heading is based on interviews with John B. Davis, Assistant Vice President, Insurance Company of North America, January 17, 1967, and C. Neville Wight, former Assistant Executive Manager, Middle Department Association of Fire Underwriters, September 22, 1966; and on a letter from George W. Clarke, General Manager, Washington (State) Surveying and Rating Bureau, October 19, 1966.

the components they replace. Should an insured purchase fire insurance with a 100 percent actual cash value coinsurance requirement, the low total premium probably would not be sufficient to restore partial losses. The insured may not wish to carry replacement cost insurance against a severe loss because the municipal building code may not allow him to replace the warehouse as originally constructed.

In each of these situations, the underwriter may refuse any coinsurance requirement and agree to coverage only at flat rates for an amount of insurance which is expected to give the insurer an adequate premium income. For the brewery, such an amount of coverage probably would be much less than its replacement cost or actual cash value. But the insurer's premium income should be enough to fully restore partial losses (total losses being almost inconceivable). For the warehouse, a suitable policy face may be only slightly greater than its theoretical actual cash value, and much less than the cost of a new warehouse. The flat rate charged for this coverage, however, should be sufficient to pay for the full replacement cost of partial losses. Thus, for the economically obsolete property, coinsurance is waived so that the policyholder need not insure beyond use value. (Furthermore, insurance in excess of economic value raises the moral hazard.) For the heavily depreciated property, coinsurance may be refused so that the flat rate can be charged to cover full replacement of partial losses. In each case, the appropriate policy face is a matter of underwriting judgment.

Property of Low Value. Below a certain amount of loss, the insurer's administrative cost of invoking a coinsurance requirement is greater than the coinsurance penalty which, on the average, might be imposed. Also, by insisting on coinsurance penalties for small losses, the insurer might incur the ill will of policyholders. For these reasons one major property insurer instructs adjusters not to inquire into any possible coinsurance deficiencies for claimed fire losses not exceeding $1,200. Although it is not clear how $1,200 was selected as the "break-even" loss, the author has been told confidentially that other companies have adopted similar critical loss values ranging from $1,000 to $1,500.

If no coinsurance penalties will be invoked for losses below, say, $1,500, it is pointless to require a coinsurance clause when the coinsurance percentage, applied to the insurable value of the property, yields an amount less than $1,500. For example, an 80 percent coinsurance requirement need not be used if the insurable value of the property is less than $1,875.

Insured's Lack of Understanding.   One platitude about percentage of value coinsurance is that the insured, particularly the homeowner, seldom understands it, and therefore coinsurance is often impractical.[22]

While coinsurance now baffles many, it can be made comprehensible to nearly all insureds. The Merritt Committee stated that the policyholder need only understand that coinsurance results in less than full indemnity if the policy face is too small.[23] One insurance agent reports that he can explain coinsurance quite effectively by saying that, in return for a rate reduction, the insured becomes a limited copartner in paying his own losses.[24] Another useful, if specious, analogy is that the insured receives coverage less expensively if he buys in sufficient "wholesale," rather than "retail," quantities.[25]

In practice, it seems that the insureds' alleged lack of understanding often has been successfully ignored. At least 80 percent

---

[22] See, for example, *Report of the Joint Committee of the Senate and Assembly of the State of New York, Appointed to Investigate Corrupt Practices in Connection with Legislation, and the Affairs of Insurance Companies, Other Than Those Doing Life Insurance Business,* Assembly Document No. 30 (Albany, N.Y., February 1, 1911), p. 90; W. J. Nichols, "The Coinsurance Clause," *The Fire Insurance Contract, Its History and Interpretation,* ed. The Insurance Society of New York (Indianapolis, Ind.: The Rough Notes Co., 1922), p. 715; *Special Bulletin No. 19; The Relation Between Co-Insurance and Premium* (New York: Insurance Bureau of the National Retail Dry Goods Association, February 15, 1926), p. 3; J. Edward Hedges, *Practical Fire and Casualty Insurance,* 5th ed. (Cincinnati, Ohio: The National Underwriter Company, 1951), p. 9; Frank Joseph Angell, *Insurance Principles and Practices* (New York: The Ronald Press Co., 1959), p. 169; C. Arthur Williams, Jr. and Richard M. Heins, *Risk Management and Insurance* (New York: McGraw-Hill Book Co., Inc., 1964), p. 195, n. 7; and Riegel and Miller, *op. cit.,* p. 495.

[23] *Report of the Joint Committee of the Senate and Assembly of the State of New York* . . . , *op. cit.,* p. 90.

[24] "Co-Insurance Explained," *Credit and Financial Management,* vol. CIV, no. 6 (June 1952), p. 34.

[25] *Ibid.*

coinsurance in fire policies has been made universally mandatory in New York City without any grave difficulties. Residents of the Gulf Coast, who experience frequent hurricane losses, understand, and seem to accept, coinsurance attached to extended coverage insurance.[26] Europeans accept 100 percent coinsurance as a matter of course.[27] The extension of the Homeowners policy to provide replacement cost coverage of structures insured to at least 80 percent of such cost suggests that insurers have not discounted entirely the effectiveness of coinsurance in promoting insurance of dwellings to high percentages of value.

TYPE OF COINSURANCE REQUIREMENT

Once the underwriter has decided to use some type of coinsurance requirement, he must choose a percentage of insurable value, a stated (or agreed) amount, or full reports of current values as a type of requirement. Unless special circumstances indicate the desirability of an agreed amount endorsement or a provisional reporting form, percentage of insurable value coinsurance should be chosen.[28]

When Agreed Amount Endorsement More Appropriate

Because, with an agreed amount endorsement, the insurer risks inadequate premium income due to rising property values and falling ratios of insurance to insurable value, many insurers are reluctant to offer this endorsement in a property insurance contract.[29] By bureau ruling in many states, the endorsement is allowed only in business interruption policies.[30] However, two fac-

---

26 Interview with C. Neville Wight, former Assistant Executive Manager, Middle Department Association of Fire Underwriters, September 22, 1966.

27 Letter from David C. Tausche, Manager for Europe, Insurance Company of North America, October 6, 1966.

28 Interview with John B. Davis, Assistant Vice President, Insurance Company of North America, December 22, 1966.

29 Ralph H. Blanchard, "Coinsurance," *Risk and Insurance and Other Papers* (Lincoln, Neb.: University of Nebraska Press, 1965), p. 142.

30 Interview with Putnam Schroeder, Research Specialist, Insurance Company of North America, September 20, 1966. But, according to Mr. Schroeder, the gradual trend toward the use of the agreed amount endorse-

tors—the bargaining power of large insureds and competition from factory mutual insurers—may force use of the agreed amount endorsement. The premium paid by the large insured may be sufficiently attractive to induce the insurer to relieve the insured of responsibility for maintaining coverage to a specified percentage of value rather than lose the account to another insurer who is willing to include an agreed amount endorsement.

When the competition comes from one of the factory mutual companies, the pressure for an agreed amount endorsement is particularly great. The factory mutuals periodically appraise each insured property, typically eliminating all types of coinsurance requirements.[31] Many of the properties insured by the factory mutuals are sprinklered risks and have other superior features with respect to fire loss.[32] The extent to which stock property insurers resort to the agreed amount endorsement in competing for properties eligible for factory mutual coverage may be indicated by the following statement, applicable to Pennsylvania and Delaware operations of stock insurers:

The Agreed Amount of Insurance clause is used in policies accounting for 70% of the premium dollar from Sprinklered Properties. . . . Unsprinklered superior non-manufacturing classes likewise are eligible.[33]

Where Provisional Reporting Form More Appropriate

The three characteristics common to all situations where a provisional reporting form should be used in lieu of a percentage of value coinsurance requirement are: (1) unpredictability of future insurable values; (2) easy, precise measurability of present insurable values; and (3) ability of the insured to appraise ac-

---

ment, evidenced by almost weekly changes in the list of properties and coverages eligible for an agreed amount endorsement, makes it almost impossible to specify states where this endorsement generally is permitted.

[31] Joseph Finley Lee, Jr., "The Functional Operation and Competitive Role of the Associated Factory Mutual Insurance Companies" (doctoral dissertation, University of Pennsylvania, 1965), p. 59.

[32] *Ibid.*

[33] Material prepared for testimony at 1965 rate hearings by the Middle Department Association of Fire Underwriters and taken from the files of the Association.

curately, and to report promptly, his current insurable values.[34]
The first circumstance makes the provisional reporting form desirable; the second and third make the form feasible.

If future insurable values cannot be predicted with fair accuracy, compliance with a percentage of value coinsurance clause is difficult. The absence of a face amount in a provisional reporting form policy, subject to a limit of liability equaling expected maximum values, gives the insured full coverage while protecting the insurer against extreme unreported increases in values.

Unpredictability of future values should be distinguished from difficulty of determining present values. When values at any given time—either before or after loss—are difficult to measure, an agreed amount endorsement is the best means of controlling insurance to insurable value because neither the insured nor the insurer could easily comply with, or effectively enforce, a percentage of value coinsurance requirement.[35] In contrast, precise determination of present insurable values is essential if a provisional reporting form is to be workable. Fluctuation of known values, rather than indeterminacy of usually stable values, points toward the use of the provisional reporting form rather than the agreed amount endorsement.

Underwriters' greatest single difficulty with provisional reporting forms is obtaining prompt reports. The insured must maintain sufficiently detailed records, kept by a clerical staff competent to file an accurate report with the insurer—usually within thirty days after the date to which the report applies. Records must be preserved during the policy period, and perhaps one to three years longer, so that the insurer may exercise its right to check reports if it desires. If these accounting standards are not met, return to a percentage of insurable value coinsurance clause or elimination of coinsurance is inevitable.

[34] "Reporting Forms—General Principles," *The Fire, Casualty, and Surety Bulletins* (Cincinnati, Ohio: The National Underwriter Company, loose-leaf, revised and supplemented periodically), Miscellaneous Fire, pp. Gd-1 to Gd-7, second printing, February, 1962.

[35] Ambrose B. Kelly, "The Insurance of Profits, Reinstatement Value, Agreed Amount and the Principle of Indemnity," *Insurance Law Journal*, no. 524 (September 1966), p. 529.

INSURED'S CHOICE OF COINSURANCE PERCENTAGE

When the underwriter has determined that a given policy must include a percentage coinsurance requirement, he must decide what choice, if any, the insured shall have among coinsurance percentages.

The theory presented in Chapter 7 suggests that the policyholder should be permitted to choose from among many coinsurance requirements, ranging from 1, 5, or 10 to 100 percent. Chapter 8 indicates that such a wide choice is currently available only with sprinkler leakage and water damage insurance. Earthquake coinsurance minimums are 40 or 50 percent. The lowest fire and extended coverage coinsurance percentages are 50 to 70 percent, depending on the type of property, except in Virginia where any risk may receive credit for 30 percent coinsurance.[36]

At one time, the range of coinsurance alternatives for fire insurance was much wider. For example, prior to 1903, the Philadelphia Fire Underwriters' Association allowed owners of "fireproof" structures to choose, and receive separate credits for, any coinsurance requirement from 10 to 100 percent in intervals of 10 percentage points. A separate schedule permitted the same range, with different credits, for nonfireproof buildings.[37] Francis C. Moore's original Universal Mercantile Schedule for fire insurance allowed any coinsurance percentage. The published rate was the 50 percent coinsurance rate with a deduction of ½ percentage point in this rate for every percentage point of coinsurance above 50 percent and a 1 percentage point increase in the published rate for each percentage point of coinsurance below 50 percent.[38]

In selecting minimum and maximum coinsurance percentages,

---

[36] Virginia Insurance Rating Bureau, *Percentage Rate Change Manual—Fire* (Richmond, Va.: The Bureau, revised and supplemented periodically), pp. 17–19, issued November, 1958.

[37] *Constitution, By-Laws, Agreement, and Rules* (Philadelphia, Pa.: Philadelphia Fire Underwriters' Association, 1908), pp. 28–29.

[38] Francis C. Moore, *Fire Insurance and How to Build* (New York: The Baker & Taylor Co., 1903), p. 709.

today's underwriter seems to rely on judgment based on four broad factors: (1) damageability of the property by the insured peril; (2) stability of the value of the insured property; (3) form of coverage (blanket or specific); and (4) the insurer's relations with insureds and mortgagees.

Damageability of Insured Property

The probable maximum property loss varies with the type of property and with the peril. Sprinkler leakage damage beyond 25 percent of insurable value is extremely rare for any type of property.[39] In contrast, it appears that over 8 percent of all fire losses to protected frame properties are total (see Table 13). Underwriters generally believe that severe fire losses to fire-resistive structures are significantly less frequent than equally severe damage to frame buildings.[40]

If probable maximum property loss is taken as the measure of "adequate" coverage, insurance to a lesser percentage of value is required for adequate protection from sprinkler leakage than from fire. Underwriters correctly reason that the minimum coinsurance requirement should not exceed the probable maximum loss. Many insureds probably would be suspicious of a requirement that they carry coverage beyond the greatest loss which the insurer itself believes is reasonably possible. The minimum coinsurance requirements reviewed in Chapter 8 generally tend to follow the estimated maximum probable loss. The coinsurance minimums are lower for the perils which cause less severe losses and, for any given peril, are lower for the types of property which appear to be less susceptible to that peril. However, the importance of judgment, apart from any estimate of probable maximum loss, can be seen in the coinsurance minimums for fire insurance in Virginia and in New York of 30 and 80 percent, respectively. Probable maximum fire loss for a particular type of

---

[39] Interview with C. Neville Wight, former Assistant Executive Manager, Middle Department Association of Fire Underwriters, September 22, 1966.

[40] Interview with John B. Davis, Assistant Vice President, Insurance Company of North America, December 22, 1966.

property does not vary 50 percentage points between these two states.

Regardless of the minimum coinsurance requirement, the maximum coinsurance requirement for any peril should always be 100 percent, with a distinct credit for each coinsurance requirement. The need for high coinsurance requirements with separate credits is particularly great for perils which generally cause small losses. For example, if the probability of a sprinkler leakage loss above 50 percent of value is negligible, the total pure premium for 100 percent sprinkler leakage coverage should equal that for 50 percentage coverage. Substantial credits should be, and are, given for sprinkler leakage coinsurance above 50 percent of value. If credits for more than 50 percent coinsurance were not available, the insured who desired 100 percent sprinkler leakage coverage would have to pay, at the 50 percent coinsurance rate, twice the premium he ought to pay if losses above 50 percent of value are thought impossible. The fact that the 100 percent sprinkler leakage coinsurance rate is not exactly half the 50 percent rate suggests that actuaries include some allowance for losses above 50 percent of value.

Stability of Insurable Values

The insurable value of almost all properties changes during a policy period due to price changes, depreciation, or changes in the amount of property insured. If a percentage of value coinsurance requirement is used instead of a provisional reporting form, the greater the fluctuation of insurable values, the lower should be the minimum coinsurance option open to the insured. As an extreme example, a merchant would have great difficulty complying with a 100 percent coinsurance requirement on his merchandise inventory. When his inventory values rise, insurance which was sufficient to meet the 100 percent coinsurance requirement becomes inadequate, and the insured faces possible coinsurance penalties. When his inventory values fall, the merchant is left with more insurance than he could collect for even a total loss. The insured has no leeway; he must know (and predict) his values precisely.

However, if the merchant can obtain insurance subject to 80 percent coinsurance, he may buy coverage for 100 percent of value, and have a 20 percentage point "cushion" to absorb increased values without being subject to coinsurance penalties. Severe losses to any increased values also probably would be paid in full. By purchasing 100 percent coverage at the 80 percent coinsurance rate, the insured is paying a higher rate than theoretically is necessary to absorb losses, but the higher rate possibly may be justified by the protection gained for possible increased values and against coinsurance penalties.

The insured can conveniently purchase this "cushion" against coinsurance penalties, without buying coverage beyond full value, only if a coinsurance requirement somewhat below 100 percent is available. Coinsurance penalties due to fluctuating values could be avoided by purchasing insurance at the flat rate, but the extra cost of doing so probably would be greater than the value to the insured of the valuation "cushion."

The assertion that the *minimum permissible* coinsurance requirement should be less than 100 percent does not conflict with the statement in the previous section that the *maximum available* coinsurance requirement should always be 100 percent.

Form of Coverage

The minimum coinsurance requirement in a blanket policy usually is higher than the minimum requirement for specific coverage of the same property. As pointed out on pages 139 and 140, blanket insurance subject to less than 100 percent coinsurance, without a pro rata distribution clause, may give the insured full protection at all locations for the cost of coverage to 80 or 90 percent (depending on the coinsurance requirement) of his aggregate values. Thus, in order to avoid unfair discrimination in favor of the holder of a blanket policy, many underwriters require that blanket insurance be subject to 90 or 100 percent coinsurance or contain a pro rata distribution clause. If 100 percent coinsurance is included, the blanket and specific rates are equal. In some states, if the blanket policy has only 90 percent coinsurance, the 80 percent specific rate is charged. The use of the higher 80 percent rate for 90 percent coverage of aggregate values compensates to some extent for full protection at many or all locations. If 80 percent coinsurance is included in the blanket policy, pro rata distribution is required, and the 80 percent rate is charged. This seems to be appropriate treatment of coinsurance requirements and credits for 80, 90, and 100 percent coinsurance in blanket policies.

It appears inappropriate, nevertheless, to stipulate that blanket insurance containing a pro rata distribution clause cannot be written subject to less than 80 percent coinsurance at the same rate as specific insurance subject to the same coinsurance requirement. Pro rata distribution converts a blanket policy to a specific policy for purposes of loss adjustment. There seems to be little reason why an insured who wishes to buy blanket protection for a small percentage of his aggregate values and accepts pro rata distribution in return for the convenience of having to buy only one policy should not receive the same credit for coinsurance which is given the insured who buys an equal amount of coverage in several specific policies.

Relations with Insureds and Mortgagees

The insurer, in order to maintain good relations with the insured and with any mortgagee, seeks to promote, without appearing to compel, insurance (particularly against fire) to a high percentage of value. If an insured, who is not faced with any coinsurance requirements and is so optimistic that he purchases fire coverage to only 30 or 40 percent of value, suffers a total loss, he often blames the insurer when the loss is not paid in full.[41] Mortgagees demand that the mortgaged property be quite fully insured against fire. This demand has been given as one reason for the popularity of 80 percent coinsurance clauses in fire policies on

[41] Interview with John B. Davis, Assistant Vice President, Insurance Company of North America, January 17, 1967.

real property.[42] An insurer who permits a mortgagor to insure against fire for less than 80 percent of value may, in case of severe loss to the mortgaged property, be confronted with a disappointed, and perhaps litigious, debtor or creditor.

However, if an insured believes that he is being unreasonably compelled to purchase unnecessary amounts of coverage, he also may become hostile. The apparent element of compulsion in coinsurance has been given as one reason for the public's lack of understanding and acceptance of it.[43] If this reason is valid, one way to reduce this hostility and to increase understanding is to offer the insured some choice of coinsurance percentages.

Historically, control of moral hazard was once advanced as a justification for not permitting full fire coverage, or at least not offering credit for 100 percent coinsurance. It was argued that the insured with full coverage had an incentive to destroy his property. Offering the actuarially justified credit for 100 percent coinsurance as a price discount would add to this incentive.[44] This belief, if it persists today, is seldom made explicit.

SUMMARY

This chapter examines the following underwriting decisions regarding coinsurance: (1) when some type of coinsurance should be used; (2) what type it should be; and (3) if percentage of value coinsurance is used, the range of the insured's choice of coinsurance percentages.

Property insurance should be subject to some type of coinsurance except where (1) all losses are at least as large as the coinsurance requirement; (2) scheduling or appraisal of the

---

[42] E. R. Hardy, "Coinsurance," *The Business of Insurance,* ed. Howard P. Dunham (New York: The Ronald Press Co., 1912), p. 179.

[43] *Report of the Co-Insurance Committee to the Board of Fire Underwriters of the Pacific on Percentage Co-Insurance and the Relative Rates Chargeable Therefor, Also on the Cost of Conflagration Hazard of Large Cities* (San Francisco, 1905), p. 3; Moore, *op. cit.,* p. 580; and Huebner, Black, and Cline, *op. cit.,* p. 94.

[44] Edward S. Gay, "Full Co-Insurance and Contribution by the Assured," address to the Underwriters' Association of the Northwest, Chicago, September 27, 1893, p. 10.

property, or the gradation of premium rates, is a more advantageous, feasible alternative; or (3) coinsurance is impractical because the insured property is of little value or is extremely obsolescent or heavily depreciated, or the insured does not adequately understand coinsurance.

Coinsurance requirements should take the form of percentages of insurable value except where (1) an agreed amount endorsement is needed because of the insured's bargaining strength, especially if the risk is eligible for factory mutual coverage, or because of the difficulty of appraising the property before or after loss; or (2) a provisional reporting form is indicated by widely fluctuating insurable values, ease of current valuation by the insured, and the insured's ability to report values accurately and promptly.

In setting the limits of the insured's choice of coinsurance percentages, the underwriter takes account of (1) the maximum probable loss to the insured property from the insured peril; (2) the stability of the insurable value of the property; (3) the form of coverage (blanket or specific); and (4) the maintenance of the insurer's good relations with insureds and mortgagees. Consideration of these factors suggests (1) that a 100 percent coinsurance requirement, with proper rate credit, should always be available; (2) that the minimum coinsurance requirement should not exceed the maximum probable loss; (3) that the minimum permissible coinsurance percentage should be less than 100 percent in order to give the insured a valuation "cushion"; and (4) that there is little theoretical objection to offering blanket insurance, subject to pro rata distribution, with the same coinsurance percentages and credits allowed for specific insurance. Perhaps consideration should be given to offering fire and extended coverage insurance subject to the low coinsurance requirements available with sprinkler leakage and water damage coverage, at least where no mortgagee's interest is involved and the insured sufficiently understands coinsurance.

CHAPTER **10**

Coinsurance and Loss Adjustment

PURPOSE

One of the assumptions of the coinsurance rate model in Chapter 8 is that all coinsurance penalties are assessed properly on the basis of the true insurable values of the loss and of the property. The purpose of this chapter is to examine the extent to which actual loss adjustments typically fulfill this assumption.

In order to apply a coinsurance provision properly in every case, the loss adjuster must determine the amount of the loss and, if the coinsurance requirement is a percentage of value, the insurable value of the property. The factors which appear to interfere with the universal application of coinsurance in the loss adjustment procedure are (1) the cost of determining insurable value, (2) policy provisions, (3) problems of property valuation, and (4) nonconcurrent apportionments involving coinsurance. This chapter discusses each of these factors in turn.

COST OF DETERMINING INSURABLE VALUE

Loss adjustment costs average 6 percent of gross premiums for all property insurers, and most of this cost is fixed for each loss.[1]

---

[1] C. Arthur Williams, Jr., *Price Discrimination in Property and Liability Insurance,* University of Minnesota Studies in Economics and Business, No. 19 (Minneapolis: University of Minnesota Press, 1959), p. 11.

Since the cost of adjusting very small losses is relatively high, insurers wish to simplify the settlement of these losses. One simplifying step is to overlook any coinsurance clause when the amount of the average coinsurance penalty which would be assessed is expected to be less than the cost of determining the insurable value of the property. According to a confidential source, one large property insurer does not investigate compliance with coinsurance requirements for losses less that $1200, while other companies set the minimum loss subject to coinsurance at $1000 to $1500.

The effect of this virtual waiver of coinsurance requirements may be estimated roughly by determining the proportion of losses which fall below the minimum to which coinsurance is applied. The absolute loss-severity function in Equation VI-4 indicates that, of all fire losses of at least $250, 36.7 percent do not exceed $1200. In 1903, F. C. Moore suggested that 68 percent of all fire losses were less than $100, in then current values.[2] Taking account of the probable number of losses less than $250, the author considers it conservative to estimate that 50 percent of all fire losses are for such small amounts that insurers find it uneconomical to invoke coinsurance requirements. However, any extra benefit received by those insureds for whom coinsurance is waived probably should not be condemned as unfair discrimination against those who suffer large losses. All insureds with equally large properties in a given class presumably have the same chance of incurring a small loss on which coinsurance is waived in practice. Furthermore, the social cost of rigorously invoking coinsurance requirements on small losses may be greater than the social benefit of the equity theoretically obtainable by doing so. The expense of collecting all coinsurance penalties might raise premium rates unduly.

In nearly all states, the Homeowners policy has been revised to make the 80 percent coinsurance requirement applicable to the smallest loss.[3] The superseded provision gave replacement cost

[2] Francis C. Moore, *Fire Insurance and How to Build* (New York: The Baker & Taylor Co., 1903), p. 709.

[3] Letter from Frank J. Caso, Manager, Personal Lines Division, Multi-Line Insurance Rating Bureau, November 18, 1966.

coverage without application of 80 percent coinsurance only for eligible losses less than the smaller of $1000 or 5 percent of the policy face.[4] This revision might be interpreted as meaning that insistence on coinsurance is profitable for the insurer on very small losses. But no evidence exists on the actuarial cost of the 5 percent-$1000 coinsurance waiver in the replacement cost extension.[5] More than one insurance company official has stated confidentially that the tightening of the coinsurance requirement was one of a series of steps taken to improve Homeowners loss experience without clear foreknowledge of the effect of each step. Insufficient time has passed to judge the impact of the policy revision.[6]

POLICY PROVISIONS AFFECTING LOSS ADJUSTMENT

Two clauses which may reduce the amount of insurance applicable to a coinsurance requirement—the pro rata distribution and pro rata liability clauses—are discussed elsewhere. Another relevant provision, the division by item of insurance clause, is taken up in Appendix 5. The clauses treated here are the waiver of inventory clause and the exclusion clause.

Waiver of Inventory Clause[7]

One current waiver of inventory clause reads:

In the event that the aggregate claim for any loss is both less than $10,000 and less than 5% of the total amount of insurance upon the property described herein at the time such loss occurs, no special inventory or appraisement of the undamaged property shall be re-

---

[4] Homeowners Policy, Form 2, Extensions of Coverage, paragraph 3a.

[5] Interview with L. H. Longley-Cook, retired Vice President and Actuary, Insurance Company of North America, September 20, 1966.

[6] Letter from Frank J. Caso, Manager, Personal Lines Division, Multi-Line Insurance Rating Bureau, November 18, 1966.

[7] Unless otherwise noted, material under this heading is drawn from "Waiver of Inventory (and Appraisement) Clause," *The Fire, Casualty & Surety Bulletins* (Cincinnati, Ohio: The National Underwriter Company, loose-leaf, revised and supplemented periodically), Fire, pp. wi-1 to wi-4, seventh printing, March and October 1953.

quired, provided, however, that nothing herein shall be construed to waive application of the first paragraph of this clause [establishing the coinsurance apportionment ratio].[8]

While this clause does not waive the coinsurance requirement, it excuses the insured from presenting detailed records which document the value of his undamaged property. This accommodation to the insured simplifies adjustment of small losses. As indicated on page 154, for many of these losses, the invoking of coinsurance is uneconomical for the insurer, and, thus, an appraisal of total values is not needed to determine the coinsurance requirement for these very small losses. For losses greater than the minimum for which invoking the coinsurance clause is practicable (approximately $1000 to $1500) but less than $10,000, the insurer may rely on valuation methods other than the insured's inventory of undamaged property.

Earlier waiver clauses did not contain the proviso which concludes the quoted clause, creating confusion as to whether the coinsurance requirement itself was waived. In the leading case construing one of these earlier clauses, the highest New York appellate court held that the waiver of inventory clause did not waive the coinsurance requirement, the court noting that opinions of experts, the insured's records, examination of the insured under oath, or a judicial proceeding could ascertain compliance with the coinsurance requirement.[9] The court did not state that the expense of these alternative valuation procedures probably would not be justified for losses less than 5 percent of the policy.

In his dissenting opinion, Justice Van Voorhis gave three objections to this interpretation. First, an explicit waiver of coinsurance for small losses had a long history. Prior to 1900, New York fire policies stipulated:

---

[8] Second paragraph of New York Standard Coinsurance Clause, Form No. 819, New York Fire Insurance Rating Organization, *General Rules* (New York: The Organization, loose-leaf, revised and supplemented periodically), p. 20, effective August 2, 1965.

[9] *New York Life Insurance Company v. Glens Falls Insurance Company,* 184 Misc. 846, 55 N.Y.S. (2d) 176 (1945), *aff'd. mem.* 86 N.Y.S. (2d) 191 (1949).

It is understood that this clause shall not apply to losses which do not exceed five per cent of the insurance.[10]

Equivalent clauses were used in two other areas of the United States[11] and in all of Canada.[12] This *New York Life* decision overruled a previous holding of the same court which construed the same clause as waiving the coinsurance requirement.[13] Second, Justice Van Voorhis reasoned that, since most insurance agents explained to insureds that the waiver of inventory clause was a waiver of coinsurance, the insurer generally would be estopped from asserting the coinsurance requirement. Third, the Justice recognized that the alternative means of enforcing coinsurance for small losses were not practical.

Another criticism of the *New York Life* decision is that the insured needs an appraisal of his undamaged property in any case where the insurer seeks to enforce a coinsurance requirement for a loss less than $10,000 or 5 percent of the amount of insurance. For these losses, the insured has no duty to provide an inventory but must do so in order to protect his interests.[14]

The waiver of undamaged inventory clause complicates the application of coinsurance to losses for which the insured is not obliged to provide a complete inventory. For losses between approximately $1200 and $10,000 (or 5 percent of the policy, if less), the insurer must find alternative means of establishing insurable value if it wishes to invoke a coinsurance requirement. The cost of pursuing these alternatives probably makes impractical the application of coinsurance where the size of the loss would justify its use if the insured's appraisal could be used as evidence

---

[10] John W. Gunn, "The Reduced Rate Average Clause," *Annual Report of Proceedings, The Fire Insurance Society of San Francisco*, vol. I (1910–1911), p. 46. For an account of the gradual introduction of the restricted waiver given at the beginning of this section, see "Average Clause Held Not to Waive Coinsurance on Small Fire Losses," *Eastern Underwriter*, vol. XLVIII, no. 43 (October 24, 1947), p. 33.

[11] Moore, *op. cit.*, p. 575. Moore does not indicate these areas.

[12] William N. Bament, "Coinsurance," address to the Insurance Society of New York, Mach 30, 1920, p. 14.

[13] *Pinsky v. Minneapolis Fire & Marine Insurance Company*, 225 App. Div. 326 at 329, 233 N.Y.S. 160 at 163 (1929).

[14] Holger de Roode, letter to the editor, *The Post Magazine and Insurance Monitor* (London), vol. LXXXVI, no. 32 (August 1, 1925), p. 1.

of insurable values. But the amount of coinsurance penalties not assessed by the insurer for lack of the insured's appraisal cannot be determined.

Exclusion Clause

At the insured's option and with the underwriter's approval, the following clause, similar to that used in other states, can be included in New York fire policies:

> If this coinsurance clause is applicable, *this policy does not cover* brick, stone or concrete foundations, piers or other supports which are below the under surface of the lowest basement floor, or, where there is no basement, which are below the surface of the ground; underground flues and pipes, underground wiring and drains.[15]

Some states provide a longer list of properties which can be excluded from coverage. Illinois, for example, also allows exclusion of brick, stone, or concrete chimneys or stacks not part of the insured building; underwater pilings; architects' fees; railroad tracks; ingots and metal scrap; ores, gravel, clay, and sand; water wheels; and the contents of certain safes and vaults, as well as other properties.[16]

An example of the effect of this clause is a building with a $100,000 insurable value—including $10,000 represented by items excluded by the New York exclusion clause—insured subject to 80 percent coinsurance. The coinsurance requirement is $72,000 (80 percent of $90,000, not of $100,000), but any loss to an excluded item is not covered.

The primary purpose of the exclusion clause is not to waive coverage on indestructible property, but to define, as accurately as is possible in general terms, the basis for determining insurable

---

15 Edwin W. Patterson and William F. Young, Jr., *Cases and Materials on the Law of Insurance,* 4th ed. (Brooklyn, N.Y.: The Foundation Press, Inc., 1961), p. 670. Emphasis supplied.

16 *Illinois Rule Book* (*Excluding Cook County*) loose-leaf, revised and supplemented periodically (Chicago: Illinois Inspection and Rating Bureau, effective May 15, 1967), pp. 49 and 50.

value for coinsurance purposes.[17] The main objective is to speed and simplify loss adjustment and only incidentally to lower the coinsurance requirement for any given coinsurance percentage. In return for the lower coinsurance requirement, the insured forgoes coverage on property which rarely suffers a severe loss from insured perils. Properly used, the exclusion clause facilitates the accurate application of coinsurance.

A once common practice,[18] no longer followed in any state,[19] was to exclude certain property from the coinsurance requirement but to include it within the policy's coverage. This procedure lowered the ratio of insurance to covered values to less than that specified in the coinsurance clause (in the above example, $72,000 of coverage meets the 80 percent coinsurance requirement but would be only 72 percent of the $100,000 covered value), especially in the case of properties with extensive stone or brick components. Excluding some property from coinsurance, but not from coverage, may make the insurer's pure premium income inadequate to pay losses and tends to discriminate against insureds with comparatively small excludable values. Fortunately, every modern policy insuring the perils selected for this study subject to coinsurance includes all covered property within the scope of its coinsurance requirement.

PROBLEMS OF PROPERTY VALUATION

Valuing properties probably is the most critical and difficult aspect of the proper application of coinsurance. Whether insurable value is the basis for establishing (1) a percentage coinsurance requirement, (2) the sum stipulated in the agreed amount endorsement, or (3) the value submitted under a periodic report-

---

[17] Morton P. MacLeod, "Coinsurance—What It Is and How It Works," *Appraisal and Valuation Manual of the American Society of Appraisers,* vol. VI (1961), p. 343.

[18] Moore, *op. cit.,* pp. 714–715.

[19] Telephone interview with Frank E. Raab, then Assistant Vice President, Policyholder Service Department—Technical, Insurance Company of North America, July 10, 1967.

ing form, this value must be known if coinsurance rates are to be adequate, reasonable, and equitable.

Yet it has been said that *exact* valuation of any property is almost impossible;[20] that neither the insurer, its agent, nor the insured can approximate closely the actual cash value of a property;[21] that property valuation is an act of "divine wisdom";[22] that valuation is a matter of philosophy, not of science;[23] and that many commercial property owners are unaware of their insurable values.[24] Indirect evidence of insurance adjusters' inability to determine exact values of properties damaged by fire is seen in the *Annual Statistical Report of the Office of the Fire Marshal of Oregon.*[25] The figures on individual losses indicate that, in a very high percentage of cases, adjusters equate insurable value ("sound value") with the amount of insurance.

Lack of careful attention to insurable values by both insureds and loss adjusters can be a serious difficulty in the practical application of coinsurance. The following sections treat one source of this difficulty—the ambiguity of various valuation standards—and the steps by which the insured can reduce the possibility that, despite the policyholder's best efforts to meet a coinsurance requirement, a panel of appraisers will find a coinsurance deficiency.

---

[20] P. D. Betterley, *Buying Insurance, A Problem of Business Management* (New York: McGraw-Hill Book Co., Inc., 1936), p. 101.

[21] A. F. Dean, *The Philosophy of Fire Insurance,* ed. W. R. Townley (Chicago: Edward B. Hatch, 1925), vol. I, pp. 125–126.

[22] William Otis Badger, "Should Co-Insurance Be Abolished?" *Best's Insurance News, Fire and Marine Edition,* vol. XXXI, no. 5 (September 20, 1930), p. 359.

[23] James C. Bonbright, *The Valuation of Property, A Treatise on the Appraisal of Property for Different Legal Purposes,* Columbia University Council for Research in the Social Sciences (New York: McGraw-Hill Book Co., Inc., 1937), vol. I, pp. 371–372.

[24] *Report of the Joint Committee of the Senate and Assembly of the State of New York, Appointed to Investigate Corrupt Practices in Connection with Legislation, and the Affairs of Insurance Companies, Other Than Those Doing Life Insurance Business,* Assembly Document No. 30 (Albany, N.Y., February 1, 1911), pp. 86–87.

[25] Salem, Ore.: State Printing, annual. See pp. 25 through 30 of each edition.

Ambiguity of Valuation Standards

If an insured and a loss adjuster are to agree on the insurable value of a property or a loss—based on "actual cash value," "replacement cost," or, occasionally, "market value"—they must agree on the meaning of these phrases.

The abstract definitions, but not practical applications, of actual cash value, replacement cost, and market value are fairly clear.[26] Replacement cost is the cost, in the insured's customary market of purchase at time of loss, of new property to replace damaged or destroyed property. For goods held by the original manufacturer, replacement cost is the cost of manufacture to the stage reached when the loss occurred, except that, when the manufacturing facilities also have been damaged heavily, replacement cost is the cost of similar finished or unfinished goods purchased from a competitor. Actual cash value is replacement cost less physical depreciation and economic obsolescence. Market value is the cost, in the insured's customary market of purchase at the time of loss, of goods in the same condition as the insured property at the time of loss.

In practice, many phrases attempting to describe valuation standards are meaningless for insurance purposes because courts, trying to adequately compensate insureds, have been very flexible in interpreting the standard valuation phrases in insurance policies.[27] Thus, some courts have defined actual cash value as market value,[28] while other courts have defined market value as actual

---

[26] Material in this paragraph is based on Bonbright, *op. cit.*, vol. I, pp. 373–384; and Edwin W. Patterson, *Essentials of Insurance Law* (New York: McGraw-Hill Book Co., Inc., 1957), pp. 136–138.

[27] Bonbright, *op. cit.*, pp. 373 and 406.

[28] *Manchester Fire Insurance Company v. Simons*, 12 Tex. Civ. App. 607, 35 S.W. 722 at 723 (1896); *Farmers' Mercantile Company v. Insurance Company*, 161 Iowa 5, 141 N.W. 447 at 454 (1913); *State Auto Mutual Insurance Company v. Cox*, 309 Ky. 480, 218 S.W. (2d) 46 at 47 (1949); *Britven v. Occidental Insurance Company*, 234 Iowa 682, 13 N.W. (2d) 791 at 793 (1944); *Gervant v. New England Fire Insurance Company*, 306 N.Y. 293, 118 N.E. (2d) 574 at 577 (1954); *Pinet v. New Hampshire Fire Insurance Company*, 100 N.H. 346, 126 Atl. (2d) 262 at 264 (1956); and *Wisconsin Screw Company v. Fireman's Fund Insurance Company*, 297 Fed. (2d) 697 at 701 (1962).

cash value.[29] In some insurance cases, actual cash value has been considered to be synonymous with replacement cost, including the substitution of new for old.[30] Other decisions state that actual cash value is replacement cost less physical depreciation.[31] Also, it has been held that actual cash value is use value to the owner.[32] A passage from a famous decision regarding the actual cash value of a brewery during Prohibition indicates the flexibility of the legal definition of actual cash value:

Where insured buildings have been destroyed the trier of fact may, and should, call to its aid, in order to effectuate complete indemnity, every fact and circumstance which would logically tend to the formation of a correct estimate of the loss. It may consider original cost and cost of reproduction; the opinions upon value given by qualified witnesses; the declarations against interest which may have been made by the assured; the gainful uses to which the buildings might have been put; as well as any other fact tending to throw light on the subject.[33]

Many courts have followed *McAnarney* in unusual cases of real estate damage.[34]

---

[29] *Niagara Fire Insurance Company v. Pool,* 31 S.W. (2d) 850 at 852 (1930); *Butler v. Aetna Insurance Company,* 64 N.D. 764, 256 N.W. 214 at 217 (1934); and *Insurance Company of North America v. McGraw,* 255 Ky. 839, 75 S.W. (2d) 518 at 520 (1928).

[30] *Fedas v. Insurance Company of the State of Pennsylvania,* 300 Pa. 555, 151 Atl. 285 at 288 (1930); *McIntosh v. Hartford Fire Insurance Company,* 106 Mont. 434, 78 Pac. (2d) 82 at 84 (1938); and *Fire Association of Philadelphia v. Coomer,* Tex. Civ. App. 158 S.W. (2d) 355 at 357 (1942).

[31] *Svea Fire and Liability Insurance Company v. State Savings and Loan Association,* 19 Fed. (2d) 134 at 135 (1927); *Dubin Paper Company v. Insurance Company of North America,* 361 Pa. 68, 62 Atl. (2d) 85 at 86 (1948); *Milwaukee Mechanics' Insurance Company v. Maples,* 37 Ala. 74, 66 So. (2d) 159 at 160 (1953); and *Knuppel v. American Insurance Company,* 269 Fed. (2d) 163 at 166 (1953).

[32] *Johnston v. Farmers' Fire Insurance Company,* 106 Mich. 96, 64 N.W. 5 at 6 (1895); and *Clift v. Fulton Fire Insurance Company,* 44 Tenn. App. 486, 315 S.W. (2d) 9 at 11 (1958).

[33] *McAnarney v. Newark Fire Insurance Company,* 247 N.Y. 176, 159 N.E. 902 at 905 (1928).

[34] James M. Guiher, "Measurement of Damages in Property Insurance Losses," *Proceedings of the American Bar Association Section of Insurance, Negligence and Compensation Law* (1965), p. 190. According to one source, court cases in twenty-one states had upheld the *McAnarney* rule as of 1969, namely, Colorado, Connecticut, Florida, Georgia, Iowa, Maryland, Massachusetts, New Hampshire, New Jersey, New York, North Carolina, Oklahoma, Pennsylvania, North Dakota, South Dakota, Tennessee, Texas,

Flexibility of valuation standards may benefit insureds in litigated cases. However, it also can create great difficulty for the insured attempting in good faith to comply with a percentage of value coinsurance requirement. He cannot be positive whether the insurer will maintain, after a loss, that the property should have been insured to the specified percentage of its historical cost, replacement cost, market value, actual cash value, or use value. The wording of the coinsurance clause may not resolve the insured's uncertainty.

Insured's Precautions against Valuation Risk

This study defines valuation risk as the probability that an insured property will be appraised at such a high value after a loss that the insured will incur a coinsurance penalty. This section outlines six methods by which the insured can treat valuation risk. These methods are: (1) assuming valuation risk; (2) avoiding percentage of value coinsurance; (3) insuring beyond the percentage requirement; (4) updating coverage; (5) maintaining accurate records of values; and (6) obtaining insurer's appraisal (available by law in three states).

Assuming Valuation Risk. The insured who assumes valuation risk under either a percentage of value coinsurance clause or a periodic reporting form ignores coinsurance and reporting requirements and assumes that after any loss he will be able to collect the full amount of the loss. He predicts that he will be able to prove that his exposed values were sufficiently low, or his loss so severe, that any coinsurance requirement will not reduce his indemnity payments. In a few litigated cases, insureds have been able to sustain this burden of proof despite insurers' claims of large insurable values and small losses.[35]

Virginia, Vermont, Washington, and Wisconsin. Harold P. Herzog, "Can Anyone Define 'Actual Cash Value'?," *Business Insurance,* vol. IV, no. 6 (March 16, 1970), p. 29.

[35] *Citizens' Savings Bank and Trust Company v. Fitchburg Mutual Fire Insurance Company,* 86 Vt. 267, 84 Atl. 970 (1912); *Smith v. Allemania Fire Insurance Company,* 219 Ill. App. 506 (1920); and *Gervant v. New England Fire Insurance Company,* 306 N.Y. 293, 118 N.E. (2d) 574 (1954).

In these disputes, the insured usually attempts to prove low values and high losses. But where the loss is an indisputable fraction of total insurable value, and this fraction is less than the coinsurance percentage, the insured should claim a large insurable value. The larger the insurable value in this type of case, the greater will be the recovery, until the policy face becomes payable. For example, if a property is insured for $60,000 subject to an 80 percent coinsurance requirement and the loss is 20 percent of insurable value, the insured should, if possible, not claim an insurable value less than $75,000 ($60,000/0.8), the maximum value for which the policy meets the 80 percent coinsurance requirement. In this case, for every $1.00 by which the value falls short of $75,000, the insured loses $0.20 of indemnity (the loss being 20 percent of value).

Avoiding Percentage of Value Coinsurance. Percentage of value coinsurance can be avoided through an agreed amount endorsement or by purchasing insurance at flat rates. For the perils selected for this study, the agreed amount endorsement is available only for limited classes of property (see page 156). Insurance without a coinsurance clause is sold only at flat rates, which generally are substantially higher than the rate for the minimum coinsurance percentage. For example, in states served by the Pacific Fire Rating Bureau, an insured with a fire-resistive building in a well-protected area pays a flat fire rate which is 155.4 percent of the 50 percent coinsurance rate.[36] It appears that many flat rates are set high to discourage coverage not subject to coinsurance, often making this method of treating valuation risk uneconomical for the insured.

Use of a periodic reporting form or the purchase of coinsurance deficiency insurance does not avoid percentage of value coinsurance. To be free of coinsurance penalties under a periodic reporting form, the insured must report 100 percent of his insurable values and the amount of any insurance not written on a reporting form. With coinsurance deficiency insurance, the insured

---

[36] Pacific Fire Rating Bureau, *Tariff Rules* (San Francisco: The Bureau, loose-leaf, revised and supplemented periodically), p. 2E, effective April 1, 1956.

must report his values and the amount of his other insurance.[37] The coinsurance deficiency insurance is subject to a coinsurance requirement very similar to the full reporting requirement in a periodic reporting form. The attraction of coinsurance deficiency insurance is that this policy permits real estate to be insured as it would be on a reporting form. The amount of coinsurance deficiency insurance written in this country probably is small. Under either a periodic reporting form or a coinsurance deficiency policy, the insured must remain mindful of his values.

Insuring beyond Percentage Requirement. If a coinsurance percentage less than 100 percent is available, the insured may agree to this lower percentage coinsurance clause, while insuring beyond what he believes is the coinsurance requirement. For example, a building which an insured believes has an insurable value of $100,000 may be insured for $90,000 subject to a 60 percent coinsurance requirement. The actual value of the building must exceed $150,000 before the insured suffers a coinsurance penalty ($0.6 \times \$150,000 = \$90,000$). The 60 percent coinsurance rate will be higher than the 90 percent coinsurance rate (42 percent higher for well-protected fire-resistive buildings in most Pacific states[38]), but a part of this higher rate may be regarded as the price for protection against coinsurance penalties caused by rising values.

Updating Coverage. An insured may attempt to keep abreast of his current insurable values and adjust his policy amounts to fulfill precisely the stated coinsurance requirement. This is a valid technique for handling valuation risk under three conditions: (1) the insured's valuation (perhaps by professional appraisal) is sufficiently authoritative to be accepted by the insurer; (2) values do not change abruptly between appraisal dates; and (3) the cost of purchasing additional insurance or canceling unnecessary insurance is not excessive.

Maintaining Accurate Records. When an insured keeps thorough, accurate records of the purchase dates and costs of his

---

[37] John H. Magee and David L. Bickelhaupt, *General Insurance*, 7th ed. (Homewood, Ill.: Richard D. Irwin, Inc., 1964), p. 927.

[38] Pacific Fire Rating Bureau, *op. cit.*, p. 2E, effective April 1, 1956.

properties, accounts accurately for depreciation, and keeps detailed inventory records, the areas in which the insurer can challenge the insured's valuations are greatly reduced. Also, such records corroborate the insured's claim of the amount of any loss.[39] Maintenance of a superior accounting system strengthens the insured's position in any negotiation with the insurer about coinsurance requirements and losses.

Obtaining Insurer's Appraisal. The statutes of Delaware, Tennessee, and Vermont require the insurer to find the insurable value of all real estate insured against fire when the coverage is written or renewed. The insured must be informed of the value determined by the insurer. Such periodic valuations seem to provide a fairly reliable basis by which the insured can judge his compliance with coinsurance requirements. These statutes are discussed more fully on pages 197–98.

PROBLEMS INVOLVING NONCONCURRENT APPORTIONMENTS

The process of adjusting a loss covered by two or more insurance policies usually involves an apportionment of the loss between or among insurers, although in some cases one policy may bear the entire loss. When all policies are substantially identical, they are said to be concurrent;[40] otherwise the policies are nonconcurrent, and the allocation of the loss among them is a nonconcurrent apportionment.

Nonconcurrent apportionments involving coinsurance can become extremely complex, both because of the importance of the exact wording of the coinsurance provision(s) involved and because of the special, somewhat arbitrary, rules which most insurers, by voluntary mutual agreement, have followed in apportioning these nonconcurrent losses. While the full spectrum of the

---

[39] Prentiss B. Reed and Paul I. Thomas, *Adjustment of Property Losses,* 3d ed. (New York: McGraw-Hill Book Co., Inc., 1969), p. 261.

[40] More precise definitions of concurrency—the "old" definition used by the National Board of Fire Underwriters and the "new" definition in the *1963 Guiding Principles*—are given below, pages 181 and 183.

intricacies of nonconcurrent apportionments with coinsurance has been reserved for Appendix 5, the broad outlines of the problem are sketched here in order to lay a foundation for a recommendation which could greatly reduce these apportionment problems.

The discussion in this section opens with a description of the procedures which have been followed in nonconcurrent apportionments involving coinsurance. Then the problems involved are demonstrated with an example of how the phrasing of a coinsurance provision is critical to the apportionment. Finally, the section closes with a recommendation which could simplify such apportionments and eliminate the need for the special rules applicable to them.

The distinction made in Chapter 4[41] between *policy to percentage of value* ("coinsurance") and *insurance to percentage of value* ("average") clauses occurs repeatedly in this discussion. A policy to percentage of value coinsurance clause limits the insurer's liability to no greater percentage of a loss than the face amount of that one policy bears to a specified percentage of the value of the insured property at the time of loss. Thus, the presence of other insurance, whether or not concurrent, cannot raise the coinsurance apportionment ratio for a policy containing a policy to percentage of value coinsurance clause. (For convenience in this context, such a clause may be given the shortened label *policy to value clause*.)

In contract, an insurance to percentage of value coinsurance clause can be more liberal to the insured because this type of clause restricts the insurer's liability to no greater proportion of any loss than the combined face amount of *all* insurance on the property bears to a specified percentage of the property value when the loss occurs. As a result, other insurance on the property may increase an insurer's limit of liability under such a clause (in this context conveniently called an *insurance to value clause*) even though that other insurance may not be concurrent with the coverage containing the insurance to value clause.

---

[41] See pages 53–55.

Procedures for Nonconcurrent Apportionments Involving Coinsurance

Before 1942, little uniformity existed in the apportionment of losses between nonconcurrent policies. From 1942 through October, 1963, most companies voluntarily followed the recommendations of the National Board of Fire Underwriters regarding these apportionments. Since November, 1963, most insurers have adhered to a simplified set of recommendations based on a new definition of nonconcurrency.

Nonconcurrent Apportionments under National Board Recommendations.[42] Under the recommendations of the National Board of Fire Underwriters—which defined policies as concurrent even though they may have differed as to face, date, insurer, or duration—three cases had to be distinguished: (1) nonconcurrency as to property covered,[43] with no policy having an insurance to value clause; (2) nonconcurrency as to property covered, with at least one policy having an insurance to value clause (four possibilities existed here); and (3) nonconcurrency only as to coinsurance provisions.

In the first case, nonconcurrency only as to property covered, the limit of liability rule applied. Each policy contributed to the loss in the ratio that its limit of liability for that loss bore to the sum of all policies' limits of liability. Each policy's limit of liability was the least of its face, the loss, or the amount it would pay

---

[42] Material under this heading from Robert P. Barbour, *The Agents Key to Fire Insurance*, 6th ed. (New York: The Spectator Co., 1949), pp. 114–119; and Prentiss B. Reed, *Adjustment of Property Losses*, 2nd ed. (New York: McGraw-Hill Book Co., Inc., 1953), pp. 213–226. For an excellent discussion of issues involved in nonconcurrent apportionments with coinsurance, see Ernest H. Minnion, *Average Clauses and Fire-Loss Apportionments*, 2nd ed. (London: Isaac Pitman & Sons, 1947), *passim*.

[43] Policies are nonconcurrent as to property covered when one policy insures some, but not all, property insured by another under one item of insurance. Thus, Policy A may insure only wheat in a warehouse, while Policy B covers all grain there. Of the nonconcurrent policies, A is specific, B is blanket. Wheat is covered by both blanket and specific insurance, and grain other than wheat has only blanket coverage.

for the loss under any other policy restrictions. If the loss exceeded the total limits of liability, each policy paid its limit.

In the second case, nonconcurrency as to property covered with at least one policy having an insurance to value clause, any one of four rules could apply, depending on the size of the loss and the coverage for the property damaged. The general rule was to interpret all insurance to value clauses as policy to value clauses (so that no policy's coinsurance deficiency could be made up by another policy) and to apply the limit of liability rule. But, in an effort to protect the insured, this general rule was followed for this type of nonconcurrency only if doing so did not reduce the total indemnity payment received by the insured to less than the total he would have received if all insurance to value clauses were applied literally. Because a policy to value interpretation of an insurance to value clause can reduce the amount of insurance available to meet a coinsurance requirement, this general rule would reduce the insurer's total liability in some cases.

When the general limit of liability rule did deprive the insured of indemnity in this type of nonconcurrency, all insurance to value clauses still were interpreted literally, but one of three special rules was applied. The first special rule, the Page Rule applicable to a loss limited to property with both specific and blanket coverage (wheat in the example in footnote 43) stipulated that the blanket policy contribute with the specific insurance in proportion to their face amounts. The second special rule applied only if the loss struck *both* property with both blanket and specific insurance *and* property with only blanket insurance (both wheat and other grain in the footnoted example). Here the Cromie Rule required the blanket policy to, first, pay the loss it alone covered and, second, contribute in proportion to its unused limit of liability to the loss which had both specific and blanket insurance. Under the third special rule, for a loss restricted to property which had only blanket coverage—grain other than wheat in the example—the face of the specific policy was applied toward meeting the blanket policy's insurance to value requirement, literally construed, even though the specific policy paid none of the loss. Throughout all three cases no policy paid more than its limit of liability under its insurance to value provision. In general, these three special rules were not favorable to insurers issuing blanket policies.

The two paragraphs immediately preceding relate only to the second broad case of nonconcurrency under the National Board recommendations, that is, nonconcurrency as to property covered with at least one policy having an insurance to value clause. In the third type of nonconcurrency, where the policies differed only in coinsurance provisions and not with respect to covered property, each policy contributed in proportion to its face amount, regardless of any coinsurance deficiencies, but no policy paid more than its limit of liability under any coinsurance provision it contained. All such provisions were applied literally.

Nonconcurrent Apportionments under the 1963 Guiding Principles.[44] Under the *1963 Guiding Principles,* policies are concurrent even though they may differ as to insurer, face, date, duration, deductibles, or coinsurance. Thus, in contrast to the National Board rules, policies may differ as to coinsurance and still be concurrent under the *Guiding Principles.* Concurrent policies share losses in proportion to their face amounts, with no policy paying more than its limit of liability under any deductible or coinsurance clause. For nonconcurrencies, the *Guiding Principles* generally follow earlier recommendations, with one major exception: blanket insurance is made excess to specific coverage, eliminating the Page and Cromie rules and making greater use of the limit of liability rule.

Because blanket coverage is excess, it pays no loss to specifically insured property until the primary coverage has paid its limit of liability. In a case with both specific and excess insurance, the following is recommended regarding coinsurance in the excess policy:

To provide the greatest recovery to the insured, the insurance declared to be excess or noncontributing under the governing Principle shall not include, in applying any coinsurance, average, or distribution

---

[44] Material under this heading from *Guiding Principles—Casualty, Fidelity, Inland Marine—First-Party Property Losses and Claims* (New York: Association of Casualty and Surety Companies, *et al.,* November 1, 1963), pp. 1–3 and 37.

clause(s) contained in any policy(ies), the value or loss on property covered under the insurance declared to be primary. However, it shall include any excess value not covered by the primary insurance and the loss unrecoverable under the primary insurance.[45]

By this procedure (1) the indemnity payment of the primary policy is subtracted from the loss to fix the loss to which the blanket policy's coinsurance apportionment ratio is applied, and (2) the primary policy's face is deducted from the full property value to set the value to which the blanket policy's coinsurance percentage is applied.

In the following passage, the *Guiding Principles* adopt the previous recommendation regarding the interpretation of insurance to value as policy to value clauses:

When a coinsurance (not reduced rate contribution or average) clause is present in any or all policies, it shall be applied as if it were a reduced rate contribution or reduced rate average clause. However, if by this procedure the insured collects less than he would collect under the terms of the coinsurance clause, the coinsurance clause shall be applied as such.[46]

An Example of a Nonconcurrent Apportionment Involving Coinsurance

Differences between policy to value and insurance to value clauses in nonconcurrent policies appear in variations of a basic example of a warehouse containing $150,000 of wheat and $50,000 of oats. The insurance consists of $110,000 Policy A on wheat only and $60,000 Policy B on all grain. The specific policy, A, has no coinsurance provision, but the blanket policy, B, is subject to an insurance to value clause reading:

It is part of the conditions of this policy, and the basis on which the rate of premium is fixed, that the Insured shall at all times maintain insurance on each item of property insured by this policy of not less than 80 per cent of the actual cash value thereof, and that, failing

---

[45] *Ibid.*, p. 3.
[46] *Ibid.* The quotation omits a footnote in the original. In this passage, a "coinsurance clause" is an insurance to value clause, and a "reduced rate contribution or average clause" is a policy to value clause.

to do so, the Insured shall be an insurer to the extent of such deficit, and in that event shall bear his, her or their proportion of any loss.[47]

Policy B has no pro rata distribution clause; if necessary for full indemnity, its whole face may be applied to any part of the grain. Only the loss, policy face, pro rata liability, and coinsurance provisions limit payments under either policy.

For a $20,000 oats loss, identically apportioned under the National Board recommendations or the *Guiding Principles,* Policy A pays nothing. Policy B pays no greater portion of the loss than the total amount of insurance on any grain ($110,000 + $60,000) bears to 80 percent of the $200,000 value of all grain ($160,000), which is 160/160 of the loss,[48] or the whole $20,000. Policy B's insurance to value clause does not reduce indemnity because Policy A restores the $100,000 coinsurance deficiency. The policy to value interpretation of an insurance to value clause, normally recommended, is not allowed here because such an interpretation would lower the insured's total indemnity to $7500 (60/160 of $20,000), all paid by Policy B. If Policy B had contained an 80 percent policy to value clause, it would have paid $7500 and left the insured a $12,500 coinsurance penalty.

Six features of this example make the insurance to value clause more liberal to the insured than is a policy to value clause: (1) the policies are nonconcurrent as to property covered; (2) the insurance to value clause is in blanket Policy B; (3) some loss (for convenience, all the loss) occurs to property (oats) with only blanket coverage; (4) the insurance to value clause in Policy B does not specify that insurance applied to its coinsurance requirement must contribute, or be concurrent, with Policy B; (5) the loss is not large enough to exhaust Policy B regardless of which type of 80 percent coinsurance clause it contains; and (6) the insurance to value clause in Policy B does not contain

---

[47] Coinsurance clause in fire insurance policies issued in the states served by the South-Eastern Underwriters Association. Quoted from Prentiss B. Reed and Paul I. Thomas, *op. cit.,* p. 404.

[48] By paying 170/160 of the loss, Policy B would violate the principle of indemnity.

a division by item of insurance provision. The effect which each of these factors has upon the apportionment is explored in Appendix 5.

A Recommendation

Because insurance to value clauses have been the source of most of the confusion and special rules surrounding nonconcurrent apportionments involving coinsurance, the author believes that insurance to value clauses should be eliminated as soon as possible and that policy to value clauses should be used in stating every percentage of value coinsurance requirement. In apportionments between concurrent or nonconcurrent policies, an insurance to value clause may increase the liability of the insurer using it, tending to upset the balance between pure premiums and expected indemnity payments achieved by equitable and just adequate coinsurance premium rates computed on the assumption that only one policy covers each loss (see page 102). When more than one policy applies, policy to value clauses minimize departures from this assumption. The National Board and the *Guiding Principles* have recommended that insurance to value clauses be interpreted as policy to value clauses whenever this does not reduce the insured's indemnity. This artificial interpretation would be unnecessary if insurance to value clauses were not used.

It seems very likely that insurance to value clauses would never have come into existence had their authors realized the problems such clauses can create. Almost without doubt, the authors of insurance to value clauses thought their provisions were equivalent to policy to value provisions but were guilty of careless draftsmanship.

In some cases, only an insurance to value clause may give full indemnity. But, when careful draftsmanship provides an easy remedy, the author does not believe that an insured merits more indemnity from *one* insurer merely because he has paid additional premium to *another* insurer for another policy, disrupting both insurers' balance between pure premium and expected indemnity.

SUMMARY

This chapter explores the extent to which exact adjustment of losses, necessary for the ideal operation of coinsurance, is hampered by (1) the cost of applying coinsurance requirements, (2) policy provisions, (3) valuation problems, and (4) problems in nonconcurrent apportionments involving coinsurance.

Because of the cost of determining insurable value in order to apply a coinsurance requirement, many adjusters do not consider coinsurance when the loss is less than $1000 to $1500, effectively waiving coinsurance for perhaps 50 percent of all fire losses to which coinsurance otherwise would apply.

The waiver of undamaged inventory clause and the exclusion clause affect the application of coinsurance. For losses above, say, $1200 but less than $10,000 or 5 percent of the policy, the insurer cannot demand that the insured report his undamaged inventory in order for the insurer to invoke any coinsurance penalty, and the insurer must resort to more expensive methods of determining compliance with coinsurance requirements. The exclusion clause simplifies the application of coinsurance by defining the types of property included in coverage and in the value on which the coinsurance requirement is computed. But if, as is no longer the case, property is excluded only from the coinsurance base and not from coverage, premium inadequacy and inequity are possible.

Ambiguous valuation standards make compliance with percentage coinsurance requirements difficult for the insured. This difficulty is somewhat reduced by adjusters' apparent tendency to equate amounts of insurance with insurable values, but this tendency distorts the statistics on losses as percentages of insurable value. Accurate statistics and precise loss adjustments are needed for proper rates. The insured can treat the risk of coinsurance penalties, some of which are due to errors in determining insurable values, by (1) assuming this valuation risk;

(2) avoiding percentage of value coinsurance; (3) insuring beyond the percentage requirement; (4) updating coverage; (5) maintaining accurate records of values; and (6) obtaining an insurer's appraisal, available by law in three states for some coverages.

In apportionments of losses among nonconcurrent policies subject to coinsurance, the presence of *insurance* to percentage of value coinsurance provisions (as opposed to *policy* to percentage of value provisions) can distort the apportionment of losses by allocating an unduly large portion of these losses to policies with insurance to value provisions. The apportionment rules of the National Board of Fire Underwriters and of the *1963 Guiding Principles,* both of which put the desirability of giving the insured full indemnity ahead of the desirability of preserving rate-making precision and the adequacy of the insurer's premium income, have recommended somewhat artificial interpretation of coinsurance provisions involved in nonconcurrent apportionments. While the author does not wish to decide the relative social priorities of the competing goals of providing insureds with full indemnity and preserving the integrity of insurers' premium rating structures, the author does recommend that policy to value coinsurance provisions replace insurance to value coinsurance clauses as soon as practicable. Doing so will greatly reduce the complexity of nonconcurrent apportionments without depriving an insured of the indemnity payment for which he has paid.

CHAPTER **11**

Regulation of Coinsurance

PURPOSE

The purpose of this chapter is to examine current state laws affecting coinsurance, there being no directly relevant federal laws. The first section of this chapter enumerates some possible objectives in the regulation of coinsurance. The second details statutes and administrative rulings bearing on coinsurance. The chapter concludes with an assessment of the effectiveness of these laws in meeting the enumerated regulatory objectives.

OBJECTIVES OF REGULATING COINSURANCE

The discussion in previous chapters suggests seven objectives which reasonably might be sought in regulating coinsurance, some of which may conflict with others. These goals are: (1) establishing equitable premium rates; (2) minimizing the cost of insurance consistent with insurers' financial strength; (3) stabilizing premium rates over time; (4) improving insureds' understanding of coinsurance; (5) minimizing insureds' difficulties in meeting coinsurance requirements; (6) minimizing uninsured losses; and (7) permitting policyholders to insure to any fraction of value at actuarially justified premium rates.

Premium Rate Equity

Adequate, reasonable, and not unfairly discriminatory premium rates are the primary objective of insurance rate regulation.[1] Properly calculated coinsurance rates are not unfairly discriminatory because they equate each insured's gross premium with his expected value of indemnity and service benefits. Hence, the desire for equitable treatment of insureds should impel legislators to allow, or even require, wide use of coinsurance unless it is impractical or can be replaced by simpler alternatives.

Lowest Cost Insurance Consistent with Insurers' Financial Strength

Widespread, accurate application of coinsurance promotes, but does not guarantee, the adequacy of insurers' premium income to pay losses. Coinsurance strengthens the financial soundness of insurers, particularly during inflationary periods when loss costs tend to rise with the price level and to create a tendency toward lower ratios of insurance to full value. At the same time, higher coinsurance requirements permit, indeed call for, lower premium rates, something to be desired during inflation. These dual effects imply that the law should favor the availability of coinsurance—especially high coinsurance requirements with the full rate credit justified by experience.

Stabilizing Premium Rates

Stability of premium rates over time adds to insurers' financial strength and gives insureds confidence in their protection.[2] By encouraging the purchase of more insurance, coinsurance is

---

[1] Spencer L. Kimball and Allen L. Mayerson, *Cases and Materials on the Law of the Insurance Enterprise* (mimeographed) (Ann Arbor, Mich., 1965), p. 297.

[2] Herbert S. Denenberg, *et al., Risk and Insurance* (Englewood Cliffs, N.J.: Prentice-Hall, Inc., 1964), p. 385; and G. F. Michelbacher, "Presidential Address: On the Use of Judgment in Rate Making," *Proceedings of the Casualty Actuarial Society*, vol. XII (1925), pp. 2–3.

said to provide a greater premium base over which fluctuating loss experience can be spread and smoothed.[3] To the extent that the stabilizing effect of coinsurance is significant, and to the extent that rate stability is preferable to flexibility of rates, public policy should encourage high coinsurance requirements.

Improving Understanding of Coinsurance

A coinsurance clause presumably becomes more effective as insureds more fully understand its provisions. Percentage of insurable value coinsurance allegedly confuses and antagonizes many insureds. Therefore, it may be proper for the law to require certain procedures which direct the insured's attention to the existence and significance of a coinsurance clause. However, if understanding and appreciation of coinsurance cannot be achieved among certain types of insureds who, as a group, consistently incur coinsurance penalties, it may be wise to forbid coinsurance clauses in policies for these insureds.

Minimizing Compliance Difficulties

If policyholders have substantial difficulty in meeting a coinsurance requirement because, for example, the "actual cash value" valuation standard is ambiguous, the law may give the insured the right to call upon the insurer to determine insurable value before loss, or the law may direct the insurer to determine this value. But, if insurers are thought to discriminate by providing appraisals to some—but not all—insureds, the law may prohibit any insurer from valuing property before loss.

Minimizing Uninsured Losses

Part of a severe loss to property not fully insured may fall directly on the property owner. Insurance can best protect the greatest number of people if complete coverage is available at

---

[3] Edward R. Hardy, *The Making of the Fire Insurance Rate* (New York: The Spectator Co., 1926), p. 281.

low cost.[4] Coinsurance requirements, particularly high coinsurance requirements, may induce policyholders to fully insure. Coverage to a high percentage of value can be made necessary to avoid coinsurance penalties. In addition, if, as expected, the insured's demand for insurance is not perfectly price inelastic, the lower premium rate for the high coinsurance requirement will prompt the purchase of more insurance. Legislators guided by this reasoning would favor high coinsurance requirements.

Allowing Purchase of Desired Amounts of Insurance

Consumer sovereignty in the insurance market presumes the availability of a wide range of types and amounts of coverage at actuarially proper rates. With respect to coinsurance, free consumer choice means that coinsurance requirements as low as 1, 5, or 10 percent, and as high as 100 percent, of insurable value should be available with proper rate differentials for every 10 percentage points of added coverage.[5] A single premium rate should not be charged for all amounts of coverage below, say, 50 percent of value because the insured with 40 percent coverage is discriminated against relative to the insured with 10 percent coverage. If consumer freedom without discrimination is an important public policy goal, the law should favor a broad range of coinsurance requirements with distinct coinsurance rates.

CURRENT LAWS AFFECTING COINSURANCE

In 33 states[6] and the District of Columbia, no statute or insurance department ruling directly affects the use of coinsurance for the perils included in this study. Regulation in the remaining

---

[4] Allan H. Willett, *The Economic Theory of Risk and Insurance* (Homewood, Ill.: Richard D. Irwin, Inc., 1951), p. 29.

[5] *Report of the Co-Insurance Committee to the Board of Fire Underwriters of the Pacific on Percentage Co-Insurance and the Relative Rates Chargeable Therefor, Also on the Cost of Conflagration Hazard of Large Cities* (San Francisco, 1905), p. 4.

[6] Alabama, Alaska, Arizona, Arkansas, California, Colorado, Connecticut, Georgia, Hawaii, Idaho, Illinois, Indiana, Kansas, Maine, Maryland, Massachusetts, Mississippi, Montana, Nebraska, Nevada, New Jersey, New Mexico,

17 states chiefly deals with procedural matters. Only Iowa, Missouri, and Texas forbid coinsurance in one or more types of policies on some properties.

Regulation of coinsurance appears to have diminished over the last several decades. One writer stated in 1925 that "at the present time laws forbidding the use of the coinsurance clause are in force" in 10 states, including Georgia.[7] Georgia does not now regulate coinsurance. In 1930, another source asserted that 19 states *"have* prohibited coinsurance *in some manner.*"[8] The Merritt Committee reported in 1911 that Michigan eased its ban on coinsurance shortly atfer adopting it, and that Missouri laws against coinsurance were ignored by common consent.[9] Maine[10] and Wyoming[11] have been said to once "restrict" and "forbid" coinsurance, but today neither state explicitly regulates coinsur-

---

New York, North Dakota, Oklahoma, Oregon, Pennsylvania, Rhode Island, South Dakota, Utah, Virginia, Washington, and Wyoming. Conclusion reached by search of *Insurance Law Index Service,* ed. Leonard S. McCombs (Jenkintown, Pa.: McCombs & Co., loose-leaf, revised and supplemented monthly through March, 1970) 6 vols. and Subcommittee of the Committee on Fire Insurance Law of the Section of Insurance, Negligence and Compensation Law, *Current Annotations of the 1943 New York Standard Fire Insurance Policy* (Chicago: American Bar Association, 1966), pp. 151–155. All statutory citations in this chapter are drawn from the texts of laws reproduced in these two sources.

[7] A. F. Dean, *The Philosophy of Fire Insurance,* ed. W. R. Townley (Chicago: Edward B. Hatch, 1925), vol. I, p. 129, n. 1. The limited scope of today's laws makes it doubtful that these prohibitions applied to all policies.

[8] F. E. Wolfe, *Principles of Property Insurance* (New York: Thomas Y. Crowell Co., 1930), p. 151, n. 9. The words for which emphasis here is supplied create ambiguities as to (1) whether the prohibitions applied in 1930 and (2) the nature of the prohibitions. Wolfe *may* have interpreted a procedural requirement, such as a written request from the insured, to be a prohibition of coinsurance. This author does not agree with this interpretation.

[9] *Report of the Joint Committee of the Senate and Assembly of the State of New York, Appointed to Investigate Corrupt Practices in Connection with Legislation, and the Affairs of Insurance Companies, Other Than Those Doing Life Insurance Business,* Assembly Document No. 30 (Albany, N.Y., February 1, 1911), p. 90.

[10] Ralph H. Blanchard, *Risk and Insurance and Other Papers* (Lincoln, Neb.: University of Nebraska Press, 1965, reprint from 1938), p. 139.

[11] Edward R. Hardy, "Co-Insurance," *The Business of Insurance,* ed. Howard P. Dunham (New York: The Ronald Press Company, 1912), vol. I, p. 178.

ance. Minnesota's 1895 prohibition of coinsurance in most policies does not stand today.[12] The 1955 Indiana legislature struck down the previously existing general ban of percentage coinsurance clauses in fire, windstorm, or sprinkler leakage policies on real property.[13] In the same year, Iowa's statutory wording of percentage coinsurance clauses was replaced by a requirement that insurers obtain the insurance commissioner's approval of the wording of any coinsurance clause.[14]

Current statutes and rulings fit into six classes, according to whether they establish (1) procedures notifying the insured of the presence of a coinsurance clause; (2) a requirement of prior approval of the wording of coinsurance clauses by the insurance commissioner; (3) standards for coinsurance rates; (4) the rights and duties of insurer and insured regarding property valuation; (5) prohibitions of coinsurance clauses; and (6) procedures under valued policy laws for adjusting *partial* losses. Some states have laws in more than one class. The full texts of the applicable statutes, described below, appear in Appendix 6.

Notification

The laws of Florida,[15] Michigan,[16] Minnesota,[17] Missouri,[18] North Carolina,[19] and South Carolina[20] outline procedures required if a percentage of insurable value coinsurance clause is included in certain policies. These procedures may be intended to notify the insured of the existence, and perhaps the significance, of a coinsurance requirement.

The Florida law applies to policies insuring against fire loss to

---

[12] Letter from Thomas L. O'Malley, Supervisor, Claims Investigation Division, State of Minnesota Insurance Division, August 18, 1965.

[13] Indiana Laws of 1955, chap. 99, repealing former sec. 39.4308, Laws of Indiana.

[14] Iowa Code of 1962, section 515.111, and comments, in *Insurance Law Index Service, op. cit.*, "Iowa" section, p. 82.

[15] Florida Statutes, as amended, section 627.0800.

[16] Michigan Compiled Laws, 1948, as amended, section 500.2840(2).

[17] Minnesota Statutes, 1953, as amended, section 65A.08(5).

[18] Revised Statutes of Missouri, 1959, as amended, section 379.155.

[19] General Statutes of North Carolina, 1943, as amended, section 58-30.1.

[20] Code of Laws of South Carolina, 1963, as amended, section 37-157.

any real or personal property. The words "coinsurance contract" must be printed or stamped on the policy face or on the form containing the clause. *If* premium rates with and without coinsurance differ, the buyer must be informed of any difference, *if* the buyer requests such information.

Under Michigan law, every coinsurance clause must be signed by the insured or his agent. Signature of the policy as a whole is not sufficient. Minnesota requires that insureds sign an application for any coinsurance clause. The content of this application is not specified.

As documented on page 199, except in limited cases Missouri does not allow coinsurance clauses in policies against fire or lightning. In these exceptional cases, the insured must sign a statement, stamped on the policy face, that the policy comes within the exceptions to the general prohibition of coinsurance in fire or lightning policies. Coinsurance clauses may be used freely in coverage against other perils, where no notification is needed.

By North Carolina law, in any policy on tangible property containing a coinsurance clause, the words "coinsurance contract" must be stamped or printed at the places and in the type sizes which the insurance commissioner may direct. *If* rate credit is given for coinsurance, and *if* the insured inquires about this credit, the insurer must describe the rate differentials.

South Carolina's law differs from North Carolina's only in that the words to be stamped or printed are "coinsurance clause."

Wording of Clause

While no statute now stipulates the exact wording of any clause,[21] the laws of Iowa,[22] Kentucky,[23] Louisiana,[24] Michigan,[25] and Texas[26] call for the prior approval or prescription of the word-

---

[21] For the text of clauses formerly set by statute in Iowa, Michigan, and South Dakota, see *Cyclopedia of Insurance in the United States,* ed. F. S. MacKay (Paterson, N.J.: The Index Publishing Co., 1965), p. 696.

[22] Iowa Code of 1962, as amended, section 515.111.

[23] Kentucky Revised Statutes, 1950, as amended, section 304.906.

[24] Louisiana Revised Statutes, 1950, as amended, section 22.694.

[25] Michigan Compiled Laws, 1948, as amended, section 500.2840(1).

[26] Insurance Laws of the State of Texas, 1951, as amended, article 5.38.

ing of coinsurance clauses, in at least some policies, by state insurance officials. These laws standardize clauses to some extent and may help to avoid misleading phrasing.

Iowa requires that coinsurance clauses in all policies on tangible property have the insurance commissioner's approval before they are used. Michigan has the same law as Iowa. Kentucky's requirement parallels Iowa's but is limited to provisions applicable to "fire or storm" losses. The Louisiana provision is the same as Iowa's except that Louisiana's law applies to policies against "fire, lightning, and windstorm."

The Texas Board of Insurance Commissioners is empowered to approve or prescribe the wording of coinsurance clauses when such clauses are permitted. The cases where Texas prohibits coinsurance are described on page 199.

In all 50 states, all policy provisions must receive the insurance commissioner's approval before use or are subject to his subsequent disapproval.[27] The singling out of coinsurance clauses for special scrutiny in these five states, therefore, may reflect particular concern for the clarity of coinsurance clauses.

Rate Standards

The statutes of Kentucky,[28] Louisiana,[29] Minnesota,[30] Missouri,[31] Texas,[32] and Wisconsin[33] mention premium rates for coverage subject to coinsurance, at least for some policies. These laws supplement the nearly universal legislation that all premium rates be adequate, reasonable, and not unfairly discriminatory. In Indiana, Kentucky, Louisiana, Minnesota, and Wisconsin,

27 Robert E. Dineen, Clifford R. Proctor, and H. Daniel Gardner, "The Economics and Principles of Insurance Supervision," *Insurance and Government*, eds. Charles C. Center and Richard M. Heins (New York: McGraw-Hill Book Co., Inc., 1962), p. 39.
28 Kentucky Revised Statutes, 1950, as amended, section 304.906.
29 Louisiana Revised Statutes, 1950, as amended, section 22.694.
30 Minnesota Statutes, 1953, as amended, section 65A.08(5).
31 Revised Statutes of Missouri, 1959, as amended, section 379.160(3).
32 Insurance Laws of the State of Texas, 1951, as amended, article 5.38.
33 Wisconsin Statutes, 1957, as amended, section 203.22.

the laws merely require "a rate reduction for a coinsurance clause." Under these statutes, coinsurance rates must be lower than flat rates. These laws do not seem to require that additional rate credit be given for each successively higher coinsurance requirement, although insurance commissioners no doubt are authorized to insist on this more stringent standard. The Indiana and Wisconsin laws apply to rates for all policies "issued by a fire insurance company."[34] In Kentucky, only insurance against fire or storm loss is within this statute. Louisiana's law pertains to coverage of fire, lightning, or windstorm damage. The Minnesota statute is not restricted as to perils or property.

In Missouri and Texas, the statutory regulation of coinsurance rates is slightly more detailed. "Fire insurance companies" operating in Missouri must file a schedule of coinsurance rates for all policies subject to coinsurance as part of the "public rating record" maintained by the superintendent of insurance. The Texas Board of Insurance Commissioners may set premium rates for all property insurance contracts issued in Texas. The Texas statute merely makes this power explicit with respect to coinsurance rates.

Property Valuation

The statutes of Delaware,[35] Tennessee,[36] and Vermont[37] specify certain cases where the insurer, either independently or at the insured's request, must appraise each insured property and

---

[34] Policies "issued by a fire insurance company" seem to encompass more than policies against the peril of fire. All the perils selected for this study are among those insured by traditional fire insurance companies. However, if a policy against fire were to be issued by a "multiple-line company"— one combining the underwriting powers of traditionally separated fire and casualty insurers—possibly this Indiana statute would not apply. The scope of these and other laws would be clarified if the laws referred to the perils insured rather than to the type of insurer.

[35] Delaware Code of 1953, as amended, sections 18.1102(2) and 18.1102(3).

[36] Tennessee Code of 1955, as amended, sections 56-1137 and 56-1139.

[37] Vermont Statutes, Annotated, 1959, as amended, section 8.3961.

advise the insured of its value. In Kentucky,[38] Missouri,[39] and Ohio,[40] insurance department rulings forbid any insurer to help any insured determine insurable value unless the insurance is subject to an agreed amount endorsement or is written on a valued form. These laws reflect different judgments as to the proper extent of the insured's responsibility for valuing his property in order to comply with a percentage coinsurance clause.

All policies insuring Delaware real property against fire, lightning, or tornado must bear an endorsement signed by the insured stating the value of the covered property. This value is binding for the application of any coinsurance clause, but the insurer may repair or replace any damage rather than pay cash for an insured loss.

The Tennessee law pertains only to fire coverage of buildings or structures. The insurer must fix the insurable value, within 90 days after coverage begins, at an amount to which the insured then agrees in writing. Otherwise, the insurable value and policy face conclusively are presumed equal, eliminating any possible coinsurance penalties.

In Vermont, insurers are required to value buildings insured against fire subject to a percentage coinsurance clause when coverage begins. This value is binding for application of the coinsurance clause.

The Kentucky, Missouri, and Ohio insurance departments have forbidden all insurers to assist insureds in complying with percentage of value coinsurance requirements, on the grounds that offering this assistance only to some insureds is discrimination and is an attempt to evade the rules on agreed amount endorsements. The rulings were prompted by memoranda sent voluntarily by some insurers to some large insureds, stating that a given amount of insurance would satisfy a percentage coinsurance requirement for the next twelve months. These memoranda were in fact agreed amount endorsements, but technically were not part of the policy.

---

[38] Letter to all admitted insurers from Kentucky Commissioner of Insurance, June, 1957. See *Insurance Law Index Service, op. cit.,* "Kentucky" section, p. 105.

[39] Missouri Division of Insurance Order, No. 14, July 27, 1964.

[40] Official Bulletin of Insurance Department of Ohio, September 21, 1959.

Prohibition of Coinsurance

Missouri[41] and Texas[42] by statute and Iowa[43] by department ruling prohibit percentage coinsurance clauses in some cases. For example, the Iowa insurance department will not approve policies covering single family dwellings, household goods, or farm buildings against fire, lightning, or windstorms if the policies have a percentage coinsurance clause.

In Missouri, coverage against fire or lightning can be subject to a percentage coinsurance requirement only if the property is personal property located in a city with 100,000 or more inhabitants. Any other peril may be insured subject to coinsurance without restriction.

Texas law forbids percentage coinsurance in coverage against any peril for (1) merchandise held for retail sale with a retail value less than $10,000 and (2) private dwelling buildings. However, the Texas Board of Insurance Commissioners may permit or *require* a coinsurance clause in policies covering any property against hail or windstorm.

Partial Losses under Valued Policy Laws

In one sense, a valued policy is one which states the value of the insured property, effectively incorporating an agreed amount endorsement.[44] In another sense, in the context of valued policy laws, a valued policy is one under which, in case of total loss, the insurer's liability is the policy face regardless of the value destroyed.[45] For partial losses—the only losses where any coinsur-

---

[41] Revised Statutes of Missouri, 1959, as amended, section 379.155.

[42] Insurance Laws of the State of Texas, 1951, as amended, article 5.38.

[43] Iowa Insurance Department Regulation T-8, adopted November 8, 1964.

[44] Ambrose B. Kelly, "The Insurance of Profits, Reinstatement Values, Agreed Amount and the Principle of Indemnity," *Insurance Law Journal*, no. 524 (September 1966), p. 529.

[45] Edwin W. Patterson, *Essentials of Insurance Law*, 2nd ed. (New York: McGraw-Hill Book Co., Inc., 1957), p. 146.

ance clause can reduce indemnity—valued policy laws usually have no effect.

Valued policy laws of some states refer to the settlement of partial losses, sometimes apparently overriding the effects of co-insurance clauses. Delaware,[46] Florida,[47] Kentucky,[48] Louisiana,[49] Minnesota,[50] New Hampshire,[51] South Carolina,[52] and West Virgina[53] have valued policy laws which require study on this point.

In Delaware, the conclusive valuation endorsed on policies covering real property against fire, lightning, or tornado seems to preclude any coinsurance penalties if (as would almost surely be the case) the policy face equals at least the coinsurance percentage of that appraised value.

Florida's valued policy statute provides that any partial fire or lightning loss to a building or structure shall be indemnified to the extent of "the actual value of such loss," not to exceed the policy face and subject to any coinsurance provision. The Florida statute thus preserves any coinsurance clause.

The Kentucky law also protects any coinsurance clause by stating that, for partial fire or storm losses to real property, the insured's recovery "shall not exceed the actual loss of the property insured." This "not exceed" wording allows coinsurance penalties.

The Louisiana valued policy law may supersede coinsurance for partial losses to "inanimate property, immovable by nature or destination" covered by a "fire policy." Here, the insurer must pay an amount "which will permit the insured to restore the damaged property to its original condition." This law recognizes certain limits to the insurer's liability, *not* including coinsurance provisions. The author has found no litigation construing this statute in relation to coinsurance.

---

[46] Delaware Code of 1953, as amended, sections 1102(a) through 1102(c).

[47] Florida Statutes, as amended, section 627.0801(2).

[48] Kentucky Revised Statutes, 1950, as amended, section 304.905.

[49] Louisiana Revised Statutes, 1950, as amended, sections 22.695(A) through 22.695(D).

[50] Minnesota Statutes, 1953, as amended, section 65A.08(5).

[51] Revised Statutes of New Hampshire, Annotated, 1955, as amended, sections 407.11(b) and 407.11(c).

[52] Code of Laws of South Carolina, 1962, as amended, section 37.154.

[53] Michie's West Virginia Code, 1955, as amended, section 3472-148.

Minnesota's valued policy law explicitly states that it does not apply to any partial loss, so coinsurance is unaffected. Similarly, the New Hampshire valued policy law stipulates that any applicable coinsurance or agreed amount clause shall be adhered to in adjusting partial losses.

References to partial losses in the valued policy laws of South Carolina and West Virginia seem to preclude coinsurance penalties. The South Carolina law applies to all fire losses, for which "the actual amount of the loss with proration between insurers" is payable. The West Virginia statute calls for payment of "the total amount of the partial loss, not exceeding the policy face," for partial losses to real property covered by a "fire insurance policy."

The only court case the author has found construing these South Carolina or West Virginia statutes in a partial loss context[54] held that the valuation fixed when the policy was issued precluded the insurer from showing an increased value, a value which would have been the basis for assessing a coinsurance penalty. Seemingly, no other reported court cases construe these statutes with respect to coinsurance.

ASSESSMENT OF REGULATION

Of the seven regulatory objectives listed on page 189, only the goals of establishing equitable premium rates, improving insureds' understanding of coinsurance, and minimizing insureds' difficulties in meeting coinsurance requirements have received meaningful legislative attention. These three areas are discussed after the limited scope of present regulation is noted.

Limited Scope of Regulation

An outstanding limitation of present regulation of coinsurance is that it often applies only to fire insurance. If the coinsurance legislation in some states is thought to promote the public interest,

---

[54] *Hunt v. General Insurance Company,* 227 S. C. 125, 87 S. E. (2d) 34 (1955).

there seems little reason why legislators in these states should not extend the regulation to all types of insurance where coinsurance is used. A few states have applied their regulations to all such policies.

The scope of existing legislation also seems to be limited by legislators' failure to consider the possible impact of coinsurance in reducing premium rates, increasing the financial strength of insurers, and reducing the number of uninsured losses. The author believes that if the beneficial effects of coinsurance in achieving these three goals were more fully appreciated coinsurance would be required, or at least freed of existing restrictions, in more states.

Premium Rate Equity

Other than filing requirements in two states, the only specific regulation of coinsurance rates is the requirement, in five states, that some credit be given for coinsurance. Such laws do little to promote equity among policyholders with insurance subject to different coinsurance requirements. Although detailed schedules of coinsurance rates probably should not be established with statutory permanence, legislatures could perfect present schedules of coinsurance rates by requiring (1) a lower premium rate for each successively higher coinsurance requirement and (2) that insurance commissioners examine, and report to the legislatures on, the actuarial basis of existing coinsurance rates.

Policyholders' Understanding of Coinsurance

Notification statutes, mandatory approval of the wording of coinsurance clauses, and prohibitions of coinsurance where the probability of misunderstanding is thought to be too great are legislative measures taken to cope with policyholders' failure to grasp the meaning of coinsurance. None of these steps appears to have been wholly successful—perhaps none can be until, as in England and Europe where coinsurance is widely understood, percentage coinsurance clauses are used in elementary or high school arithmetic texts dealing with fractions and percentages. But many insureds might better understand percentage of value coinsurance if they had to sign the following statement after personally filling in its blanks.

I believe that the actual cash value/replacement cost (underline proper one) of property here insured is $... This policy is subject to a .... percent coinsurance clause. If my estimate of the value of the property here insured is correct, the coinsurance clause requires that the face amount of this policy be at least $.... in order for losses up to the face of the policy to be paid fully. But the insurer will never be liable for more than $.... on any loss. If the value of the property here insured at the time of a loss is greater than I have now estimated, *the loss may not be paid in full.* If the value of the property here insured increases by $...., to a total of $...., I should increase the amount of this policy by $...., to a total of $.... to comply with the .... percent coinsurance clause. *Otherwise, any loss may not be paid in full.*

Completing this statement should make the insured aware of (1) the importance of current and changing values; (2) the difference between actual cash value and replacement cost; (3) the arithmetic of coinsurance; and (4) the need for more coverage as values increase. The knowledge required to complete this form is no greater than that which an insurance salesman should give every insured whose policy is subject to coinsurance.

Property Valuation

Of three logically possible statutory modifications of insureds' responsibility for meeting a percentage coinsurance requirement —(1)requiring insurer appraisal, sometimes conclusive, of each property when first insured; (2) giving each insured the right, at his expense, to an insurer's appraisal; and (3) forbidding insurers to value property before loss—only the second appears desirable. The first type of requirement forces the insurer to incur administrative expenses which premium rates may not allocate equitably among insureds. When the valuation is conclusive, the coinsurance clause may be negated. The third alternative creates an artificial restriction with which compliance seems difficult and which may antagonize insureds honestly attempting to meet coinsurance requirements. Only the second alternative—the insurer's valuation at the request and expense of the insured without making the appraisal binding on the insurer—gives the insured reliable valuation advice, at no extra cost to other policyholders, while preserving the insured's responsibility to comply with a coinsurance clause.

SUMMARY

This chapter enumerates possible objectives in the regulation of coinsurance, and details and appraises existing regulation. Coinsurance might be regulated in order to (1) establish equitable premium rates; (2) minimize the cost of insurance consistent with insurers' financial strength; (3) stabilize premium rates; (4) improve insureds' understanding of coinsurance; (5) minimize insureds' difficulties in meeting coinsurance requirements; (6) minimize uninsured losses; and (7) permit policyholders to insure to any fraction of value at actuarially justified rates.

Current statutes and insurance department rulings affect coinsurance in 17 states. Regulation can be categorized as to whether it establishes (1) procedures notifying the insured of the presence of a coinsurance clause; (2) requirements of the insurance commissioner's approval of phrasing in coinsurance clauses; (3) standards for coinsurance rates; (4) rights and duties of insurer and insured with respect to valuation before loss; (5) prohibition of coinsurance clauses; or (6) procedures for settling partial losses under valued policy laws.

Current regulation often is limited illogically to fire insurance, and its scope suggests that many legislators are unaware of the ways in which coinsurance can reduce premium rates, increase insurers' financial strength, and minimize uninsured losses. In each of the areas which regulation now emphasizes—(1) reducing rates where coinsurance is used, (2) making insureds aware of coinsurance clauses, and (3) reducing insureds' difficulties in meeting coinsurance requirements—it seems that regulation could be improved.

CHAPTER **12**

Conclusions and Recommendations

PURPOSE

This chapter presents this author's conclusions and recommendations in the form of answers to the questions posed in Chapter 1 about various aspects of coinsurance. The author's broad purpose has been to present the best possible answers to these questions, pointing out areas which insurers and insurance students should investigate further.

CONCLUSIONS

In order to compute a pure premium rate which equates each insured's periodic pure premium with his expected periodic indemnity payments when some losses may be less than the policy face, an insurer must know—along with the frequency and severity of losses—the extent to which each property is insured or can be assumed to be insured. Insurance to value exists when each property is insured exactly to the extent which the insurer assumes in computing the premium rate. Insurance to value may be much less than insurance to 100 percent of value. Since the pure premium rate should fall[1] as the actual policy face increases, insur-

---

[1] At a decreasing rate if small losses predominate, at an increasing rate if large losses predominate, and at a constant rate if losses of all sizes are equally likely.

ance to value is significant because, without some corrective measure, (1) aggregate premiums tend to be inadequate if underinsurance is prevalent; (2) aggregate premiums tend to be excessive if overinsurance is common; and (3) unless all policyholders insure to the same extent, insureds with more complete protection suffer some price discrimination when all insureds facing equal hazard pay the same premium rate.

The extent of overinsurance or underinsurance is difficult to determine from present data, but differences in ratios of insurance to value—sources of discrimination, unless corrected—almost certainly exist. Coinsurance can correct deviations from insurance to value by reducing the expected indemnity payments of underinsured policyholders in proportion to their underinsurance, but coinsurance can do nothing to correct price discrimination against insureds with coverage exceeding a particular coinsurance requirement. Although numerous methods, both within and outside the policy, can discourage insurance beyond full value or to only small fractions of value, these devices do not balance pure premiums with indemnity payments as effectively as does coinsurance.

Coinsurance seems best defined as an apportionment of losses between an insurer and its insured such that the insurer pays, within other policy restrictions, a fraction of each loss equal to the ratio (called the coinsurance apportionment ratio) of a designated amount of insurance to (1) a stated sum or (2) the whole, or a specified percentage, of the value of the insured property. The designated insurance may be (1) the face amount of the policy requiring coinsurance, (2) the total face amounts of the insured's applicable policies, or (3) under provisional reporting form policies, full insurance on the property values last reported before loss. While this definition perhaps is too lengthy for a rudimentary explanation of coinsurance, it is useful in more rigorous analysis.

Clauses embodying coinsurance can be classified by the components of their coinsurance apportionment ratios. Alternative ratios are: (1) face of policy requiring coinsurance to stated amount; (2) total of all insurance to stated amount; (3) policy face to percentage of value (in an "average" clause); (4) total insurance to percentage of value (in a "coinsurance" clause); and (5) in provisional reporting form policies, which lack a fixed face amount, the value last reported before loss to the true value at the reporting date.[2] A few clauses specify coinsurance requirements of either a stated sum or a percentage of value, depending on the circumstances of the loss. These various ratios can have different effects on the insured's indemnity payment and on the sharing of liability among insurers whose concurrent policies contain different types of coinsurance clauses.[3]

By balancing the pure premiums with the expected indemnity payments of each policyholder whose coverage does not exceed the coinsurance requirement, coinsurance directly serves the objectives of equity among insureds and adequacy of the insurer's premium income.[4] The socially desirable goal of insurance to a high fraction of value may be promoted by offering only high coinsurance requirements, but this limited offer restricts consumer freedom. Responsibility for maintaining insurance to value may be placed entirely on the insured by means of a percentage of value coinsurance requirement, or may be shared between insurer and insured by means of a stated sum coinsurance requirement or a provisional reporting form policy. A final objective of coinsurance may be to gain a competitive price advantage for the insurer which uses coinsurance clauses in order to lower rates for coverage which other insurers sell without coinsurance.

The key to theoretically correct premium rates for coverage subject to coinsurance is a distribution of losses by size for the insured class of property. The severity of losses must be expressed

---

[2] The face amount of any insurance not written on a provisional reporting form is subtracted from both the value last reported and the true value at the reporting date.

[3] By current definition, concurrent policies may contain different types of coinsurance clauses, and some may contain none.

[4] Except with various retrospective rating plans, the equity and adequacy of a premium rate charged at the beginning of the policy period for protection during the policy period should be judged on the basis of each insured's *expected* indemnity during the policy period, *not* what he *actually* receives because of a fortuitous loss. But past actual losses can influence future expected losses.

in the same terms as the coinsurance requirement[5] in order for precise distribution of losses not greater than the coinsurance requirement and the total percentage of losses greater than the coinsurance requirement to be found. Very little is known about dollar or percentage loss severity. Study of 2680 fire losses to Oregon frame-protected properties indicates that (1) properties not exceeding $10,000 in sound value before loss suffer a greater proportion of losses equal to or greater than any fraction of value than do larger properties; and (2) total losses, comprising about 8 percent of all losses in the sample, are more frequent than all partial losses above 50 percent of value.

Given a loss-severity distribution applicable to the property and peril in question, equitable and just adequate pure premium coinsurance rates can be derived by equating each insured's periodic pure premium with his expected indemnity payments during that period. Loss frequency determines the general level of pure premium rates, but the relativities (i.e., ratios) among pure premium rates are determined only by the size distribution of losses. When appropriate margins for administrative expenses, contingencies, and profits are added to the pure premium coinsurance rates,[6] different gross premium coinsurance rates should (1) apply to a wide range of finely graduated coinsurance requirements; (2) contain no reversals (in which the percentage decrease in the coinsurance rates between two coinsurance requirements is greater than the percentage increase in coverage between the two requirements, thus implying a negative marginal cost of insurance); (3) decrease at a decreasing rate for larger coinsurance requirements;[7] (4) be presented in the format which most strongly encourages insurance to an adequate percentage of value; and (5) establish different coinsurance rate *relativities* for classes of properties whose distinguishing characteristics significantly affect loss severity.

---

[5] Dollars of loss for stated sum coinsurance requirements and losses as percentages of property value for percentage coinsurance requirements.

[6] Allocation of these loadings is beyond the scope of this study.

[7] Because small losses (dollar or percentage of value) are more frequent than large ones and expense margins are either a constant or decreasing percentage of pure premiums.

In practice, rates for stated amount coinsurance requirements (not often used with insurance against the perils selected for this study) are negotiated between insurers and insureds. Credits for percentage coinsurance requirements are products of judgment. The schedules of sprinkler leakage, water damage, and earthquake coinsurance credits, uniform throughout the nation,[8] meet the above five criteria somewhat more fully than do the schedules of fire and extended coverage coinsurance credits in seven representative regions and states. These latter schedules, applying uniform flat rates for all coverage below 50 percent (often 80 percent) of value, force some discrimination in favor of insureds who buy very small amounts of coverage relative to their property values. Frame structures in unprotected areas usually can be insured against fire only at high, flat rates, despite evidence (see pages 87–90) that the high concentration of small percentage losses to such properties justifies coinsurance credits for substantial coverage. Few schedules of coinsurance rates for any peril properly treat coinsurance in blanket policies. Another common weakness is the use of the same percentage coinsurance rate *relativities* for properties whose losses appear to differ in severity. For example, no weight is given to the differing damageability of different types of property in the schedules of coinsurance credits for sprinkler leakage, water damage, or earthquake insurance, even though some types of property are much more susceptible to severe losses from these perils than are others. No schedule of credits for any peril included in this study explicitly differentiates risks by size, although small buildings, which experience a greater proportion of losses above 50 percent of value than do large buildings, deserve less credit for a given percentage of coinsurance than do large buildings. Some fire coinsurance rate schedules implicitly assume that loss severity is independent of loss frequency; others assume interdependence of these factors.

Coinsurance underwriting decisions concern three variables: first, whether some form of coinsurance clause should be used;

---

[8] A separate schedule of earthquake credits applies in eight Pacific states.

second, if so, whether it should be an agreed amount clause, a percentage coinsurance clause, or a full reporting requirement in a provisional reporting form policy; and, third, if a percentage coinsurance clause is appropriate, how much latitude should be given the insured in choosing a coinsurance percentage. In property insurance, some form of coinsurance requirement should be used unless (1) all losses are at least as large as the policy face; (2) a preferable alternative for maintaining insurance to value (such as appraisal, scheduling, or graded rates) is feasible; or (3) insureds' widespread misunderstanding of coinsurance makes it impracticable. The author believes that these exceptions are less frequent than often is thought. Given the need for some type of coinsurance, a percentage coinsurance requirement should be used except when (1) the size of the risk (usually many properties), the insured's bargaining power (particularly among competing insurers), or the difficulty of determining current values (such as for rare objects) call for an agreed amount endorsement; or (2) fluctuating values, which the insured can measure easily and report accurately and promptly, suggest use of a provisional reporting form policy. The insured should, and almost always does, have the choice of a 100 percent coinsurance requirement and coinsurance rate. The minimum available coinsurance percentage is low for perils characteristically causing slight damage, is higher for blanket than for specific coverage, and typically is high enough to encourage insurance sufficient to protect creditors' interests.

Aspects of loss adjustment which can interfere with the precise operation of coinsurance are the cost of loss adjustment, the waiver of undamaged inventory for small losses, and the complexity of property valuation. Because the cost of invoking coinsurance on small losses is greater than the average coinsurance penalty assessed on such losses, some insurers, the author has been confidentially informed, do not apply coinsurance on fire losses claimed to be less than $1000 or $1500 depending on the insurer. In effect, this cost barrier waives coinsurance on perhaps 50 percent of the number of fire losses. Because insureds usually are not required to report the sound value of undamaged insured property when a fire loss does not exceed the lesser of $10,000 or 5 percent of the policy, inventories supplied by the insured cannot be used to check compliance with coinsurance requirements for these losses, and insurers must incur the added cost of other checks if coinsurance is to be applied. The greatest source of friction arising from percentage of value coinsurance is the difficulty of property valuation. Most of this difficulty stems from honest differences of opinion as to value and from the ambiguity of "actual cash value." Although both the insured and the insurer's representatives act in good faith, valuation difficulties may cause the well-intentioned insured to incur a coinsurance penalty when none is deserved or the insurer's representative to forgo assessing a proper coinsurance penalty.

Seventeen states in some way regulate coinsurance in some policies, but only Iowa, Missouri, and Texas expressly forbid coinsurance clauses in one or more types of policies.[9] Laws pertaining to coinsurance may be classified according to whether they establish (1) procedures notifying insureds of the presence of coinsurance clauses in their policies; (2) requirements of the insurance commissioner's approval of wording of coinsurance clauses; (3) standards for coinsurance rates; (4) rights and duties of insurers and insureds with respect to valuation before loss ;(5) prohibition of coinsurance clauses; or (6) procedures for settling partial losses under valued policy laws. The objectives of these laws are to make insureds aware of coinsurance, to provide for some measure of equity and reasonableness in premium rates by requiring some rate credit for coinsurance, and to forbid coinsurance among classes of policyholders when many of them may be misled by coinsurance clauses. The limited scope of coinsurance regulation (confined mostly to fire policies on real property) suggests that some legislators do not realize the extent to which coinsurance can establish quite precise equity among insureds, enhance insurers' financial strength, reduce the cost of insurance, and stabilize premium rates over time.

---

[9] Valued policy laws in Louisiana, South Carolina, and West Virginia *may* be interpreted as barring coinsurance penalties.

RECOMMENDATIONS

The primary recommendation growing out of this study is that more statistics be compiled on distributions of losses from various perils as percentages of value for different classes of property. In a few years the statistics of the National Insurance Actuarial and Statistical Association may permit comparison of fire loss experience between policies with and without coinsurance clauses,[10] but these data may be inadequate to establish the necessary distributions. With full distributions, it may be possible to determine (1) whether coinsurance credits generally are too high or too low; (2) what factors (such as protection, construction,[11] occupancy, size, and loss frequency) influence percentage loss severity and should, therefore, be made the basis for classifying risks for coinsurance so that each class has a distinct set of actuarially justified coinsurance rate relativities. Such statistics also may indicate whether frame-unprotected structures and other properties are entitled to fire coinsurance credits now usually denied them. Loss-severity distributions are the theoretical heart of coinsurance; these distributions do not now exist.

This study points toward a number of improvements which could be incorporated into the revision of coinsurance rate schedules which should follow the compilation of loss-severity statistics. First, a 100 percent coinsurance requirement, with a distinct rate credit, always should be available. A coinsurance credit promotes premium rate equity and adequacy only for insureds with coverage not exceeding the specified coinsurance requirement. Insureds wishing full coverage should not be charged an inequitably high premium rate which is proper only for ratios of insurance to value less than 100 percent.

Second, percentage coinsurance requirements for all perils included in this study should not be more than 10 percentage points apart. Any wider interval is likely to cause undue price discrimi-

---

[10] Interview with LeRoy J. Simon, General Manager, National Insurance Actuarial and Statistical Association, August 30, 1966.

[11] Or damageability for property other than buildings.

nation if insureds with, say, 75 percent coverage must pay the 50 percent coinsurance rate because their coverage is insufficient to meet the next higher, perhaps 80 percent, coinsurance requirement.

Third, for fire and extended coverage insurance, minimum coinsurance percentages should be reduced so that the range of coverage for which the flat rate is charged is narrowed. According to the Oregon fire loss data, the 10 percent fire coinsurance pure premium rate should be 84 percent higher than the 70 percent rate. If 80 percent is the minimum coinsurance requirement, an insured with only 10 percent coverage is favored over the insured with 70 percent coverage, because both pay the same premium rate if their properties are substantially identical. In principle, flat rates encourage very low ratios of insurance to value and promote inequity, and the insurer's financial strength may be threatened if many insureds purchase very small amounts of flat coverage. Coinsurance theory suggests offering a 10 percent coinsurance requirement at an equitable, just adequate (and probably prohibitive) coinsurance rate. When small percentage losses are more frequent than large ones, coinsurance rates should decrease at a decreasing rate instead of at the constant rate found in many schedules. Greater appreciation of the mathematics of coinsurance will lead to this improvement.

Fourth, coinsurance rates in blanket policies should follow three rules. First, the 100 percent blanket coinsurance rate should equal the 100 percent coinsurance rate for specific insurance on the same property. Second, the 90 percent blanket coinsurance rate should be higher than the 90 percent specific coinsurance rate for the same property, the blanket rate perhaps equaling the 80 percent specific coinsurance rate. Third, with 80 percent or less blanket insurance (including flat blanket insurance) a pro rata distribution clause should be required, but the specific coinsurance rate for that coinsurance percentage (or the flat rate) for the same type of property should apply. The first rule recognizes that, with 100 percent coinsurance, the insured with a blanket policy must buy full coverage in order to get full protection and merits the coinsurance credit given insureds with equal coverage in specific policies. The second rule is necessary because, with blanket insurance of 90 percent of his aggregate values, the insured who is able to apply all his insurance to one location in order to cover a loss may have full protection and should pay a higher rate than the specifically insured policyholder who does not get full protection with 90 percent coverage. Alternatively, 90 percent blanket insurance could be subject to pro rata distribution. The third rule reflects the fact that blanket insurance subject to pro rata distribution is equivalent to specific insurance in the prorated amount and should be available at the specific coinsurance rate. Any other rules for coinsurance in blanket policies discriminate either in favor of or against holders of specific policies.

The findings regarding nonconcurrent apportionments support the recommendation that *insurance* to percentage of value clauses ("coinsurance" clauses) should be eliminated in favor of *policy* to percentage of value clauses ("average" clauses) for all percentage of value coinsurance requirements. With insurance to value clauses, some insurers' liabilities are unpredictably increased, the balance of pure premiums with expected indemnity payments is upset for all insurers, and, in principle, the financial strength of insurers using "coinsurance" clauses is reduced.

The regulation of coinsurance should be improved in several ways. First, the prohibitions of coinsurance in Iowa, Missouri, and Texas should be removed. The author believes that any evils which these prohibitions were meant to counter can be controlled more directly without depriving insureds and insurers of the benefits of coinsurance. Similarly, states with valued policy laws referring to partial losses should amend their laws, if necessary, to explicitly permit coinsurance penalties.

Second, legislators and insurance departments can do more to promote proper coinsurance credits. Present rate regulation, where it does deal directly with coinsurance, seems to require only that rates for all coinsurance percentages be lower than the flat rate for the same property. There is no requirement that, for example, the 80 percent rate be lower than the 70 percent rate. A more effective, yet flexible, law would go further to stipulate that each successively higher coinsurance requirement carry a lower premium rate. As an additional step to refine the equity, adequacy, and reasonableness of coinsurance rates, each legislature might direct its insurance commissioner to report to it periodically on the actuarial basis for the coinsurance rate credits the commissioner has approved. The commissioner, in turn, may request such actuarial justification from insurers.

Third, the statutory procedures of a few states, by which insureds must be informed of the presence of coinsurance clauses in their policies, should be strengthened and enacted in all states. Believing that the notification requirement is sound but that merely calling for the signature of the insured on a separate form is not sufficient, the author has proposed a form to be completed in longhand by every insured whose policy contains a coinsurance clause. Completing this form, one copy of which would be attached to the insured's copy of his policy, should force the insured to understand, or inquire into, the mechanics of coinsurance. The use of this form would complicate the sale of policies subject to coinsurance, but coinsurance should not be used except where insureds have sufficient knowledge of coinsurance to complete the form.

Finally, legislators should consider giving each insured the statutory right to ask at any time for his insurer's valuation of property insured subject to percentage of value coinsurance. If this valuation were performed at the insured's expense, such a law would ease the insured's difficulty of complying with any coinsurance requirement, would improve public understanding of coinsurance, presumably would reduce coinsurance penalties, and would not raise premiums for those insureds not using this valuation service. The law should provide that any valuation by the insurer prior to loss would not be binding in loss adjustment.

In sum, the author has tried to show that coinsurance *can* be a relatively simple, mathematically precise method for properly pricing insurance on property subject to losses less than the face amount of insurance. He also has sought to demonstrate that coinsurance *will* achieve this goal only when accurate statistics on loss severity are the basis for actuarially justified coinsurance rates and when insurers, insurance regulators, and insureds understand and appreciate the importance of coinsurance in determining the proper cost of insurance.

The Policy Face and the Pure Premium Rate

This appendix demonstrates arithmetically that, for a very small increase in the policy face, the pure premium rate changes by the factor

$$-\frac{f \int_0^F Ls(L)dL}{F^2} .$$

If a building, with a value of 100 units, averages one loss every 50 policy periods ($f = 1/50$), and the size distribution of losses (L, measured in the same units as value) follows the function

$$s(L) = \frac{1}{100}$$

with all sizes of loss being equally probable for simplicity, then

$$fs(L) = \frac{1}{5000} .$$

The $s(L)$ function is a complete distribution of the unconditional probabilities of losses from one to 100 units because

$$\int_0^{100} \frac{1}{100} dL = \left[\frac{1}{100} L \right]_0^{100} = \frac{100}{100} = 1.$$

The $fs(L)$ function is not a complete probability distribution because the probability of no, or zero, loss (in this example, 0.98) is not defined by the $s(L)$ function.

The expected value of a loss of L units is $L/5000$. The expected value of all losses not exceeding any face amount, $F(\leqq 100$ units) is

$$\int_0^F \frac{L}{5000}\, d(L) = \left.\frac{L^2}{10,000}\right|_0^F = \frac{F^2}{10,000}.$$

Indemnity payments for losses greater than the policy face but not exceeding 100 have an expected value of

$$F\left(1 - \int_0^F \frac{1}{5000}\right) = \left.F - \frac{L}{5000}\right|_0^F = F\left(1 - \frac{F}{5000}\right).$$

Thus, the pure premium rate equation in this example is

$$R = \frac{\dfrac{F^2}{10,000} + F\left(1 - \dfrac{F}{5000}\right)}{F}.$$

Specifically, for 12 units of coverage the rate is

$$R_{12} = \frac{\dfrac{144}{10,000} + 12\left(1 - \dfrac{12}{5000}\right)}{12} = 0.0098$$

units per unit of insurance. For 13 units, the pure premium rate per unit is

$$R_{16} = \frac{\dfrac{169}{10,000} + 13\left(1 - \dfrac{13}{5000}\right)}{13} = 0.0097$$

units, or a discrete decrease of 0.0001.

The expression

$$-\frac{f\int_0^F Ls(L)dL}{F^2},$$

evaluated midway between 12 and 13, equals − 0.0001. For each policy,

$$f \int_0^F Ls(L)dL = \frac{F^2}{10,000}.$$

The left-hand side integral is numerically approximated as

$$- \frac{12^2 + 13^2}{(10,000 \times 2)/(12 \times 13)} = -0.0001.$$

Therefore, evaluation of the integral and comparison of the two pure premium rate equations give the same rate change.

APPENDIX 2

Coinsurance Clauses and Deductibles

This appendix shows that the recommendation of the *1963 Guiding Principles*—that a per loss deductible be subtracted from the loss payment after coinsurance has been applied—is less liberal to the insured with a coinsurance deficiency than is the alternative of subtracting the deductible first and then applying coinsurance. Under the *Guiding Principles*, the indemnity paid for any loss is smaller, until the policy face is paid, and the minimum loss for which the policy face is paid is larger than under the alternative method.

Let

L_G = dollar amount of indemnity paid under the *Guiding Principles*.

I_A = dollar amount of indemnity paid under the alternative method.

D = dollar amount of per loss deductible.

L, F, and C retain their previous meanings. The two indemnity formulas are:

$$I_G = \frac{FL}{C} - D$$

and

$$I_A = \frac{F(L - D)}{C},$$

provided that no indemnity payment exceeds the lesser of the loss or the policy face.

For the insured with a coinsurance deficiency $(F < C)$, indemnity under the *Guiding Principles* is less than that under the alternative method (unless the face is payable) because I_A minus I_G is positive:

$$I_A - I_G = \frac{F(L - D)}{C} - \left(\frac{FL}{C} - D\right) = D\left(1 - \frac{F}{C}\right).$$

Since $F < C$, the solution is positive.

As an example, if

$$C = \$80,000$$
$$L = 21,000$$
$$F = 60,000$$
$$D = 1,000$$

then

$$I_G = \frac{(60,000)\,(21,000)}{80,000} - 1,000 = \$14,750$$

and

$$I_A = \frac{60,000(21,000 - 1000)}{80,000} = \$15,000.$$

Therefore,

$$I_A - I_G = 15,000 - 14,750 = \$250 = 1000\left(1 - \frac{60,000}{80,000}\right).$$

The least loss for which the policy face is payable is higher under the *Guiding Principles* than under the alternative method. Let L_G and L_A, respectively, equal the least loss for which $L = F$ under each method. From

$$I_G = \frac{FL}{C} - D$$

by substitution

$$F = \frac{FL_G}{C} - D$$

and

$$L_G = C + \frac{CD}{F} \; .$$

For the alternative,

$$I_A = \frac{F(L - D)}{C}$$

$$F = \frac{(FL_A - D)}{C}$$

$$L_A = C + D.$$

L_G is larger than L_A. Specifically,

$$L_G - L_A = \left(C + \frac{CD}{F} \right) - (C + D) = D \left(\frac{C}{F} - 1 \right).$$

Since $F < C$, this solution is positive.

Numerically, if

$$C = \$80{,}000$$

$$F = 60{,}000$$

$$D = 1{,}000,$$

under the *Guiding Principles*

$$F = \frac{FL_G}{C} - D$$

by substitution,

$$60{,}000 = \frac{60{,}000 L_G}{80{,}000} - 1000 = \$81{,}333.$$

Under the alternative,

$$F = \frac{(FL_A - D)}{C}$$

$$60,000 = \frac{60,000(L_A - 1000)}{80,000}$$

$$L_A = 80,000 + 1000 = \$81,000.$$

L_G is greater than L_A by \$333, and

$$\$333 = D\left(\frac{C}{F} - 1\right) = 1000\left(\frac{80,000}{60,000} - 1\right).$$

Under the alternative procedure, the insurer absorbs a part $\left(1 - \frac{F}{C}\right)$ of the deductible, unless the policy face is payable.

The *Guiding Principles* procedure apparently was selected so that the insured would bear the whole deductible.

APPENDIX 3

From Loss Severity to Rate Relativities

This appendix shows that, if the same size distribution of losses applies to two risks, the pure premium coinsurance rate *relativities* for each risk are the same, even though one risk has more frequent losses than the other.

Assume that losses to Risk A and Risk B, each worth $10,000, adhere to the following hypothetical distribution:

Size of Loss $X_1 < L \leqq X_2$		Arithmetic Mean Loss	Percentage of Losses
X_1	X_2		
$ 0	$ 2,000	$ 500	40
2,000	4,000	3,000	30
4,000	6,000	5,000	10
6,000	8,000	7,000	5
8,000	10,000	9,500	15

Risk A belongs to a class in which each property averages one loss in 25 years. A property in Risk B's class averages one loss in ten years. Hence, the relative frequencies of losses are: $f_A = 0.04$, and $f_B = 0.10$.

The general pure premium rate equation for percentage coinsurance rates is

$$R/\$100 = f \left(\frac{\int_0^F Ls(L)dL + F\left[1 - \int_0^F s(L)dL\right]}{F/100} \right).$$

224

For coinsurance rate computation the policy face is assumed to equal the coinsurance requirement. For Risk *A*, this equation gives the following rates per $100 of coverage:

$$R_{2000} = 0.04 \left(\frac{(0.40)500 + (0.60)2000}{20} \right) = 2.800$$

$$R_{4000} = 0.04 \left(\frac{(0.40)500 + (0.30)3000 + (0.30)4000}{40} \right) = 2.3000$$

$$R_{6000} = 0.04 \left(\frac{(0.40)500 + (0.30)3000 + (0.10)5000}{60} \right) +$$

$$0.04 \left(\frac{(0.20)6000}{60} \right) = 1.8666$$

$$R_{8000} = 0.04 \left(\frac{(0.40)500 + (0.30)3000 + (0.10)5000}{80} \right) +$$

$$0.04 \left(\frac{(0.05)7000 + (0.15)8000}{80} \right) = 1.5750$$

$$R_{10,000} = 0.04 \left(\frac{(0.40)500 + (0.30)3000 + (0.10)5000}{100} \right) +$$

$$0.04 \left(\frac{(0.05)7000 + (0.15)9500}{100} \right) = 1.3500.$$

For Risk *B*, the factor 0.10 replaces 0.04 as the first element in the right-hand side of the equations. Thus, each coinsurance rate for Risk *B* is 2.5 times (0.10/0.04) the corresponding rate for Risk *A*, or $R_{2000} = 7.0000$; $R_{4000} = 5.7500$; $R_{6000} = 4.6666$; $R_{8000} = 3.9375$; and $R_{10,000} = 3.3750$.

For both risks, the pure premium coinsurance rate *relativities* (i.e., each rate expressed as a percentage of one of the rates) are identical. For both risks, the five rates, as percentages of the 100 percent ($10,000) rate, are: $R_{2000} = 207.41$ percent; $R_{4000} = 170.37$ percent; $R_{6000} = 138.27$ percent; $R_{8000} = 116.67$ percent; and $R_{10,000} = 100.00$ percent.

In general, loss frequency determines pure premium rate levels; the distribution of losses by size determines pure premium rate relativities.

From Rate Relativities to Loss Severity

This appendix shows that, if the relativities among all coinsurance rates and the arithmetic mean losses among all coinsurance requirements are known, the percentages of losses between each two coinsurance requirements can be determined.

The hypothetical distribution of losses in Appendix 3 indicates that, for a $10,000 building, the coinsurance rate relativities for $2,000, $4,000, $6,000, $8,000, and $10,000 of coverage are 207.41, 170.37, 138.27, 116.67, and 100.00, respectively. The arithmetic mean losses within each $2,000 layer of coverage are $500, $3,000, $5,000, $7,000, and $9,500.

From this information, it can be deduced that 40 percent, 30 percent, 10 percent, 5 percent, and 15 percent of the losses fall within each $2,000 layer of coverage, regardless of the level of premium rates.

From an assumed pure premium rate of $1.00 per $100 for $10,000 of coverage, five equations, each equating pure premiums and expected indemnity payments for a particular policy face, can be formulated. The unknowns in these equations are p_1, p_2, p_3, p_4, and p_5, the unconditional probabilities (f times s values) of some loss between each two coinsurance requirements. Because of the rounding of the coinsurance rate relativities, the ratio $p_1 : p_2 : p_3 : p_4 : p_5$ will only approximate 40 : 30 : 10 : 5 : 15. The five equations are:

1. $20(2.0741) = 500p_1 + 2{,}000p_2 + 2{,}000p_3 + 2{,}000p_4 + 2{,}000p_5$

2. $40(1.7037) = 500p_1 + 3{,}000p_2 + 4{,}000p_3 + 4{,}000p_4 + 4{,}000p_5$

3. $60(1.3827) = 500p_1 + 3{,}000p_2 + 5{,}000p_3 + 6{,}000p_4 + 6{,}000p_5$

4. $80(1.1667) = 500p_1 + 3{,}000p_2 + 5{,}000p_3 + 7{,}000p_4 + 8{,}000p_5$

5. $100(1.0000) = 500p_1 + 3{,}000p_2 + 5{,}000p_3 + 7{,}000p_4 + 9{,}500p_5$

These equations can be solved by repeated substitutions and subtractions. For example, Equation 5 minus Equation 4 gives

$$100.0000 - 93.3360 = 1{,}500p_5$$

$$p_5 = 0.0044426.$$

This value, substituted into the difference between Equation 4 and Equation 3, gives

$$10.3740 = 1000p_4 + 2000(0.0044426)$$

$$p_4 = 0.0041888.$$

Continuing this process yields:

$$p_1 = 0.0118304$$

$$p_2 = 0.0089008$$

$$p_3 = 0.0029512.$$

The ratio $p_1 : p_2 : p_3 : p_4 : p_5$ is $39.9 : 30.1 : 10.0 : 5.0 : 15.0$.

Using an IBM 7040 computer, the author applied this technique in order to extract the distributions of losses as percentages of value implicit in the relativities of several fire coinsurance rate schedules now in use (see Chapter 7). Insurance of 10, 20, 30, and so on up to 100 percent of value was assumed, with arithmetic mean losses of 5, 15, 25, and so on up to 95 percent of value in each 10 percentage-point interval for a 10-equation model. In order to test each schedule, an 80 percent rate of $0.40 was assumed. It was further assumed that expense loadings were a constant percentage of pure premiums.

Each loss distribution produced by the computer corresponded to the set of p's in the above example. Each distribution contained alternately positive and negative values, i.e., p_1 positive,

p_2 negative, p_3 positive, and so on up to negative p_{10}. Although these are mathematically correct and unique solutions, the negative values are inadmissible because they imply negative unconditional probabilities of loss. The author believes that the reason for these results is the application of a constant flat rate, usually for all coverages up to at least 50 percent of value (80 percent in some schedules). If the same rate applies to 10 and 50 percent coverage and if rates are equitable and just adequate, losses below 50 percent of value must be impossible (have a total expected value of zero), as shown in Equation 2-4, page 16. But if the flat rate for 10 percent coverage is less than the 60 percent coinsurance rate, some loss below 60 percent of value must have a positive expected value, again as shown by Equation 2-4. Faced with the requirement that losses for percentages of value which are less than the minimum coinsurance percentage have probabilities summing to zero (in order to justify the flat rate) and that some of these small losses be possible (in order to justify the rate reduction for the minimum coinsurance requirement), the computer apparently hit upon alternately positive and negative probabilities *throughout*. The impossibility of negative probabilities leads one to question the equity of flat rates.

Coinsurance in Nonconcurrent Apportionments

This appendix explores how a nonconcurrent apportionment involving a policy with an insurance to percentage of value coinsurance provision is affected by the characteristics of the loss being apportioned. To achieve this objective the appendix examines variations of the illustrative loss situation introduced in Chapter 10.

The basic situation to be used involves a warehouse containing $150,000 of wheat and $50,000 of oats. The insurance consists of $110,000 Policy A on wheat only and $60,000 Policy B on all grain. The specific policy, A, has no coinsurance provision, but the blanket policy, B, is subject to an insurance to value clause reading:

It is part of the conditions of this policy, and the basis on which the rate of premium is fixed, that the Insured shall at all times maintain insurance on each item of property insured by this policy of not less than 80 per cent of the actual cash value thereof, and that, failing to do so, the Insured shall be an insurer to the extent of such deficit, and in that event shall bear his, her or their proportion of any loss.

Policy B has no pro rata distribution clause; if necessary for full indemnity, its whole face may be applied to any part of the grain. Only the loss, policy face, and pro rata liability and coinsurance provisions limit payments under either policy.

For a $20,000 oats loss, identically apportioned under the National Board recommendations or the *Guiding Principles,* Policy A pays nothing. Policy B pays no greater portion of the loss than the total amount of insurance on any grain ($110,000 + $60,000) bears to 80 percent of the $200,000 value of all grain ($160,000), which is 160/160 of the loss,[1] or the whole $20,000. Policy B's insurance to value clause does not reduce indemnity because Policy A restores the $100,000 coinsurance deficiency. The policy to value interpretation of an insurance to value clause, normally recommended, is not allowed here, because such an interpretation would lower the insured's total indemnity to $7500 (60/160 of $20,000), all paid by Policy B. If Policy B had contained an 80 percent policy to value clause, it would have paid $7500 and left the insured a $12,500 coinsurance penalty.

Six features of this example make the insurance to value clause more liberal to the insured than is a policy to value clause: (1) the policies are nonconcurrent as to property covered; (2) the insurance to value clause is in blanket Policy B; (3) some loss (for convenience, all the loss) occurs to property (oats) with only blanket coverage; (4) the insurance to value clause in Policy B does not specify that insurance applied to its coinsurance requirement must contribute to, or be concurrent with, Policy B; (5) the loss is not large enough to exhaust Policy B regardless of which type of 80 percent coinsurance clause it contains; and (6) the insurance to value clause in Policy B does not contain a division by item of insurance provision.

In the following sections, each of these features is altered, and the loss is adjusted under the National Board recommendations, assuming first an insurance to value, and second a policy to value, clause. Finally, changes introduced by the *1963 Guiding Principles* are noted.

---

[1] By paying 170/160 of the loss, Policy B would violate the principle of indemnity.

NONCONCURRENCY AS TO PROPERTY

Assume that both policies cover all grain, with all other facts the same as in the basic example. The National Board recommended that policies nonconcurrent only as to coinsurance share losses in the ratios of their face amounts, no policy paying more than its limit of liability under any coinsurance or other restriction. Since Policy B's 80 percent insurance to value requirement is met, such a requirement does not limit the policy's liability. But a policy to value clause limits Policy B's liability to 37.5 percent (60/160) of the loss. Prorating liability by face amount with Policy A, Policy B is liable for no more than 35.3 percent (60/170) of the loss, a lesser limit than that under the policy to value clause. Thus, no 80 percent coinsurance clause limits Policy B's liability to less than the $7,058.82 which it contributes with Policy A's $12,941.18 (110/170 of $20,000) to give full indemnity.

But, if Policy A is only $90,000, Policy B is liable for 60/150 (40 percent) of the loss under its pro rata liability clause, 150/160 (93.75 percent) of the loss under an 80 percent insurance to value clause, and 60/160 (37.5 percent) of the loss under an 80 percent policy to value clause. With an 80 percent insurance to value clause in Policy B, Policy A pays 90/150 of the loss, and Policy B, under its pro rata liability clause, pays 60/150 of the loss, giving full indemnity. With the policy to value clause, Policy A, under its pro rata liability clause, again pays 90/150 of the loss, or $12,000, Policy B, under its policy to value clause, pays 60/160 of the loss, or $7500, and the coinsurance penalty is $500.[2]

These results are the same under the *1963 Guiding Principles,* where policies differing only as to coinsurance are concurrent and apportion losses by face amounts, no policy paying more than permitted by any coinsurance or other clause.

---

[2] See Prentiss B. Reed, *Adjustment of Property Losses,* 2nd ed. (New York: McGraw-Hill Book Co., Inc., 1953), p. 224, example 2, for an analogous case.

CLAUSE IN SPECIFIC POLICY

Assume that $110,000 Policy A, specifically covering wheat alone, is subject to some 80 percent coinsurance provision and that $60,000 Policy B on all grain is free of coinsurance. Values remain at $150,000 of wheat and $50,000 of oats, but the $20,000 loss is limited to wheat in order to have a loss subject to coinsurance. Policy A's coinsurance requirement is 80 percent of the wheat's value, or $120,000.

The National Board here recommended the limit of liability rule with policy to value interpretation of any insurance to value clause or, if this interpretation reduced indemnity, the Page Rule with insurance to value clauses literally construed. Whether Policy A contains an 80 percent policy to value clause or an 80 percent insurance to value clause construed as a policy to value clause, the loss is fully paid. Policy A's limit of liability is $18,333.33 (110/120 of the whole loss, less than the loss or Policy A's face). Policy B's limit of liability is the $20,000 loss. Since the total of the limits of liability, $38,333.33, exceeds the loss, Policy A pays 18,333.33/38,333.33 of the loss, or $9,565.21, and Policy B pays the remaining $10,434.79. Here, the recommendation that insurance to value clauses be taken as policy to value clauses eliminates differences between the two provisions.

Under the *1963 Guiding Principles,* interpretation of insurance to value clauses as policy to value clauses also eliminates these distinctions, but the *Guiding Principles,* by declaring blanket Policy B to be excess coverage, put more of the loss on Policy A. Policy A pays its $18,333.33 limit of liability before Policy B pays the remaining $1666.67.

If Policy A's insurance to value clause had been interpreted literally, the $170,000 of insurance available for wheat losses would have met the $120,000 coinsurance requirement, and, under the *Guiding Principles,* Policy A would have paid all the loss. Under the National Board method, by which each policy's limit of liability would have been the loss, each policy would have borne half the loss.

LOSS WITH ONLY BLANKET COVERAGE

Assume that in the basic example the $20,000 loss occurs to wheat, property with both blanket and specific coverage. In contrast to the immediately preceding example, the only coinsurance clause is an 80 percent requirement in Policy B. The other facts of the basic example are retained.

Whether Policy B has a policy to value or an insurance to value clause, the National Board recommended a policy to value interpretation under the limit of liability rule, unless, as is not the case here, the Page Rule with literal interpretation of insurance to value clauses would give more indemnity. Policy A's liability is limited by the $20,000 loss. Policy B's liability is limited by its 80 percent policy to value clause (actual or by interpretation) on all grain to 60/160 of the loss, or $7500. The sum of these limits ($27,500) being more than the loss, Policy A pays 20,000/27,500 of the loss ($14,545.45), and Policy B pays 7500/27,500 of the loss ($5454.55). Here, by interpretation, no differences remain between policy to value and insurance to value clauses. Without this interpretation, however, an 80 percent insurance to value clause in Policy B would be fulfilled, and each policy, with a limit of liability equal to the loss, would pay $10,000.

Under the *1963 Guiding Principles*, Policy B is excess to Policy A. Not subject to coinsurance, Policy A pays the whole $20,000 wheat loss. Any coinsurance clause in Policy B is irrelevant because Policy B pays nothing. But, for a $130,000 wheat loss, Policy B may be liable for part or all of the $20,000 *excess* loss, depending on whether it contains an 80 percent insurance or policy to value clause. In this case, the coinsurance requirement is $72,000, or 80 percent of the difference between the $200,000 value of all grain and Policy A's $110,000 face. The $60,000 face of Policy B obliges it to pay only 60/72 of the $20,000 excess loss under a policy to value clause. With an insurance to value clause, Policy A's additional $110,000, helping to meet the coinsurance requirement on all grain, obligates Policy B to pay the whole excess loss. Here, an insurance to value clause is taken literally because a policy to value construction would reduce the insured's total indemnity.

SPECIFICATION OF CONTRIBUTING OR CONCURRENT INSURANCE[3]

Assume that, in the basic example, Policy B's coinsurance clause limits the insurer's liability to no more than that portion of any loss which the amount of insurance contributing (or concurrent) with Policy B, together with the face amount of Policy B, bears to 80 percent of the value of all grain.[4] In the basic example, Policies A and B are not concurrent, and Policy A is not contributing with Policy B for losses to oats. Once, it was hoped that requiring contributing insurance would eliminate differences between policy to value and insurance to value clauses,[5] but, since not all contributing insurance is concurrent, only a limitation to concurrent insurance makes the coinsurance clauses equivalent.

Concurrent policies are identical to the extent specified by the

---

[3] An early court decision, still followed, holds that all other insurance covering any portion of the property insured subject to a coinsurance requirement can be applied to meet that requirement if the coinsurance provision does not specify concurrent or contributing insurance and if the other insurance does not declare itself excess. See *Northwestern Fuel Company v. Boston Insurance Company*, 131 Minn. 19, 154 N.W. 513 (1915). "Insurance," *Corpus Juris Secundum* (Brooklyn, N.Y.: American Law Book Co., 1946), vol. 44, p. 1167, n. 12, cites *Northwestern Fuel* on this point as ruling law. The *1969 Cumulative Annual Pocket Part for Volume 44 of Corpus Juris Secundum* contains no modification of this point.

[4] Several modern insurance to value clauses limit applicable coverage to contributing insurance. See Western Actuarial Bureau clause in Illinois Inspection and Rating Bureau, *Illinois Rule Book (Excluding Cook County)* (Chicago: the Bureau, loose-leaf, revised and supplemented periodically), p. 22, effective January 5, 1953 (quoted on p. 56 above); and New York clause in New York Fire Insurance Rating Organization, *General Rules* (New York: the Organization, loose-leaf, revised and supplemented periodically), p. 20, effective August 2, 1965 (quoted on p. 49 above). Clauses specifying concurrent insurance are rare, but, for a Canadian example, see William N. Bament, "Co-Insurance" address to the Insurance Society of New York, March 30, 1920, pp. 5 and 7.

[5] J. J. Fitzgerald, "Coinsurance Is Much Misunderstood," *Journal of American Insurance*, vol. IV, no. 6 (June 1927), p. 29.

National Board or the *1963 Guiding Principles.* Contributing insurance is merely insurance which pays a portion of a loss which would have been paid by another policy in the absence of the contributing policy.[6] For example, with the $130,000 wheat loss, nonconcurrent Policy A is contributing insurance from the standpoint of Policy B, because Policy A lowers Policy B's payment. But Policy B is not contributing from the standpoint of Policy A because, for wheat losses under the *Guiding Principles,* Policy A pays its limit of liability before Policy B pays anything.

In the unchanged basic example of a $20,000 loss to oats, either an 80 percent concurrent or an 80 percent contributing insurance to value clause in Policy B achieves the same results as a policy to value clause under either the National Board recommendations or the *Guiding Principles.* Policy A, not insuring oats, is not concurrent with Policy B, contributes nothing, and cannot raise Policy B's coinsurance apportionment ratio above the 60/160 which obliges Policy B to pay $7500.

But, under the *Guiding Principles,* for the $130,000 wheat loss ($20,000 excess loss for Policy B), only a concurrent insurance to value clause limits Policy B's liability to that payable under a policy to value clause. The coinsurance requirement in this case is $72,000, which is met only if Policy A is applied to it. Nonconcurrent Policy A contributes with Policy B by reducing the excess loss Policy B must pay. Therefore, the only coinsurance clauses which can exclude Policy A and keep Policy B's coinsurance apportionment ratio at 60/72 are an 80 percent policy to value clause and an 80 percent concurrent insurance to value clause.

LOSS NOT REQUIRING PAYMENT OF POLICY FACE

If, in the basic example, the loss is so large that Policy B must pay its face under an 80 percent policy to value clause, it must pay its face under an 80 percent insurance to value clause (which

---

[6] Insurance Department of the Chamber of Commerce of the United States, *Dictionary of Insurance Terms* (Washington, D.C.: The Chamber, 1949), p. 18.

is more liberal to the insured), and any differences between the coinsurance clauses in Policy B disappear. A basic characteristic of all coinsurance clauses is that they do not reduce indemnity for losses at least as great as the coinsurance requirement. With nonconcurrency and contribution, however, the minimum loss for which a policy to value (and, therefore, insurance to value) clause does not reduce indemnity differs under the National Board recommendations from that under the *Guiding Principles.*

Under neither the National Board procedures nor the *Guiding Principles* does even a total loss in the basic example exhaust $60,000 Policy B when it is subject to an 80 percent policy to value clause. By the National Board's Cromie Rule, Policy B pays 60/160 (37.5 percent) of the $50,000 oats loss, or $18,750, leaving a $41,250 unspent limit of liability to contribute pro rata with Policy A's $110,000 face amount in paying the $150,000 wheat loss. Since the total limits of liability for wheat ($151,250) exceed the loss, neither Policy A nor Policy B pays its limit. Policy B pays an additional $40,909.09 (about 27 percent of the wheat loss, less than Policy B's 37.5 percent coinsurance limit of liability for wheat). Under the *Guiding Principles,* Policy B also pays $18,750 for a $50,000 loss to oats. Of the $150,000 total loss to wheat, only $40,000 is excess to Policy A's $110,000 face. For wheat, Policy B's coinsurance requirement is $72,000, and 60/72 of $40,000 is $33,333.33. In all, under the *Guiding Principles,* Policy B pays $52,083.33 for a total loss; under the National Board method, it pays $59,159.09. An 80 percent policy to value clause still is a binding limit on the insurer's liability.

As a case where a severe loss exhausts Policy B when it contains an 80 percent policy to value clause, assume that the $200,000 value of all grain is composed of $10,000 of oats and $190,000 of wheat, the other facts remaining as in the basic example. Under the Cromie Rule, loss of all oats and of at least $166,250 of wheat eliminates the effect of 80 percent coinsurance. Policy B pays 60/160 of $10,000, or $3750, for the oats, leaving a $56,250 limit of liability. A loss of $166,250 of wheat exhausts both Policy A (paying 110,000/166,250 of the loss) and Policy B (paying 56,250/166,250 of the loss). Policy B pays approximately 34 percent of the wheat loss, less than its 37.5 percent co-insurance limit of liability.

Under the *Guiding Principles,* if all the oats and at least $177,500 of the wheat are destroyed, Policy B pays its face under any type of 80 percent coinsurance requirement. After paying 60/160 of the oats loss, Policy B again has an unspent limit of liability of $56,250. Since, for wheat, Policy B pays 60/72 of the loss, the least *excess* loss which calls forth $56,250 from Policy B is $67,500 (72/60 of $56,250). Since the primary Policy A first pays $110,000 for wheat, the least loss which exhausts Policy B is $177,500 ($110,000 + $67,500).

If Policy B had been subject to an 80 percent insurance to value clause, smaller losses would have been needed to force Policy B to pay its face under either the National Board method or the *Guiding Principles.* Furthermore, these examples of least losses for which no 80 percent coinsurance clause reduces indemnity are only two of an infinite number which could be produced with various combinations of wheat and oats values totaling $200,000 and with various policy faces.

DIVISION BY ITEM OF INSURANCE CLAUSE

Assume the same facts as in the basic example, but with a division by item of insurance provision as the second sentence of an insurance to value clause reading:

It is part of the conditions of this policy, and the basis on which the rate of premium is fixed, that the Insured shall at all times maintain insurance on each item of property insured by this policy of not less than 80 percent of the actual cash value thereof, and that, failing to do so, the Insured shall be an insurer to the extent of such deficit, and in that event shall bear his, her or their proportion of any loss. If the insurance under this policy be divided into two or more items, the foregoing shall apply to each item separately.[7]

---

[7] The first sentence of this clause is the same as the entire clause in the basic example (page 49). The second sentence of this clause is the final sentence of the current New York Standard Coinsurance Clause, New York Fire Insurance Rating Organization, *General Rules, op. cit.,* p. 20, effective August 2, 1965.

The division is by item of insurance, not item of insured property. For example, five bulldozers and five trucks may be covered under one item of insurance ("$500,000 on heavy equipment"), two items of insurance ("$300,000 on bulldozers, $200,000 on trucks"), or ten items of insurance ("$60,000 on Bulldozer A," etc.). Division by item of insurance provisions are added to insurance to value clauses in policies containing more than one item of insurance, perhaps in order to prevent an insured, otherwise facing a coinsurance penalty, from contending that, for example, the item of insurance on bulldozers should be applied to the coinsurance deficiency under the item of insurance on trucks in a two-item policy. Division by item of insurance generally reduces the indemnity payment under an insurance to value clause, thus bringing it closer to that payable under a policy to value clause.

In the basic example, assume that Policy B—instead of containing only one item of insurance on grain—insures, under two items, $25,000 on oats and $35,000 on wheat. The other facts are unchanged. For the $20,000 oats loss, the coinsurance requirement is reduced to 80 percent of the value of the oats, or $40,000. Since, with the division by item provision, only coverage on oats can be applied to this requirement, the $110,000 of Policy A does not raise Policy B's coinsurance apportionment ratio above 25/40, the same ratio that would exist under a $25,000 policy on oats subject to an 80 percent policy to value clause. Under the National Board recommendations or the *Guiding Principles,* Policy B pays five-eighths of the loss, or $12,500, instead of the whole loss it pays in the basic example.

A division by item of insurance provision in an insurance to value clause also can *increase* a policy's loss payment, under the National Board procedures or the *Guiding Principles,* if the division excludes underinsured property from the settlement of a loss to more fully insured property. In the basic example, assume that Policy B contains two items of insurance: $60,000 on grain and $40,000 on the warehouse, which is worth $75,000. With the division by item of insurance clause, the 80 percent coinsurance requirement on all grain is $160,000. Policies A and B, both applicable to grain, provide $170,000 of coverage, and Policy B pays the whole $20,000 oats loss as before. But, without the division by item of insurance provision, a one-item Policy B, insuring "$100,000 on warehouse and contents," is subject to a coinsurance requirement of 80 percent of the $275,000 combined value of the grain and the warehouse, or $220,000. For a $20,000 loss to oats, only Policy B provides coverage, but all the $210,000 of insurance (Policy A plus Policy B) on any part of the warehouse or its contents may be applied to the coinsurance requirement. Thus, without division by item of insurance, the one-item Policy B is liable for only 21/22 of the loss, not the full loss which it bears with the division by item provision in the two-item policy.

APPENDIX **6**

Statutes Applicable to Coinsurance

Organized alphabetically by state and numerically by statute section numbers within states, this appendix presents the texts of statutes applicable to coinsurance. Regulation of coinsurance is the subject of Chapter 11.

DELAWARE

1102

Valued Policy. (a) Whenever any policy of insurance shall be issued to insure any real property in this State against loss by fire, tornado, or lightning, and the property insured shall be wholly destroyed without criminal fault on the part of the insured, or his assigns, the amount of the insurance stated in such policy (except policies with blanket coverage provided for in section 1103 of this title) shall be taken conclusively to be the true value of the property insured and the true amount of loss and measure of damages, subject to the proviso in subsection (b) of this section.

(b) Every such policy, whether hereafter issued or renewed, shall have endorsed across the face of it the following: "It is agreed by the insurer and insured that the value of the real property insured is the sum of $_____."

(c) The amount of the agreed value stated in the endorsement shall be binding on both parties as to value, but nothing contained in this section shall, in case of loss, prevent the company insuring from adjusting the loss by replacing the property destroyed. In case any owner shall effect any subsequent insurance on the same property upon any larger value than so agreed, all such insurance, that existing as well as that subsequently obtained, shall become void.

FLORIDA

627.0800

No property insurer shall issue any policy or contract of fire insurance covering either real or personal property in this state which contains any clause or provision requiring the insured to take out or maintain a larger amount of fire insurance than that expressed in such policy; nor in any way provide that the insured shall be liable as a co-insurer with the insurer issuing the policy for any part of the loss or damage which may be caused by fire to the property described in such policy; and any such clause or provision shall be null and void, and of no effect unless there is printed or stamped on the face of such policy or on a form attached thereto the words: "CO-INSURANCE CONTRACT. The rate charged in this policy is based upon use of a co-insurance clause attached hereto, with the consent of the insured." The rate for the insurance with and without the co-insurance clause shall be furnished the insured upon request.

627.0801(2)

In the case of partial loss by fire or lightning of any such property the insurer's liability, if any, under the policy shall be for the actual amount of such loss but not to exceed the amount of insurance specified in the policy as to such property and such perils.

IOWA

515.111

Contracts of insurance against loss or damage by fire or other perils may contain a coinsurance or contribution clause or clause having similar effect, provided the form setting up the terms of the same has been approved by the commissioner of insurance.

KENTUCKY

304.905

Except as provided in KRS 304.906, insurers that take fire or storm risks on real property in this state shall, in case of total loss thereof by fire or storm, be liable for the full estimated value of the property insured, as the value thereof is fixed on the face of the policy, except that the estimated value of the property insured may be diminished to the extent of any depreciation in the value of the property occurring between the date of the policy and the loss. In case of partial loss of the property insured, the liability of the insurer shall not exceed the actual loss of the party insured. The insured shall be liable for any fraud he may practice in fixing the value of the property, if the insurer is misled thereby.

[Coinsurance clause of a storm policy was held to be of no avail, and although the value of the building damaged by a storm was several times greater than the amount of the policy, yet the insurer is liable for the full amount. *Hartford Fire Insurance Co. v. Henderson Brewing Co.*, 168 Ky. 715, 182 S. W. 852.]

304.906

Insurers of property against fire or storm may contract with the insured that the insured shall, during the life of the policy, maintain insurance upon the property so insured to the extent of an agreed proportion of the actual cash value of the property at the time of loss, and that if the insured fails to do so, the insured shall be a co-insurer to the extent that the insurance then in force is less than the amount of the agreed proportion, and shall bear his part of any loss, as co-insurer, to that extent. The acceptance of a policy containing such a provision shall be at the option of the insured, and a reduced premium rate shall apply to the policy. No such provision shall be valid unless the form setting up the terms of the provision has been approved by the commissioner of insurance.

LOUISIANA

22.694

No policy of fire, lightning or windstorm insurance covering property or risks in this state shall contain any clause or provisions requiring the insured to take out or maintain a larger amount of insurance than that covered by such policy or providing in any way that the insured shall be liable as a co-insurer with the insurer unless such clause has been approved by the fire insurance division and there has been a consideration allowed in the rate of premium charged for such policy.

22.695(B)

Under any fire insurance policy, which may be written hereafter, and which is intended to take effect, at or after 12 o'clock noon, Central Standard Time, on the first day of August, 1964, on any inanimate property, immovable by nature or destination, situated within the state of Louisiana, the insurer shall pay to the insured, in case of partial damage, without criminal fault on the part of the insured or the insured's assigns, such amounts, not exceeding the amount for which the property is insured, at the time of such partial damage, in the policy of such insurer, as will permit the insured to restore the damaged property to its original condition; provided, however, that for any loss of an insured object which would constitute a total loss under Section A of this provision but which loss is covered by a blanket-form policy of insurance, Section B of this provision shall apply, and the insurer shall pay to the insured an amount equal to the actual cash value at the time of the loss of each insured object so destroyed, not exceeding the total amount of the insurance.

MICHIGAN

2840

(1) Any person may obtain from any insurer authorized to do business within the state of Michigan, a coinsurance clause to be attached to or included in any policy issued by such insurer insuring the interest of the insured in any real or tangible or intangible personal property against direct, indirect or consequential loss or damage, and the insurer shall have the right to issue such coinsurance clause, providing the form of the same has first been approved by the commissioner.

Any such insurance policy or the coinsurance endorsement attached thereto shall be signed by the insurer or its authorized agent.

MINNESOTA

65A.08(5)

Any policy may contain a coinsurance clause, if the insured requests the same, in writing, of which fact such writing shall be the only evidence, and if, in consideration thereof, a reduction in the rate of premium is made by the company. When so demanded and attached to the policy, this agreement shall be binding upon both the insured and the company, and, in case of loss, the actual cash value of the property so insured at the time of the loss, including the buildings, shall be the basis for determining the proper amount of the coinsurance, and the amount of loss, notwithstanding any previous valuation of the building.

MISSISSIPPI

5693

No insurance company shall knowingly issue any fire insurance policy upon property within this State for an amount which, together with any existing insurance thereon, exceeds a fair value of the property, nor for a longer term than five years. When buildings and structures insured against loss by fire, and situated within this State, are totally destroyed by fire the company shall not be permitted to deny that the buildings or structures insured were worth at the time of the issuance of the policy the full value upon which the insurance is calculated and the measure of damages shall be the amount for which the buildings and structures were insured. No insurance company or agent thereof shall be permitted to attach a three-quarter value clause to insurance of this kind and any fire insurance company or agent thereof who violates this section shall be guilty of a misdemeanor and shall upon conviction be fined not less than two hundred ($200.00) dollars, nor more than one thousand ($1000.00) dollars for each offense.

MISSOURI

379.140

In all suits brought upon policies of insurance against loss or damage by fire hereafter issued or renewed, the defendant shall not be permitted to deny that the property insured thereby was worth at the time of the issuing of the policy the full amount insured therein on said property; and in case of total loss of the property insured, the measure of damage shall be the amount for which the same was insured, less whatever depreciation in value, below the amount for which the property is insured, the property may have sustained between the time of issuing the policy and the time of the loss, and the burden of proving such depreciation shall be upon the defendant; and in case of partial loss, the measure of damage shall be that portion of the value of the whole property insured, ascertained in the manner prescribed in this chapter, which the part injured or destroyed bears to the whole property insured.

379.155

No fire insurance policy which may be issued after this section takes effect shall contain any clause or provision requiring the assured to take out or maintain a larger amount of insurance than that covered by such policy, nor in any way providing that the assured shall be liable as coinsurer with the company issuing the policy for any part of the loss or damage which may be occasioned by fire or lightning to the property covered by such policy, nor making provisions for a reduction of such loss or damage, or any part thereof, by reason of the failure of the assured to take out and maintain other insurance upon said property. And all clauses and provisions in fire policies, issued after the taking effect of this section, in contravention of the prohibitions in this section contained, shall be ab initio void and of no effect; provided, that the provisions of this section shall not apply to policies issued upon personal property in cities which now contain or which may hereafter contain one hundred thousand inhabitants or more whenever the insured signs an agreement indorsed across the face of said policy to be exempt from the provisions thereof.

379.160(3)

The appearance of an adjuster of any company at the place of fire and loss in which said company is interested by reason of an insurance on such property, shall be considered evidence of notice and to be held as a waiver of the same on the part of the company, provided, that on any policies issued upon property, real or personal, or real and personal, there may be attached a coinsurance clause; and provided further, that when a coinsurance clause is attached to any policy a reduction in rate shall be given therefor, in accordance with coinsurance credits that are now or may hereafter be filed as a part of the public rating record in the office of superintendent of insurance in this state, by fire insurance companies, that have been or shall hereafter be approved by the superintendent of insurance; provided further, that in all suits brought upon policies of insurance against loss or damage by fire hereafter issued or renewed, the defendant shall not be permitted to deny that the property insured thereby was worth at the time of the isuing of the policy the full amount insured therein on said property covering both real and personal property; and provided further, that nothing in this section shall be construed to repeal or change the provisions of section 379.140.

NORTH CAROLINA

58-30.1

No insurance company or agent licensed to do business in this State may issue any policy or contract of insurance covering property in this State which shall contain any clause or provision requiring the insured to take or maintain a larger amount of insurance than that expressed in such policy, nor in any way provide that the insured shall be liable as a coinsurer with the company issuing the policy for any part of the loss or damage to the property described in such policy, and any such clause or provision shall be null and void, and of no effect: Provided, the coinsurance clause or provision may be written in or attached to a policy or policies issued when there is printed or stamped on the filing face of such policy or on the form containing such clause the words "coinsurance contract," and the Commissioner may, in his discretion, determine the location of the words "coinsurance contract" and the size of the type to be used. If there be a difference in the rate for the insurance with and without the coinsurance clause, the rates for each shall be furnished the insured upon request.

NEW HAMPSHIRE

407.11(b)

If an insured building is only partially destroyed by fire or lightning, the insured shall be entitled to the actual loss sustained not exceeding the sum insured.

407.11(c)

Nothing contained in paragraphs (a) and (b) of this section shall be construed as prohibiting the use of coinsurance, or agreed amount.

SOUTH CAROLINA

37.154

No company writing fire insurance policies, doing business in this State, shall issue a policy for more than the value stated in the policy or the value of the property to be insured, the amount of insurance to be fixed by the insurer and insured at or before the time of issuing the policy. In case of total loss by fire the insured shall be entitled to recover the full amount of insurance, and in case of a partial loss the insured shall be entitled to recover the actual amount of the loss, but in no event more than the amount of the insurance stated in the contract. But if two or more policies are written upon the same property, they shall be deemed and held to be contributive insurance, and if the aggregate sum of all such insurance exceeds the insurable value of the property, as agreed by the insurer and the insured, each company shall, in the event of a total or partial loss, be liable for its prorata share of insurance. Nothing in this section shall be held to apply to insurance on chattels or personal property.

37.157

No insurance company or agent licensed to do business in this State may issue any policy or contract of insurance covering property in this State which shall contain any clause or provision requiring the insured to take or maintain a larger amount of insurance than that expressed in such policy, nor in any way provide that the insured shall be liable as a coinsurer with the company issuing the policy for any part of the loss or damage to the property described in such policy, and any such clause or provision shall be null and void and of no effect. But such a clause or provision may be used if there is stamped on the filing face of such policy or printed in bold type at the top of such clause, the words "coinsurance clause." If there be a difference in the rate for insurance with and without the coinsurance clause, the rates for each shall be furnished the insured upon request.

TENNESSEE

56.1137

Every agent, within ninety (90) days after making or writing any contract of fire insurance on any building or structure in this state, shall cause the same to be personally inspected; and no company, and no officer or agent thereof, and no insurance broker, shall knowingly issue, negotiate, continue or renew or cause to permit to be issued, negotiated, continued or renewed any fire insurance policy upon property or interests therein within the state of an amount which, with any existing insurance thereon, exceeds the fair value of the property.

56.1139

If the agent fails to place a reasonable value on any such insured property within the ninety (90) days, as provided in sec. 56.1137, and which is agreed to by the insured, and a loss occurs, in that event the value as shown by the policy or application shall be conclusively presumed to be reasonable, and settlement shall be made on that basis.

TEXAS

5.38

No company subject to the provisions of this sub-chapter may issue any policy or contract of insurance covering property in this State, which shall contain any clause or provision requiring the assured to take out or maintain a larger amount of insurance than expressed in such policy, nor in any way providing that the assured shall be liable as a co-insurer with the company issuing the policy for any part of the loss or damage which may be caused by fire to the property described in such policy, and any such clause or provisions, except as herein provided, shall be null and void, and of no effect; provided, co-insurance clauses and provisions may be inserted in policies written upon cotton, grain, or other products in process of marketing, shipping, storing or manufacturing.

Provided, further, it shall be optional with an insured to accept a policy or contract of insurance containing such clause or provision covering other classes of property, except private dwellings, and except stocks of merchandise offered for sale at retail when of a value less than Ten Thousand ($10,000.00) Dollars, when a reduction in the rate is allowed for such policy, and said clause in such policy shall be valid and binding; and the Board of Insurance Commissioners shall have power to name the rates to apply when such co-insurance clause or provision shall be used.

Provided, further, that by appropriate order the Board of Insurance Commissioners may authorize, and in its discretion require the use of any form of co-insurance clauses on or in connection with insurance policies covering against the hazards of tornado, windstorm and hail, on any or all classes of property;

the Board to make such rules and regulations with reference to such clauses and the use thereof, as well as credits in premium rates for the use thereof on policies covering against the hazards mentioned as it may deem proper.

VERMONT

8.3961

Whenever a fire insurance company shall write a policy covering a building in this state and shall attach thereto the so-called co-insurance clause, or any similar clause requiring the insured to carry insurance in amount equal to any percentage of the value of such building, the insured may ask for a valuation of such building insured, which valuation may be agreed upon in writing by the insuring company and the insured, and shall be the valuation of the property insured for the purpose of fixing the liability of the company during the life of the policy.

WEST VIRGINIA

3472.148

All insurers issuing policies providing fire insurance on real property situate in West Virginia, shall be liable, in case of total loss by fire or otherwise, as stated in the policy, for the whole amount of insurance stated in the policy, upon such real property; and in case of partial loss by fire or otherwise, as aforesaid, of the real property insured, the liability shall be for the total amount of such partial loss, not to exceed the whole amount of insurance upon such real property as stated in the policy. This section shall not apply where such insurance has been procured from two or more insurers covering the same interest in such real property.

WISCONSIN

203.22

Except as otherwise provided by law, no fire insurance company shall issue any policy in this state containing any provision limiting the amount to be paid in case of loss below the actual cash value of the property, if within the amount for which the premium is paid, unless, at the option of the insured, a reduced rate shall be given for the use of a coinsurance clause made a part of the policy. Any company may, by so providing in the policy, distribute the total insurance in the manner and upon as many items as specified therein, or limit the amount recoverable upon any single item, article or animal to an amount not exceeding the cost thereof, or to an amount specified in the policy. Any company, officer or agent violating any provision of this section shall upon conviction thereof, be punished by a fine of not less than $100 nor more than $500 and the license of such agent and company may be suspended for a period not exceeding one year.

Bibliography

Books

American Mutual Insurance Alliance. *Study Kit for Students of Insurance—Casualty, Fire, Marine, Life.* Chicago: The Alliance, n.d.

Angell, Frank Joseph. *Insurance Principles and Practices.* New York: The Ronald Press Co., 1959.

Appleman, John Allan. *Insurance Law and Practice.* Kansas City, Mo.: Vernon Law Book Co., 1942.

Athearn, James L. *Risk and Insurance.* New York: Appleton-Century-Crofts, Inc., 1962.

Athearn, James L., and Toole, Cameron S. *Questions and Answers on Insurance.* 2nd ed. Englewood Cliffs, N.J.: Prentice-Hall, Inc., 1960.

Barbour, Robert P. *The Agents Key to Fire Insurance.* 6th ed. New York: The Spectator Co., 1949.

Bell, H. S. *Average and Contribution in Fire Insurance.* London: Charles and Edwin Layton, 1911.

Best's Fire and Casualty Aggregates and Averages. New York: Albert M. Best Co., annual.

Betterley, P. D. *Buying Insurance, A Problem of Business Management.* New York: McGraw-Hill Book Co., Inc., 1936.

Black, Henry Campbell. *Black's Law Dictionary.* 4th ed. St. Paul, Minn.: West Publishing Co., 1951.

Bonbright, James C. *The Valuation of Property, A Treatise on the Appraisal of Property for Different Legal Purposes.* 2 vols. Published under the auspices of the Columbia University Council for Research in the Social Sciences. New York: McGraw-Hill Book Co., Inc., 1937.

Chamber of Commerce of the United States, Insurance Department. *Dictionary of Insurance Terms.* Washington, D.C.: The Chamber, 1949.

Corpus Juris Secondum. Brooklyn, N.Y.: American Law Book Co., 1946.

Couch, George J. *Cyclopedia of Insurance Law.* vol. 9. Edited by Ronald A. Anderson. Rochester, N.Y.: The Lawyers Co-operative Publishing Co., 1962.

Current Annotations of the 1943 New York Standard Fire Insurance Policy. Prepared by the Subcommittee of the Committee on Fire Insurance Laws of the Section of Insurance, Negligence and Compensation Law. Chicago: American Bar Association, 1966.

Cyclopedia of Insurance in the United States. Edited by F. S. MacKay. Paterson, N.J.: The Index Publishing Co., 1965.

Dean, A. F. *The Philosophy of Fire Insurance.* 3 vols. Edited by W. R. Townley. Chicago: Edward B. Hatch, 1925.

Denenberg, Herbert S., *et al. Risk and Insurance.* Englewood Cliffs, N.J.: Prentice-Hall, Inc., 1964.

Dickerson, O. D. *Health Insurance.* Rev. ed. Homewood, Ill.: Richard D. Irwin, Inc., 1963.

Elliott, Curtis M. *Property and Casualty Insurance.* National Association of Insurance Agents—McGraw-Hill Insurance Bookshelf. New York: McGraw-Hill Book Co., Inc., 1960.

The Fire, Casualty and Surety Bulletins. Cincinnati, Ohio: The National Underwriter Company, loose-leaf, revised and supplemented periodically.

Gordis, Philip. *Property and Casualty Insurance, A Guide Book for Agents and Brokers.* 14th ed. rev. Indianapolis, Ind.: The Rough Notes Co., Inc., 1966.

Goshay, Robert C. *Corporate Self-Insurance and Risk Retention Plans.* Homewood, Ill.: Richard D. Irwin, Inc., 1964.

Greene, Mark R. *Risk and Insurance.* 2nd ed. Cincinnati, Ohio: South-Western Publishing Co., 1968.

Hardy, Edward R. *The Making of the Fire Insurance Rate.* New York: The Spectator Co., 1926.

Hartford Fire Insurance Company. *The Coinsurance Clause.* Hartford, Conn.: The Company, 1909.

Hedges, J. Edward. *Practical Fire and Casualty Insurance.* 5th ed. Cincinnati, Ohio: The National Underwriter Company, 1951.

Huebner, S. S., and Black, Kenneth, Jr. *Property Insurance.* 4th ed. New York: Appleton-Century-Crofts, Inc., 1957.

Huebner, S. S., Black, Kenneth, Jr., and Cline, Robert S. *Property and Liability Insurance.* New York: Appleton-Century-Crofts, Inc., 1968.

Insurance Information Institute. *Sample Insurance Policies for Property and Liability Coverages.* New York: The Institute, n.d.

Insurance Law Index Service. 6 vols. Edited by Leonard S. McCombs. Jenkintown, Pa.: McCombs & Co., Inc., supplemented through March 1970.

Ketcham, Edward A., and Ketcham-Kirk, Murray. *Essentials of the Fire Insurance Business.* Madison, Wis.: by the authors, 1922.

Kimball, Spencer L., and Mayerson, Allen L. *Cases and Materials on the Law of the Insurance Enterprise.* Mimeographed. Ann Arbor, Mich., 1965.

Kulp, C. A. *Casualty Insurance.* 3rd ed. New York: The Ronald Press Co., 1956.

Kulp, C. A., and Hall, John W. *Casualty Insurance.* 4th ed. New York: The Ronald Press Co., 1968.

Lee, Joseph Finley, Jr. "The Functional Operations and Competitive Role of the Associated Factory Mutual Insurance Companies." Doctoral dissertation, University of Pennsylvania, 1965.

MacDonald, Donald L. *Corporate Risk Control.* New York: The Ronald Press Co., 1966.

McGill, Dan M. *Life Insurance.* Rev. ed. Homewood, Ill.: Richard D. Irwin, Inc., 1966.

Magee, John H., and Bickelhaupt, David L. *General Insurance.* 7th ed. Homewood, Ill.: Richard D. Irwin, Inc., 1964.

Magee, John H., and Serbein, Oscar N. *Property and Liability Insurance.* 4th ed. Homewood, Ill.: Richard D. Irwin, Inc., 1967.

Mayerson, Allen L. *Introduction to Insurance.* New York: The Macmillan Co., 1962.

Mehr, Robert I., and Cammack, Emerson. *Principles of Insurance.* 4th ed. Homewood, Ill.: Richard D. Irwin, Inc., 1966.

Mehr, Robert I., and Hedges, Bob A. *Risk Management in the Business Enterprise.* Homewood, Ill.: Richard D. Irwin, Inc., 1963.

Minnion, Ernest H. *Average Clauses and Fire-Loss Apportionments.* 2nd ed. London: Sir Isaac Pitman & Sons, Ltd., 1947.

Moore, Francis C. *Fire Insurance and How to Build.* New York: The Baker & Taylor Co., 1903.

Mowbray, Albert H., and Blanchard, Ralph H. *Insurance, Its Theory and Practice in the United States.* 5th ed. New York: McGraw-Hill Book Co., Inc., 1961.

Mowbray, Albert H., Blanchard, Ralph H., and Williams, C. Arthur, Jr. *Insurance, Its Theory and Practice in the United States.* 6th ed. New York: McGraw-Hill Book Co., Inc., 1969.

Neter, John, and Wasserman, William. *Fundamental Statistics for Business and Economics.* 2nd ed. Boston: Allyn & Bacon, Inc., 1961.

Patterson, Edwin W. *Essentials of Insurance Law.* New York: Mc-Graw-Hill Book Co., Inc., 1957.

Patterson, Edwin W., and Young, William F., Jr. *Cases and Materials on the Law of Insurance.* 4th ed. Brooklyn, N.Y.: The Foundation Press, Inc., 1961.

Pfeffer, Irving. *Insurance and Economic Theory.* Homewood, Ill.: Richard D. Irwin, Inc., 1956.

Pierce, John Eugene. *Development of Comprehensive Insurance for the Household.* Homewood, Ill.: Richard D. Irwin, Inc., 1958.

Reed, Prentiss B. *Adjustment of Property Losses.* 2nd ed. New York: McGraw-Hill Book Co., Inc., 1953.

Reed, Prentiss B., and Thomas, Paul I. *Adjustment of Property Losses.* 3rd ed. New York: McGraw-Hill Book Co., Inc., 1969.

Report of the Co-Insurance Committee of the Board of Fire Underwriters of the Pacific on Percentage Coinsurance and the Relative Rates Chargeable Therefor, Also on the Cost of Conflagration Hazard of Large Cities. San Francisco, 1905.

Report of the Joint Committee of the Senate and Assembly of the State of New York, Appointed to Investigate Corrupt Practices in Connection with Legislation, and the Affairs of Insurance Companies, Other Than Those Doing Life Insurance Business. Assembly Document No. 30. Albany, N.Y., February 1, 1911.

Richards, George. *Law of Insurance.* 4th ed. Edited by Rowland H. Long. New York: Baker, Voorhis & Co., 1932.

Riegel, Robert, and Loman, H. J. *Insurance Principles and Practices.* Rev. ed. New York: Prentice-Hall, Inc., 1942.

Riegel, Robert, and Miller, Jerome S. *Insurance Principles and Practices.* 5th ed. Englewood Cliffs, N.J.: Prentice-Hall, Inc., 1966.

Rodda, William H. *Fire and Property Insurance.* Englewood Cliffs, N.J.: Prentice-Hall, Inc., 1956.

————. *Inland Marine and Transportation Insurance.* 2nd ed. Englewood Cliffs, N.J.: Prentice-Hall, Inc., 1958.

————. *Property and Liability Insurance.* Englewood Cliffs, N.J.: Prentice-Hall, Inc., 1966.

Schlaifer, Robert. *Introduction to Statistics for Business Decisions.* New York: McGraw-Hill Book Co., Inc., 1961.

Schultz, Robert E., and Bardwell, Edward C. *Property Insurance.* New York: Rinehart & Co., 1959.

Standard Mathematical Tables. 12th ed. Edited by Robert C. Weast, Samuel M. Selby, and Charles D. Hodgman. Cleveland, Ohio: The Chemical Rubber Publishing Co., 1959.

Vance, William R. *Handbook on the Law of Insurance.* 3rd ed. Edited by Buist M. Anderson. St. Paul, Minn.: West Publishing Co., 1951.

Vickrey, William S. *Microstatics.* New York: Harcourt, Brace & World, Inc., 1964.

Walford, Cornelius. *The Insurance Cyclopaedia.* 2 vols. London: Charles and Edwin Layton, 1871.

Webster's New International Dictionary of the English Language. 2nd ed., unabridged. Springfield, Mass.: G. & C. Merriam Co., 1958.

Willett, Allan H. *The Economic Theory of Risk and Insurance.* Homewood, Ill.: Richard D. Irwin, Inc., 1951.

Williams, C. Arthur, Jr. *Price Discrimination in Property and Liability Insurance.* Minneapolis: University of Minnesota Press, 1959.

Williams, C. Arthur, Jr., and Heins, Richard M. *Risk Management and Insurance.* New York: McGraw-Hill Book Co., 1964.

Winter, William D. *Marine Insurance, Its Principles and Practices.* 3rd ed. New York: McGraw-Hill Book Co., Inc., 1953.

Wolfe, F. E. *Principles of Property Insurance.* New York: Thomas Y. Crowell Co., 1930.

Yamane, Taro. *Mathematics for Economists.* Englewood Cliffs, N.J.: Prentice-Hall, Inc., 1962.

Pamphlets

Chamber of Commerce of the United States, Insurance Department. "Insurance Facts for Policyholders: Coinsurance." *Insurance Bulletin Number Six.* Washington, D.C., October, 1961.

Guiding Principles—Casualty, Fidelity, Fire, Inland Marine—First-Party Property Losses and Claims. New York: Association of Casualty and Surety Companies, *et al.*, November 1, 1963.

Lumbermen's Mutual Casualty Company. *A Study of Under-Insurance in American Industry,* n.p.: The Company, 1951.

Martin, Charles J. *The Co-Insurance Clause or Average Clause in Fire Insurance.* New York: Frank B. Jordan, General Insurance Broker, n.d.

National Retail Dry Goods Association, Insurance Bureau. *The Relation Between Co-Insurance and Premium.* New York: The Association, February 15, 1926.

Oregon, State of, Office of the Fire Marshal. *Annual Statistical Report.* Salem, Ore.: State Printing, 1953–1966.

The Philadelphia Contributionship for the Insurance of Houses from Loss by Fire. *Co-Insurance Briefly Explained.* Philadelphia: The Contributionship, n.d.

Wilmerding, Herbert. *Graded Co-Insurance.* Philadelphia: no publisher shown, 1902.

Wingo, H. W. *Coinsurance—When Your Client Asks "Why?"* Hartford, Conn.: Hartford Fire Insurance Co., 1965.

Woolley, J. K. *The Principles and Mechanics of Fire Insurance Rating as Incorporated in General Basic Schedule.* Seattle, Wash.: Washington (State) Surveying and Rating Bureau, 1937.

Articles

Adam, John, Jr. "Underwriting in Fire Insurance." In *Property and Liability Insurance Handbook,* edited by John D. Long and Davis W. Gregg, pp. 190–205. Homewood, Ill.: Richard D. Irwin, Inc., 1965.

"Adequate Insurance to Value Would Have Put Homeowners in the Black." *The National Underwriter* LXVIII, no. 45 (November 6, 1964): 1, 33–36.

"Attention to Co-Insurance on Small Losses is Vital." *Loss Research* VIII, no. 3 (April, 1951): 3–4.

"Average Clause Held Not to Waive Coinsurance on Small Fire Losses." *Eastern Underwriter* XLVIII, no. 43 (October 24, 1947): 33–34.

Badger, William Otis. "Should Co-Insurance Be Abolished?" *Best's Insurance News, Fire and Marine Edition* XXXI, no. 5 (September 20, 1930): 359, 374.

Bament, William N. "Co-Insurance." Address to the Insurance Society of New York, March 30, 1920.

Behlmer, Sidney G. "Other Consequential Loss Insurance." In *Property and Liability Insurance Handbook,* edited by John D. Long and Davis W. Gregg, pp. 130–143. Homewood, Ill.: Richard D. Irwin, Inc., 1965.

Benchert, Lars-G., and Sternberg, Ingvar. "An Attempt to Find an Expression for the Distribution of Fire Damage Amount." *Proceedings of the XVth International Congress of Actuaries* II (1957): 288–294.

Bishop, Avard L. "The Co-Insurance Clause." *Journal of American Insurance* VI, no. 3 (March, 1929): 5–6ff.

Blades, John R. "Coinsurance." *Best's Insurance News, Fire and Casualty Edition* XLII, no. 2 (June, 1941): 35–39.

Blanchard, Ralph H. "Coinsurance." In *Risk and Insurance and Other Papers,* pp. 138–143. Lincoln, Neb.: University of Nebraska Press, 1965.

"Catastrophic Cover Gap Called Widespread." *The Journal of Commerce and Commercial* (May 7, 1969): 9.

Clutter, James E. "How INA Modernized Property Valuation Procedures." *Best's Review* (Property and Liability Edition) LXX no. 7 (November, 1969): 74–77.

"Coinsurance, Contribution or Average Clause." *Rough Notes Monthly Policy, Form & Manual Analyses* (August, 1963): 1–2.

"Co-Insurance Explained," *Credit and Financial Management* CIV no. 6 (June, 1952): 33–34.

Commission on Insurance Terminology of the American Risk and Insurance Association. *Bulletin* II, no. 1 (March, 1966): 3–4.

Degener, Robert F. "Inland Marine Insurance—Floaters." In *Property and Liability Insurance Handbook*, edited by John D. Long and Davis W. Gregg, pp. 391–401. Homewood, Ill.: Richard D. Irwin, Inc., 1965.

de Roode, Holger. Letter to the editor, *The Post Magazine and Insurance Monitor* (London) LXXXVI, no. 32 (August 1, 1925): 1.

Dineen, Robert E., Proctor, Clifford R., and Gardner, H. Daniel. "The Economics and Principles of Insurance Supervision." In *Insurance and Government*, edited by Charles C. Center and Richard M. Heins, pp. 5–91. New York: McGraw-Hill Book Co., Inc., 1962.

Durand, David. "A Simple Method for Estimating the Size Distribution of a Given Aggregate Income." *The Review of Economic Statistics* XXV, no. 4 (November, 1943): 227–230.

Elink-Schuurman, W. H. A. "Über die Prinzipien einer Feuerschadenstatistik." *Reports, Memoirs and Proceedings of the Sixth International Congress of Actuaries* II (1909): 269–287.

Falls, Laurence E. "Coinsurance." *Best's Insurance News, Fire and Casualty Edition* XLIX, no. 6 (October, 1948): 25–26, 92–94.

"Fire Companies Progressing in Requiring Insurance to Value," *Insurance Advocate* LXXII, no. 3 (April 1, 1961): 14–16.

Fitzgerald, J. J. "Coinsurance Is Much Misunderstood." *Journal of American Insurance* IV, no. 6 (June, 1927): 21, 29.

"Further Description of Co-Insurance Clause," *Eastern Underwriter* XXIII, no. 43 (October 13, 1922): 19–20.

Gay, Edward S. "Full Co-Insurance and Contribution by the Assured." Address to the Underwriters' Association of the Northwest, Chicago, September 27, 1893.

Greene, Mark R. "Allied Lines Insurance." In *Property and Liability Insurance Handbook*, edited by John D. Long and Davis W. Gregg, pp. 100–118. Homewood, Ill.: Richard D. Irwin, Inc., 1965.

————. "The Effect of Insurance Settlements in a Disaster." *The Journal of Risk and Insurance* XXXI, no. 3 (September, 1964): 381–392.

Guiher, James M. "Measurement of Damages in Property Insurance Losses." *Proceedings of the American Bar Association Section of Insurance, Negligence and Compensation Law* (1965): 187–201.

Gunn, John W. "The Reduced Rate Average Clause." *Annual Report of Proceedings, The Fire Insurance Society of San Francisco* I (1910–1911): 45–49.

Hardy, E. R. "Co-Insurance." In *The Business of Insurance*, edited by Howard P. Dunham, vol. I, pp. 173–184. New York: The Ronald Press Co., 1912.

Herzog, Harold P. "Can Anyone Define 'Actual Cash Value'?" *Business Insurance* IV, no. 6 (March 16, 1970): 29–30.

"HO Coverage Increased 10 PC." *The Journal of Commerce and Commercial* (January 30, 1969): 8.

Johansen, Paul. "On Fire Insurance of Rural Buildings." *Transactions of the XVth International Congress of Actuaries* II (1957): 211–215.

Kaplan, Charles N. "Burglary, Theft and Robbery Insurance Rates." In *Examination of Insurance Companies*, vol. V, pp. 111–126. New York: New York State Insurance Dept., 1955.

Kelly, Ambrose B. "The Insurance of Profits, Reinstatement Value, Agreed Amount and the Principle of Indemnity," *Insurance Law Journal*, no. 524 (September, 1966): 517–530.

————. "Insurance and Inflation." *Best's Review* (Property and Liability Edition) LXX, no. 9 (January, 1970): 24–28.

Kulp, C. A. "Non-Insured and Non-Insurable Loss." *Journal of American Insurance* V, no. 6 (June, 1928): 11–13ff.

Longley-Cook, L. H. "Problems of Fire Insurance Rate Making." *Proceedings of the Casualty Actuarial Society* XXXVIII, part I (November, 1951): 94–102.

Louis, William A. "Some Observations on Co-Insurance." *Proceedings of the Fifteenth Annual Meeting of the Fire Underwriters' Association of the Pacific*, San Francisco, 1926, pp. 130–141.

MacLeod, Morton P. "Coinsurance—What It Is and How It Works." *Appraisal and Valuation Manual of the American Society of Appraisers* VI (1961): 335–349.

Michelbacher, G. F. "Presidential Address: On the Use of Judgment in Rate Making." *Proceedings of the Casualty Actuarial Society* XII (1925): 1–20.

"National Board's Program to 'Lick' the Under-Insurance Problem." *The Local Agent* XVIII, no. 3 (March, 1946): 15–16.

Nichols, W. J. "The Coinsurance Clause," In *The Fire Insurance Contract, Its History and Interpretation*, edited by The Insurance Society of New York, pp. 697–715. Indianapolis, Ind.: The Rough Notes Co., Inc., 1922.

"Note: Valuation and Measure of Recovery under Fire Insurance Policies." *Columbia Law Review* XLIX, no. 6 (June, 1949): 818–836.

Parker, Kent H. "Ratemaking in Fire Insurance." In *Property and Liability Insurance Handbook,* edited by John D. Long and Davis W. Gregg, pp. 169–189. Homewood, Ill.: Richard D. Irwin, Inc., 1965.

Phelan, John D. "Business Interruption Insurance." In *Property and Liability Insurance Handbook,* edited by John D. Long and Davis W. Gregg, pp. 119–129. Homewood, Ill.: Richard D. Irwin, Inc., 1965.

Picone, Alexander. "Homeowners Need Insurance to Avoid Damaging Effects of Underinsurance, Inflation." *The Journal of Commerce and Commercial* (August 14, 1969): 7.

————."Retail Credit Co. Introduces New Residential Replacement Cost Reporting Service in 4 States." *The Journal of Commerce and Commercial* (March 19, 1969): 10.

Potter, F. P. O. "Insurance to Value." *The Casualty and Surety Journal* IX, no. 9 (November, 1948): 9–15.

Proceedings of the National Association of Insurance Commissioners, I (1965): 208–209.

Riegel, Robert. "Coinsurance." *Journal of American Insurance* XXII, no. 6 (June, 1945): 4–5, 19–22.

Roane, John D. C. "Appraisals and Underinsurance." Address before a meeting of Maryland Insurance Agents, Ocean City, Maryland, June, 1952.

Rodda, William H. "Multiple Line Underwriting: Rating Methods." In *Readings in Property and Casualty Insurance,* edited by H. Wayne Snider, pp. 351–362. Homewood, Ill.: Richard D. Irwin, Inc., 1959.

Roome, A. B. "Coinsurance under Fire Policies." *Annual of American Insurance Thought: Fire, Casualty, Surety.* 6th ed., pp. 182–185. New York: Convention Yearbook Co., 1926.

Rutledge, George F. "Farm and Crop Insurance." In *Property and Liability Insurance Handbook,* edited by John D. Long and Davis W. Gregg, pp. 144–157. Homewood, Ill.: Richard D. Irwin, Inc., 1965.

Salzmann, Ruth E. "Rating by Layer of Insurance." *Proceedings of the Casualty Actuarial Society,* L (1963): 15–26.

Sloan, E. J. "The Average and 80% Clauses of Fire Insurance Policies." *Proceedings of the Insurance Institute of Hartford,* I (1908–1909): 67–75.

Traver, George G. "Under-Insurance a Vital Matter that Agents Fail to Stress." *The Weekly Underwriter* CLIV, no. 7 (February 16, 1946): 435ff.

"Underinsurance Trend Is Accented by Sampling." *The National Underwriter* LVI, no. 37 (September 11, 1952): 14.

"Vital Reasons for Insurance to Specified Percentage of Value." *Eastern Underwriter XXXIII*, no. 20 (May 13, 1932): 31.

Whitney, A. W. "The Actuarial Theory of Fire Insurance Rates as Depending upon the Ratio of Insurance to Sound Value hence a Determination of the Rates for Use with a Coinsurance Clause," *Reports, Memoirs and Proceedings of the Sixth International Congress of Actuaries* II (1909): 395–403.

————. "The Co-Insurance Clause." Paper read before the Fire Underwriters' Association of the Pacific, San Francisco, January 13, 1904.

————. "The Conflagration Hazard and Co-Insurance." *Proceedings of the Thirteenth Annual Meeting of the Fire Underwriters' Association of the Pacific*, San Francisco, 1906, pp. 73–78.

Zangerle, Joseph M. "Inflationary Pressures on Homeowners Insurance." *Best's Review* (Property and Liability Edition) LXX, no. 6 (October, 1969): 20–28.

Rate Manuals

Fire Insurance Research and Actuarial Association. *Manual of Rates, Rules and Clauses for Earthquake and Volcanic Eruption Insurance*. New York: The Association, 1950, Revision No. 2–1957.

————. *Manual of Rates, Rules and Clauses for Water Damage Insurance*. New York: The Association, 1963.

Georgia Inspection and Rating Bureau. *Extended Coverage Manual*. Atlana: The Bureau, loose-leaf, revised and supplemented periodically.

————. *Georgia Rule Book*. Atlanta: The Bureau, loose-leaf, revised and supplemented periodically.

Illinois Inspection and Rating Bureau. *Illinois Rule Book (Excluding Cook County)*. Chicago: The Bureau, loose-leaf, revised and supplemented periodically.

Middle Department Association of Fire Underwriters. *Rule Book*. Philadelphia: The Association, loose-leaf, revised and supplemented periodically.

Mountain States Inspection Bureau. *Colorado Rule Book*. Denver, Colo.: The Bureau, loose-leaf, revised and supplemented periodically.

————. *New Mexico Rule Book*. Denver, Colo.: The Bureau, loose-leaf, revised and supplemented periodically.

National Bureau of Casualty Underwriters. *Burglary Insurance Manual*. New York: The Bureau, 1958.

New England Insurance Rating Association. *Manual of Rates, Rules and Forms for Extended Coverage, Vandalism and Malicious Mischief, Special Extended Coverage, Builders' Risk Special Extended Coverage, Windstorm and Hail—Massachusetts.* Boston: Recording & Statistical Corp., loose-leaf, revised and supplemented periodically.

————. *Manual of Rules and Clauses.* Boston: Recording & Statistical Corp., loose-leaf, revised and supplemented periodically.

New York Fire Insurance Rating Organization. *General Rules.* New York: The Organization, loose-leaf, revised and supplemented periodically.

————. *Rules for Extended Coverage Endorsement.* New York: The Organization, loose-leaf, revised and supplemented periodically.

Pacific Fire Rating Bureau. *Tariff Rules.* San Francisco: The Bureau, loose-leaf, revised and supplemented periodically.

Philadelphia Fire Underwriters' Association, *Constitution, By-Laws, Agreement, and Rules.* Philadelphia: The Association, 1908.

Virginia Insurance Rating Bureau. *Percentage Rate Change Manual—Fire.* Richmond, Va.: The Bureau, loose-leaf, revised and supplemented periodically.

Washington (State) Surveying and Rating Bureau. *General Rules.* Seattle, Wash.: The Bureau, loose-leaf, revised and supplemented periodically.

Court Cases

Aetna Insurance Company v. Eisenberg, 188 F. Supp. 415 (1960).

American Insurance Company v. Iaconi, 47 Del. 167, 89 Atl. (2d) 141 (1952).

Britven v. Occidental Insurance Company, 234 Iowa 682, 13 N.W. (2d) 791 (1944).

Buse v. National Ben Franklin Insurance Company of Pittsburgh, Pa., 164 N.Y.S. 1088, 123 N.E. 858 (1916).

Butler v. Aetna Insurance Company, 64 N.D. 764, 256 N.W. 214 (1934).

Citizens' Savings Bank and Trust Company v. Fitchburg Mutual Fire Insurance Company, 86 Vt. 267, 84 Atl. 970 (1912).

Clift v. Fulton Fire Insurance Company, 44 Tenn. App. 486, 315 S.W. (2d) 9 (1958).

Commodity Credit Corporation v. American Equitable Assurance Company, 198 Ark. 1160, 133 S.W. (2d) 443 (1939).

Commonwealth Insurance Company v. O. Henry Tent and Awning Company, 287 Fed. (2d) 316 (1961).

Dahms & Sons Company v. German Fire Insurance Company, 153 Iowa 168, 132 N.W. 870 (1911).

Dubin Paper Company v. Insurance Company of North America, 361 Pa. 68, 62 Atl. (2d) 85 (1948).

Farmers' Feed Company v. Scottish Union and National Insurance Company, 173 N.Y. 241, 65 N.E. 1105 (1903).

Farmers' Mercantile Company v. Insurance Company, 161 Iowa 5, 141 N.W. 447 (1913).

Fedas v. Insurance Company of the State of Pennsylvania, 300 Pa. 555, 151 Atl. 285 (1930).

Fire Association of Philadelphia v. Coomer, Tex. Civ. App. 158 S.W. (2d) 355 (1942).

Fireman's Fund Insurance Company v. Pekor, 106 Ga. 1, 31 S.E. 779 (1898).

Gervant v. New England Fire Insurance Company, 306 N.Y. 293, 118 N.E. (2d) 574 (1954).

Harper v. Penn Mutual Fire Insurance Company, 199 F. Supp. 663 (1961).

Home Insurance Company v. Eisenson, 181 Fed. (2d) 416 (1950).

Hunt v. General Insurance Company, 227 S.C. 125, 87 S.E. (2d) 34 (1955).

Insurance Company of North America v. McGraw, 255 Ky. 839, 75 S.W. (2d) 518 (1928).

Johnston v. Farmers' Fire Insurance Company, 106 Mich. 86, 64 N.W. 5 (1895).

Knuppel v. American Insurance Company, 269 Fed. (2d) 163 (1953).

McAnarney v. Newark Fire Insurance Company, 247 N.Y. 176, 159 N.E. 902 (1928).

McIntosh v. Hartford Fire Insurance Company, 106 Mont. 434, 78 Pac. (2d) 82 (1938).

Manchester Fire Insurance Company v. Simons, 12 Tex. Civ. App. 607, 35 S.W. 722 (1896).

Milwaukee Mechanics' Insurance Company v. Maples, 37 Ala. 74, 66 So. (2d) 159 (1953).

New York Life Insurance Company v. Glens Falls Insurance Company, 184 Misc. 846, 55 N.Y.S. (2d) 176 (1945), *aff'd. mem.* 86 N.Y.S. (2d) 191 (1949).

Niagara Fire Insurance Company v. Pool, 31 S.W. (2d) 850 (1930).

Northwestern Fuel Company v. Boston Insurance Company, 131 Minn. 19, 154 N.W. 513 (1915).

Oppenheim v. Fireman's Fund Insurance Company, 119 Minn. 417, 138 N.W. 777 (1912).

Pinet v. New Hampshire Fire Insurance Company, 100 N.H. 346, 126 Atl. (2d) 262 (1956).

Pinsky v. Minneapolis Fire & Marine Insurance Company, 225 App. Div. 326, 233 N.Y.S. 160 (1929).

Ranallo v. Hinman Brothers Construction Company, et al., 49 F. Supp. 920 (1942).

Smith v. Allemania Fire Insurance Company, 219 Ill. App. 506 (1920).

State Auto Mutual Insurance Company v. Cox, 309 Ky. 480, 218 S.W. (2d) 46 (1949).

Stephenson v. Agricultural Insurance Company, 116 Wis. 277, 93 N.W. 19 (1903).

Svea Fire and Liability Insurance Company v. State Savings and Loan Association, 19 Fed. (2d) 134 (1927).

Templeton v. Insurance Company of North America, 201 S.W. (2d) 784 (1947).

Texas City Terminal Railway Company v. American Equitable Assurance Company of New York, 130 F. Supp. 843 (1955).

United Services Automobile Association v. Russom, 241 Fed. (2d) 296 (1957).

Wisconsin Screw Company v. Fireman's Fund Insurance Company, 297 Fed. (2d) 697 (1962).

Letters

Blanchard, Ralph H., Professor Emeritus of Insurance, Graduate School of Business, Columbia University. Letter to the author, May 4, 1967.

General Adjustment Bureau, Inc. Letter to the author from G. M. Lynch, National Manager, Education, September 29, 1966.

Illinois Inspection and Rating Bureau. Letter to the author from R. J. Nagel, Assistant Manager, September 5, 1967.

Insurance Company of North America. Letter to the author from David C. Tausche, Manager for Europe, October 6, 1966.

Middle Department Association of Fire Underwriters. Letter to the author from H. Reed Mullikin, Executive Manager, December 21, 1966.

Minnesota, State of, Insurance Division. Letter to the author from Thomas L. O'Malley, Supervisor, Claims Investigation Division, August 18, 1965.

————. Letter to the author from A. C. Richter, Manager, Rating Division, November 15, 1966.

Multi-Line Insurance Rating Bureau. Letter to the author from Frank J. Caso, Manager, Personal Lines Division, November 18, 1966.

New England Insurance Rating Association. Letter to the author from Robert H. Stocker, Executive Manager, June 1, 1967.

New Hampshire Board of Underwriters. Letter to the author from W. H. Ferris, Manager, Inspection and Rating, September 15, 1966.

Oregon, State of, Office of the Fire Marshal. Letter to the author from Norbert J. Lecher, Statistician, September 9, 1966.

Pacific Fire Rating Bureau. Letter to the author from R. Williams, Executive Secretary, December 8, 1966.

The Philadelphia Contributionship for the Insurance of Houses from Loss by Fire. Letter to the author from Edwin C. Miller, Assistant Treasurer, August 6, 1965.

Safeco Insurance Company of America. Interoffice correspondence to Northwest Division agents, May 18, 1966.

St. Paul Fire and Marine Insurance Company. Letter to the author from James P. White, Superintendent, Property-Personal Lines Department, October 20, 1966.

South-Eastern Underwriters Association. Letter to the author from R. L. Gatewood, Secretary, December 14, 1966.

State Farm Fire and Casualty Company. Letter to the author from P. G. Buffinton, Vice President, October 21, 1966.

Washington (State) Surveying and Rating Bureau. Letter to the author from George W. Clarke, General Manager, October 19, 1966.

Western Actuarial Bureau. Letter to the author from Edwin N. Searl, General Manager, April 28, 1967.

Interviews

American Institute for Property and Liability Underwriters, Inc. Telephone interview with Edwin S. Overman, President, November 17, 1966.

Fire Insurance Research and Actuarial Association. Personal interview with P. R. Bechtolt, Manager, January 31, 1967.

Insurance Company of North America. Personal interview with Edward B. Black, Secretary-Underwriting, January 17, 1966.

―――――. Personal interviews with John B. Davis, Assistant Vice President, December 22, 1966, and January 17, 1967.

―――――. Personal interview with L. H. Longley-Cook, then Vice President and Actuary, September 20, 1966.

―――――. Telephone interview with Frank E. Raab, Assistant Vice President, Policyholder Service Department—Technical, July 10, 1967.

―――――. Personal interview with Putnam Schroeder, Research Specialist, September 20, 1966.

Life Insurance Company of North America. Personal interview with Ruth E. Salzmann, then Actuary, Treaty Reinsurance Department, May 4, 1967.

Middle Department Association of Fire Underwriters. Personal interview with C. Neville Wight, then Assistant Executive Manager, September 22, 1966.

National Insurance Actuarial and Statistical Association. Personal interview with LeRoy J. Simon, General Manager, August 30, 1966.

University of Pennsylvania. Personal interviews with Dorothy S. Brady, Research Professor of Economics, August 5, 1966, October 3, 1966, and December 19, 1966.

Index

*This book has been set in 10 point Caledonia,
leaded 3 points, and 9 point Caledonia, leaded
2 points. Chapter numbers are in 12 point
Craw Clarendon Book and 24 point Craw
Clarendon; chapter titles are in 18 point Craw
Clarendon. The size of the type page is 24 by
41½ picas.*